IMAGES
of America

ALONG THE DAMARISCOTTA

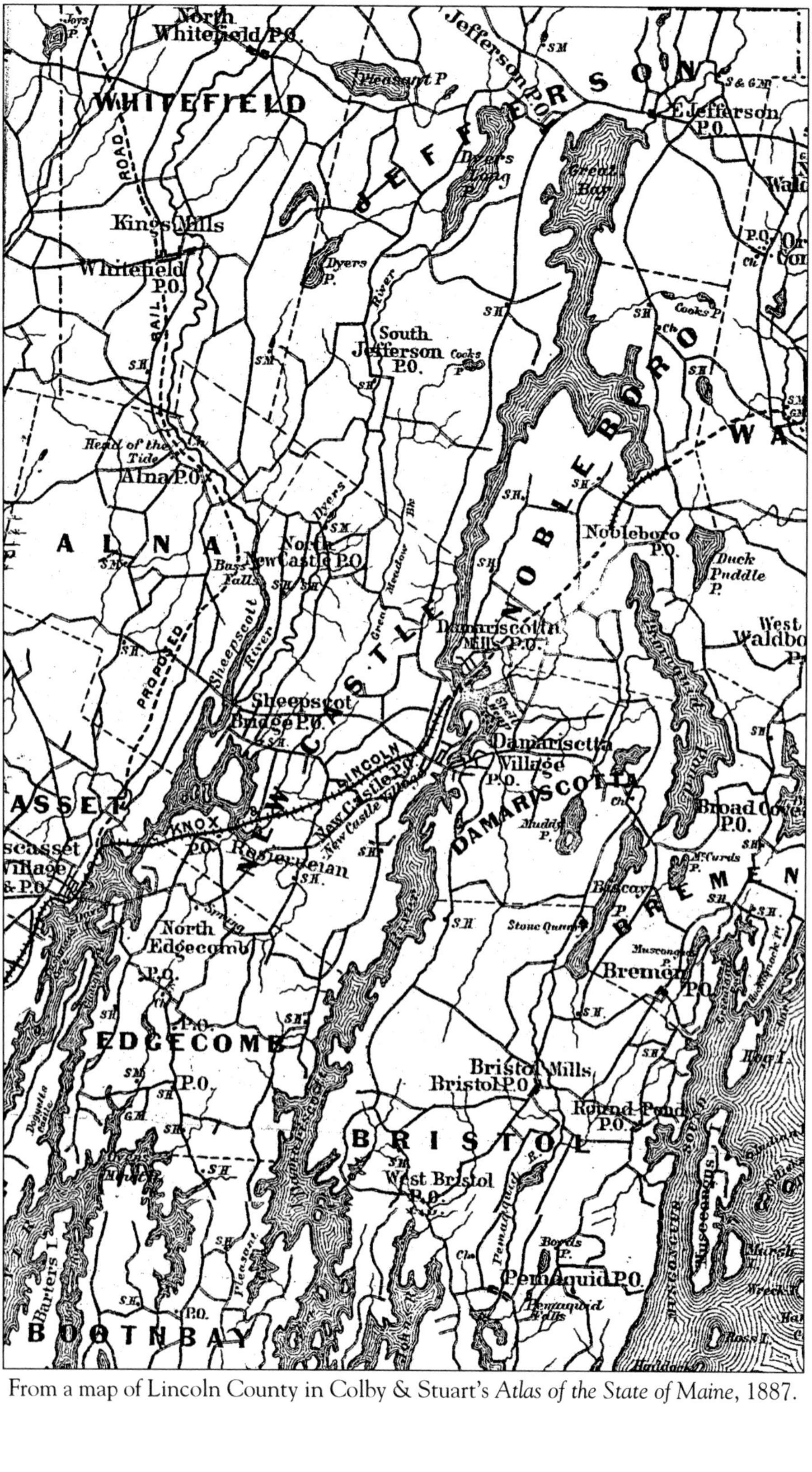

From a map of Lincoln County in Colby & Stuart's *Atlas of the State of Maine*, 1887.

IMAGES
of America

ALONG THE DAMARISCOTTA

Compiled by
Dorothy A. Blanchard

ARCADIA
PUBLISHING

ISBN 978-0-7385-8981-7

Published by Arcadia Publishing
Charleston, South Carolina

Printed in the United States of America

For all general information contact Arcadia Publishing at:
Telephone 843-853-2070
Fax 843-853-0044
E-mail sales@arcadiapublishing.com
For customer service and orders:
Toll-Free 1-888-313-2665

Visit us on the Internet at www.arcadiapublishing.com

OTHER PUBLICATIONS BY DOROTHY A. BLANCHARD

"Into the Heart of Maine: A Look at Dexter's Franco-American Community." *Maine Historical Society Quarterly*, Vol. 33, No. 1 (Summer 1993).

This book is dedicated to
the memory of my mother and father.

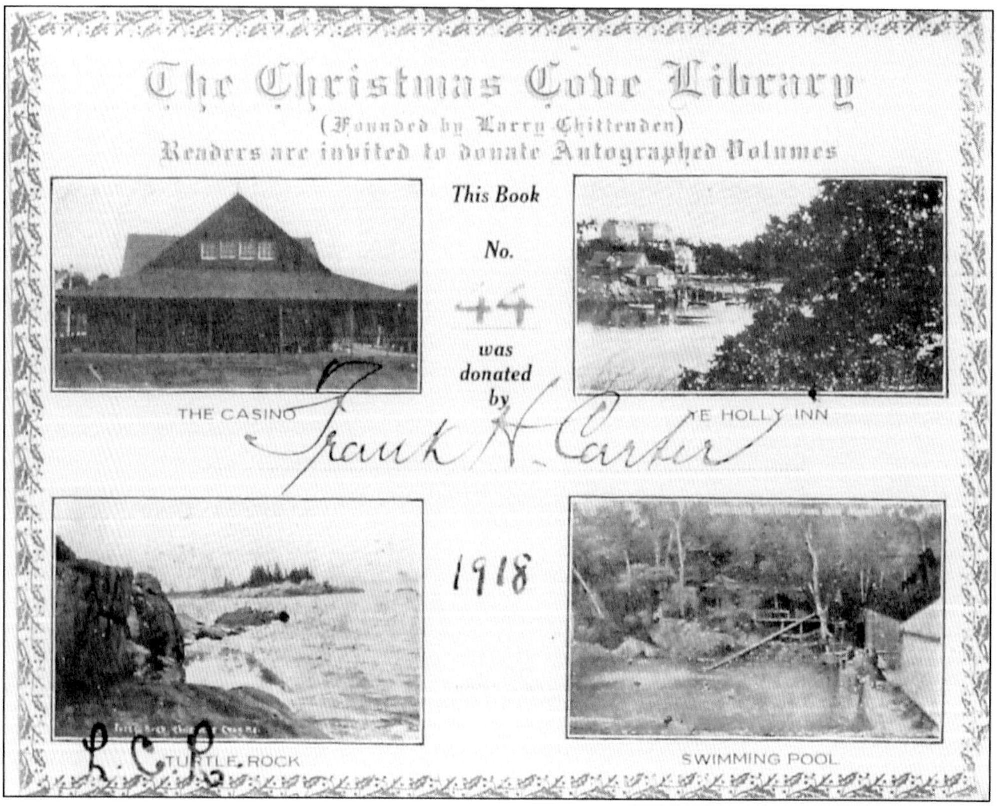

Contents

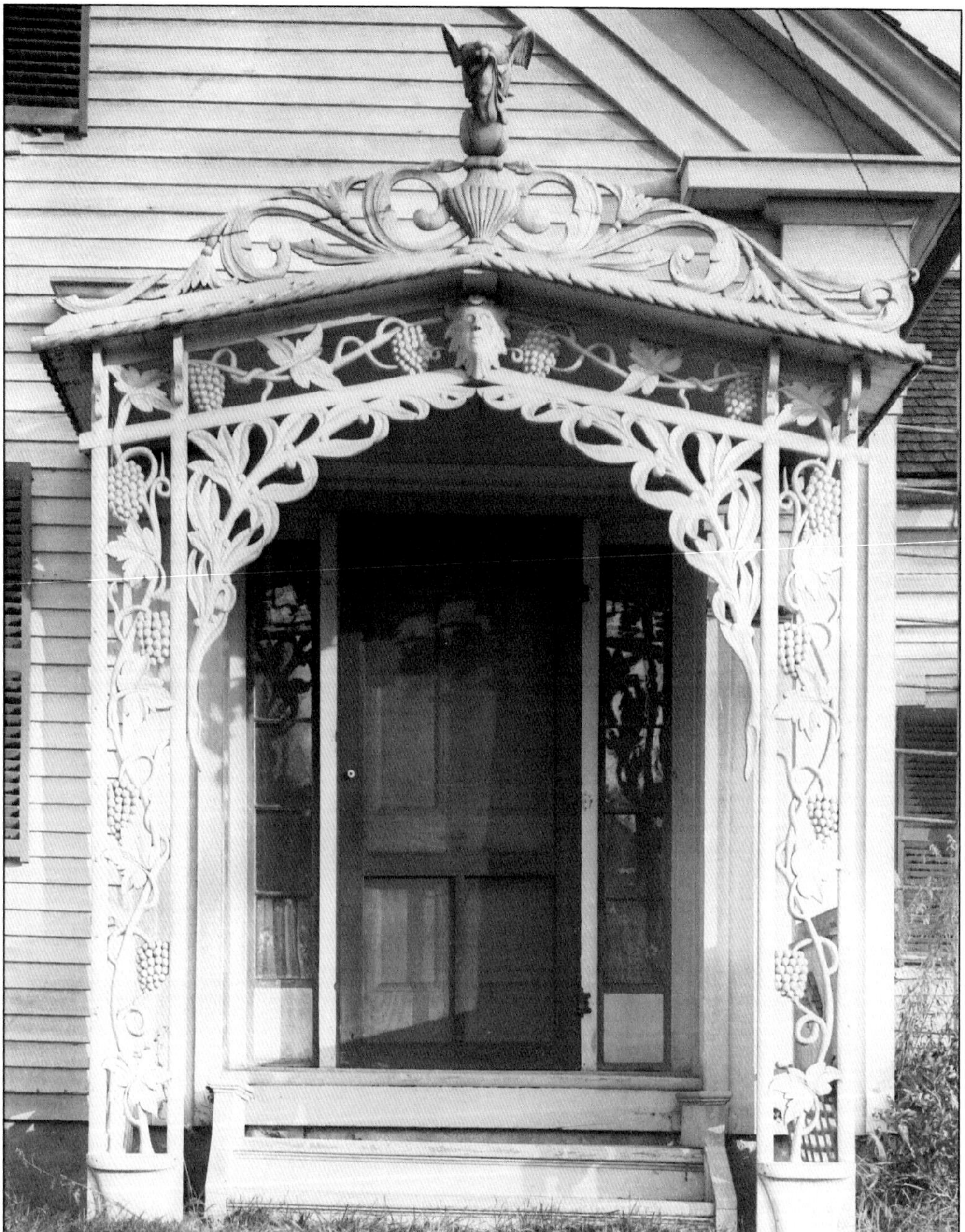

Edbury Hatch was an accomplished woodcarver. Unfortunately, his apprenticeship to a Newcastle figurehead carver in 1870 coincided with the decline of large wooden sailing vessels, and he found few opportunities to practice his craft. But he continued to carve in his spare time and when he moved back to Newcastle after the turn of the century his work began to appear in porticos, signs, and ornaments around the town. This beautifully carved entrance to his home is an invitation to recall another era and to explore the maritime traditions and rich history of the Damariscotta River. (Nobleboro Historical Society, Ivan Flye Collection)

Introduction

Few rivers in Maine have the physical evidence of antiquity found along the Damariscotta. Shell middens dating from prehistoric times are still visible today, proof of the bounty yielded to Native Peoples by this productive waterway. The name itself, "Damariscotta," is said to be derived from a Native American word meaning "abundance of little fishes," a reference to the annual alewife run at Damariscotta Mills. With the arrival of Europeans the river continued to play a vital role, providing opportunities for the shipbuilding, brickmaking, fishing, and lumbering industries which were the backbone of the area's early economy. Hundreds of vessels of every size and description were built along the river, and bricks, ice, alewives, and lumber products were shipped to distant markets in the boom years of a thriving economy.

Given such impressive beginnings it is understandable that when those industries collapsed or were drastically altered in the late nineteenth century, the towns along the river went through a period of transition. As the brickyards, shipyards, and mills shut down, and family farms were divided up or abandoned, new opportunities in commerce, recreation, and tourism took their place. How did residents adapt to such change? What was life like fifty to one hundred and twenty-five years ago? What were the social, cultural, and recreational activities of a people working through a transitional time? And most importantly, how did the river and lake continue to influence their lives? This era, sometimes neglected by historians, is a vital link between the area's Golden Age and modern Lincoln County. It is fortunate that the development of photography occurred simultaneously with these changes, and that many wonderful images remain to remind us of our recent past.

Compared to Maine's mighty rivers, the Damariscotta is short, a mere 26 miles (including the lake) from Jefferson to Christmas Cove, but packed into such a short distance is a rich and diverse history. The eight towns bordering the waterway—Jefferson, Nobleboro, Damariscotta, Newcastle, Edgecomb, Boothbay, Bristol, and South Bristol—developed independently and each has a distinctive heritage, fascinating in its own right. The common bond linking them is the river, a body of water so adaptable to multiple uses that it has served the needs of lumbermen, farmers, shipbuilders, brickmakers, fishermen, cottage owners, schoolchildren, and tourists. It was used for food, transportation, business, pleasure, and recreation; and as the photographs, postcards, and ephemera in this book reveal, the river was an integral part in the lives of those who worked on it and lived beside it.

The photographs have been organized in an orderly progression along the length of the waterway, as though the reader were taking a cruise from Jefferson to Christmas Cove. It starts on Davis Stream at the head of the lake and meanders along both shores into the coves and past summer camps, continues through the bustle of activity at Damariscotta Mills, the salt bay, and the towns nestled along the river, and ends with a glimpse of life at the shipyards and cottage communities of the lower river. It is meant to be a journey through time and place to another era, simpler perhaps, but still one of transition and uncertainty to those who lived through it. Perhaps it will bring back memories to those who can recall some of the people and events; and to those who view the images for the first time, I hope it will be a voyage of discovery. In any case, enjoy the trip!

Dorothy A. Blanchard
February 1995

Acknowledgments

A research project usually involves the efforts of more than one individual. And although I have collected the photographs and composed the text that follows, none of it would have been possible without the cooperation and genuine helpfulness of a number of local people. Their willingness to share their time and knowledge has not only made it easier to assemble the information, but says a great deal about the people who live in this part of Maine. I am sincerely grateful to several Lincoln County individuals and institutions who not only loaned me their photographs and postcards, but who shared historical anecdotes and family stories so that this book could have a human content as well as a historical one.

Special thanks to: Ralph and Priscilla Bond, Arthur Jones, George Dow, Marjorie and Calvin Dodge, Carolyn Reny, Beryl Hunt, Nancy and Dick Kennedy, the Nobleboro Historical Society, Hudson Vannah, David Page, David Belknap, Lillian Hale, Norman Kelsey, Mac Blanchard, Phyllis Tonry, Dot Hathorne, Robert Brown, Howie Davison, George Campbell, Bill Kelsey, the Gamage Shipyard, Barbara Rumsey, and The Boothbay Region Historical Society.

Thanks also to Mark Biscoe who allowed me to use material on shipbuilding in Damariscotta and Newcastle from his recently published book, *No Plucker Set of Men Anywhere*, and to the Skidompha Library staff, Carroll Dinsmore, Jim Stevens, Margaret Morton, Kim Kelsey, Margaret House, Dr. Fred Hinck, Tom Brooke, and John Robert MacDonald who not only tolerated my endless questions, but provided leads, information, direction, advice, and cross-checked my historical references.

One

The Lake

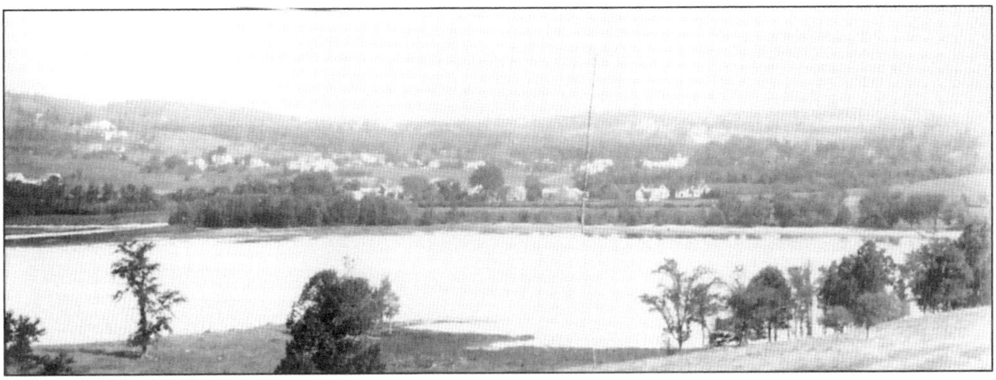

The village at Jefferson with its neat farms and fields forms a picturesque backdrop for the headwaters of the Damariscotta. Early settlers were attracted by the valuable timber along the shores of the lake, convenient water transportation for rafting logs to the mills, abundant water power along feeder streams, and the fertile soil. Originally called Balltown in honor of John Ball, one of the earliest settlers, the village sent men into battle during the Revolutionary War and into the skirmishes of the backcountry agrarian revolt that followed it. Fiercely independent settlers acted to protect their new farms from the legal claims of the wealthy and powerful Kennebec Proprietors and to defend their populist understanding of the Revolution. This Jeffersonian ideal probably gave the town its present name. Nineteenth-century Jefferson—the town was incorporated in 1801—witnessed a continuation of its farming and lumbering industries as well as the start of a tourist industry centered on the natural beauty of the lake. (Ralph Bond)

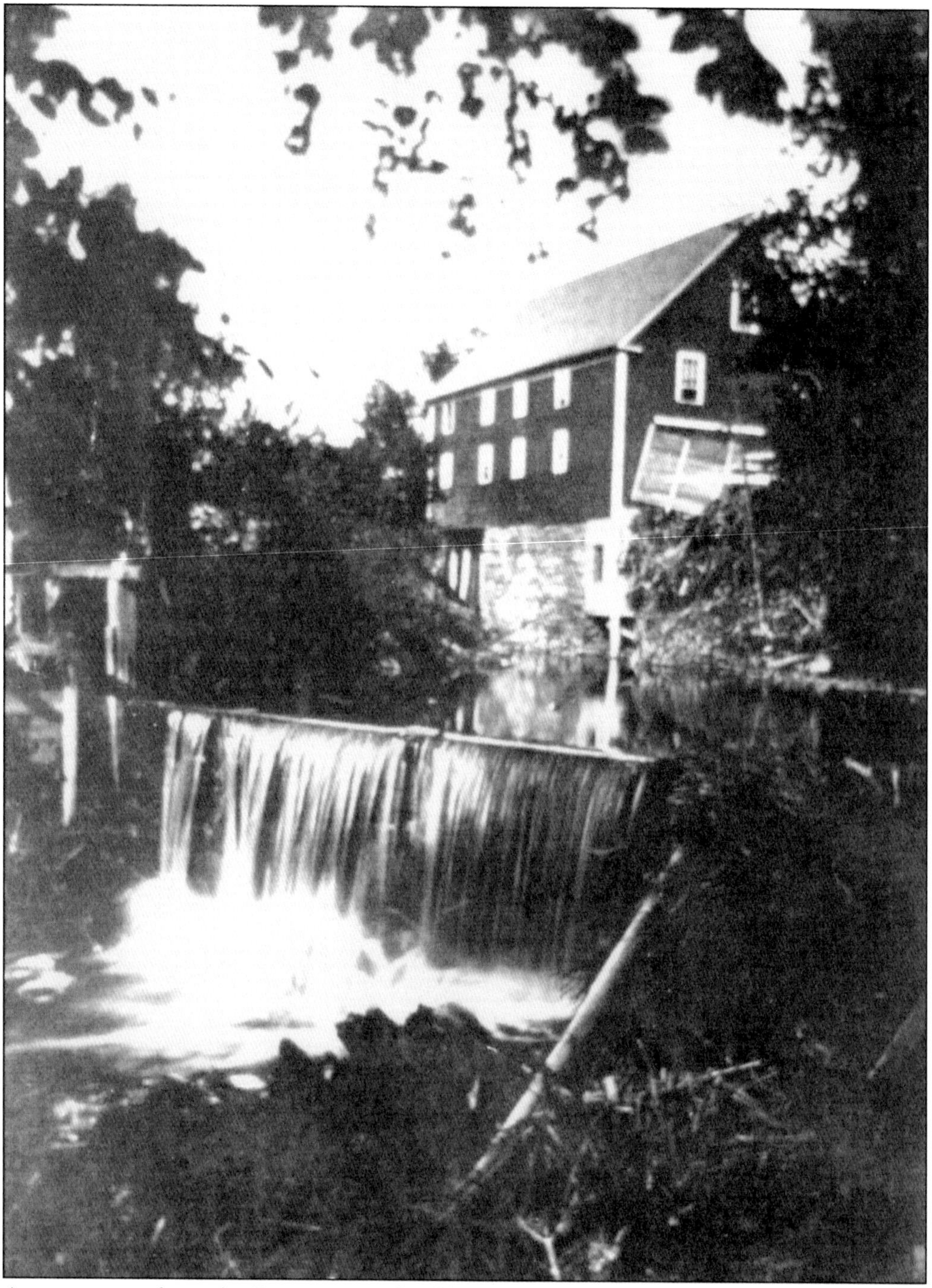

Any excursion down the Damariscotta should begin on Davis Stream. The major inlet at the head of the lake, its source lies in the towns of Somerville and Washington. By the time it flowed through the village at Jefferson, it was large enough to provide water power for several sawmills. The Davis Mill on the East Branch was built in 1902 and used two water wheels to turn out barrel staves and heads. The operation was short-lived, however, as fire destroyed the mill in 1909. (Ralph Bond)

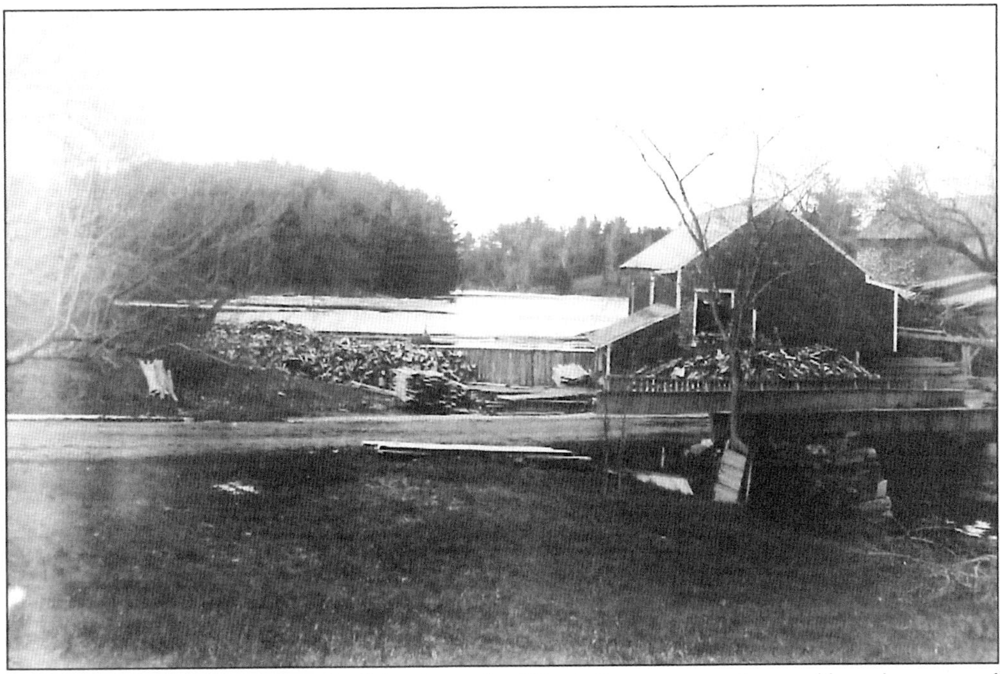

The Merserve Mill located on the West Branch of Davis Stream manufactured barrel staves and heads as well as shingles, laths, and custom lumber. At the turn of the century men earned 75¢ bundling shingles for a ten-hour shift; the sawyer was paid $1. (Ralph Bond)

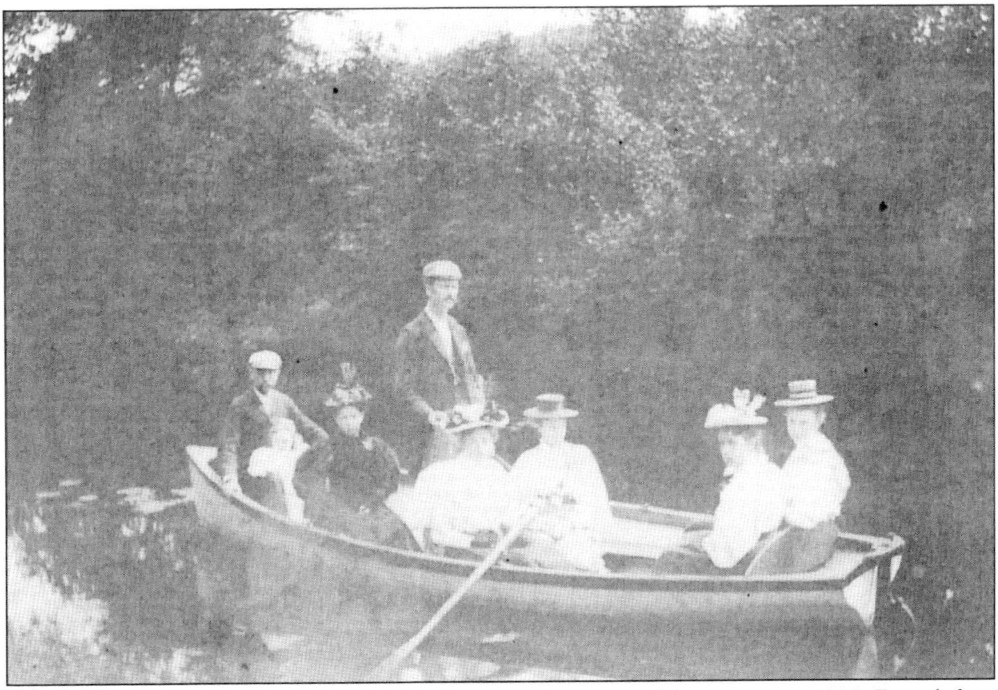

The Witham family enjoying a boat ride on the calm waters of the stream, c. 1890. From left to right are: William Witham (holding Melvin), Elizabeth Witham, Charles (standing), Amanda, Kate, Fossie R., and unknown. (Ralph Bond)

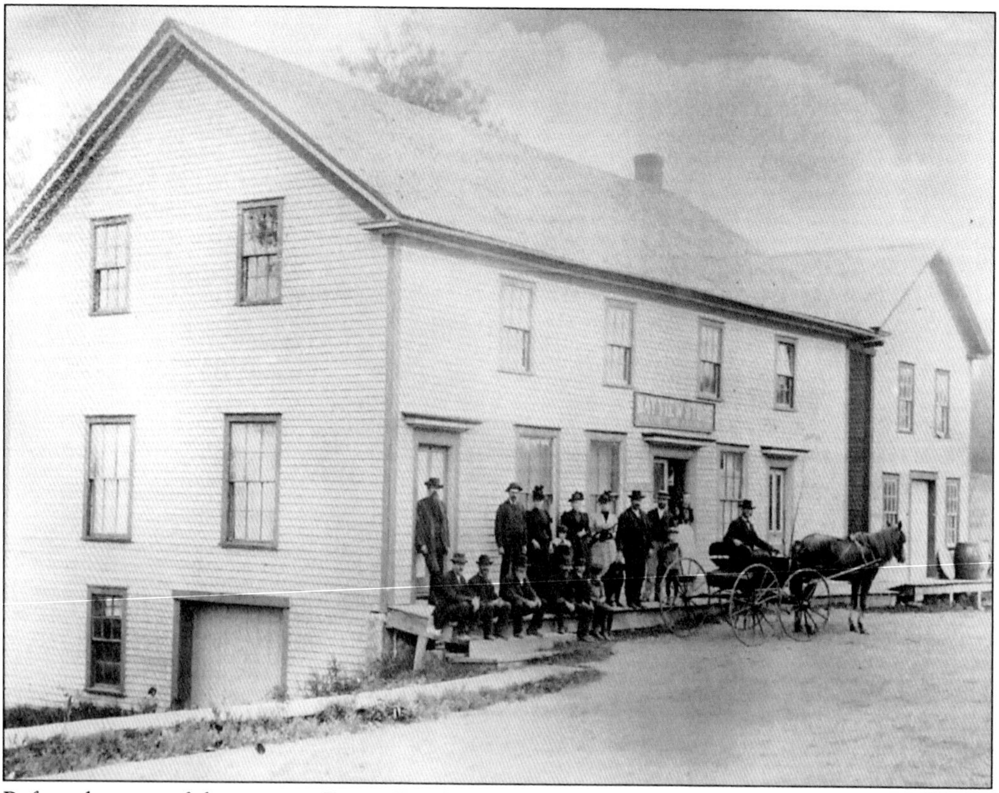

Before the turn of the century Briggs Farnham operated the Bayview Store, located at the east end of the bridge. The second floor was used for meetings, dances, plays, and minstrel shows. (Ralph Bond)

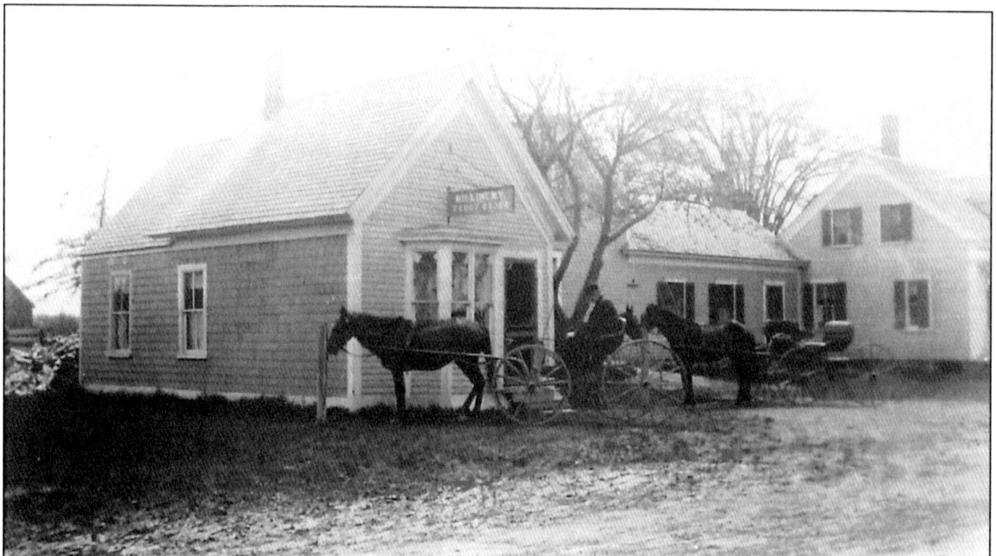

Miss Daisey Sedgley's millinery shop advertised "millinery, underwear, hosiery, skirts, shirt waists, wrappers, fancy work and novelties." The building was later moved on the ice to be used as a private residence for Max Belz. (Ralph Bond)

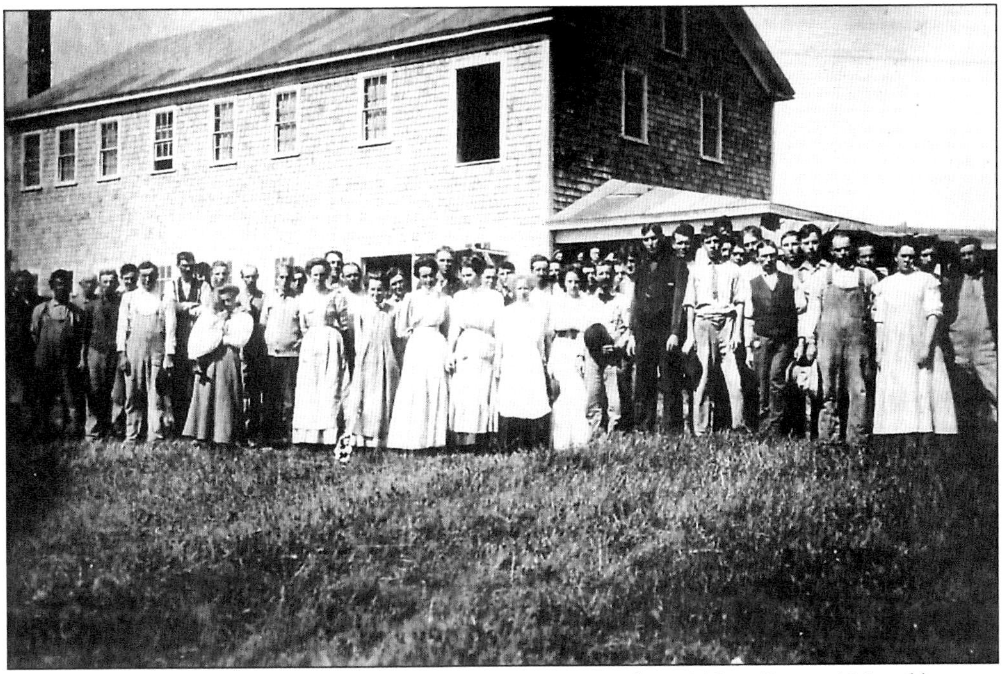

The Twitchell and Champlin Corn Canning Factory opened in 1908 on Route 126 and became the town's largest employer. The business employed about fifty people and operated ten years in Jefferson before it moved to New Sharon. (Ralph Bond)

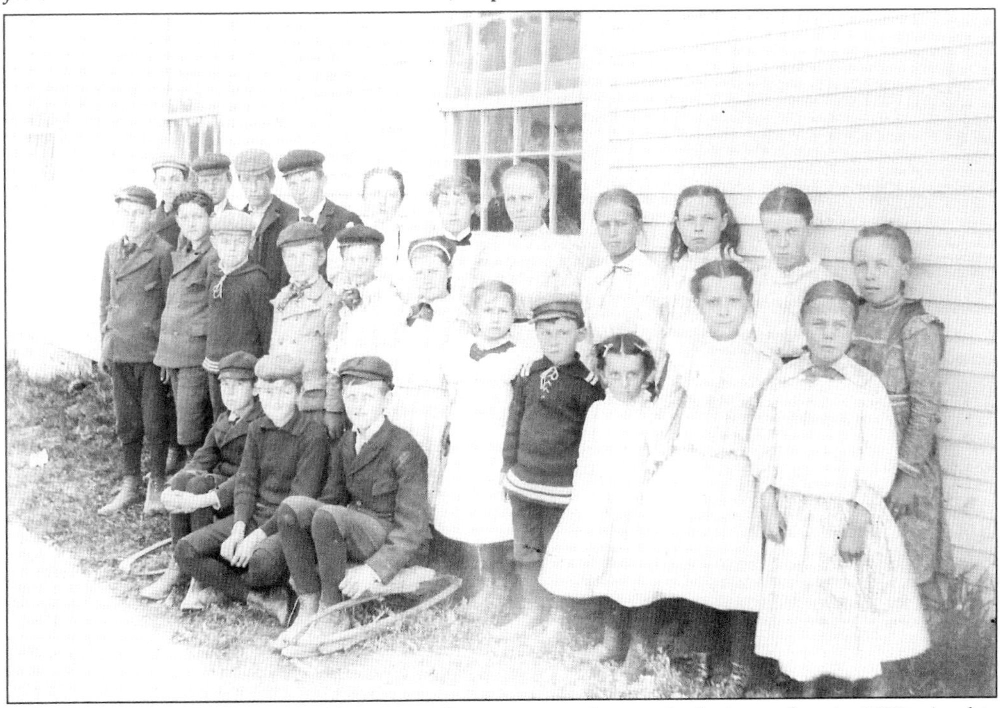

Children at the Village School having a class picture taken with their teacher in 1899. At this time there were seventeen school districts in Jefferson, each with its own building. The Village School was the largest, and in some years had as many as fifty pupils. (Ralph Bond)

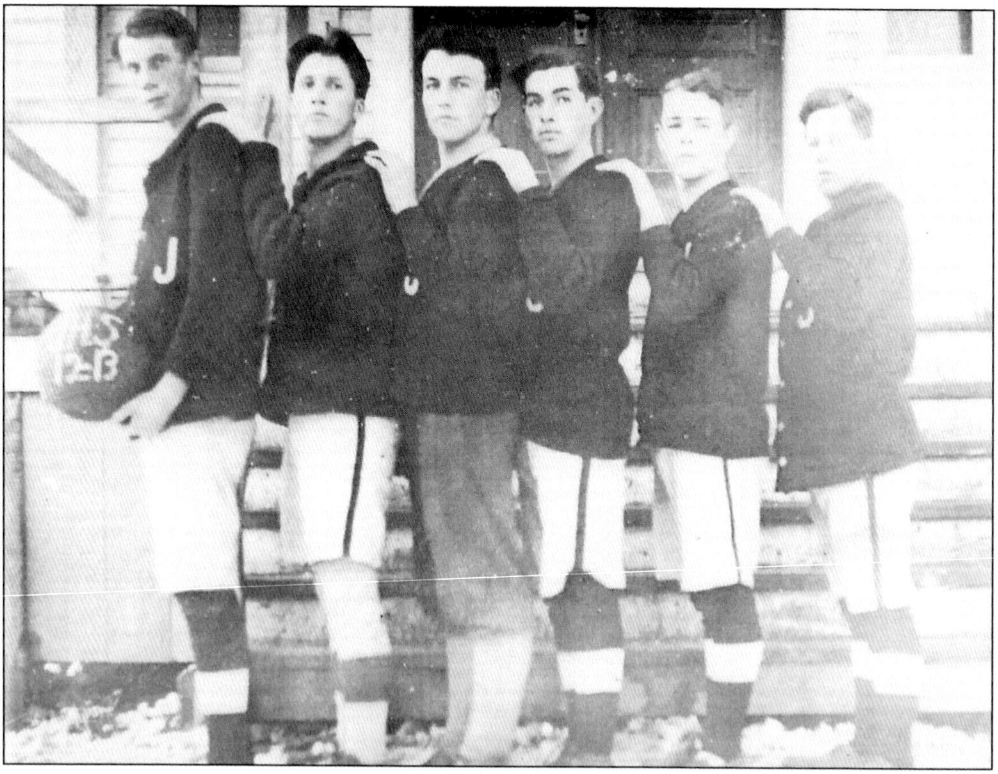
J
12-13

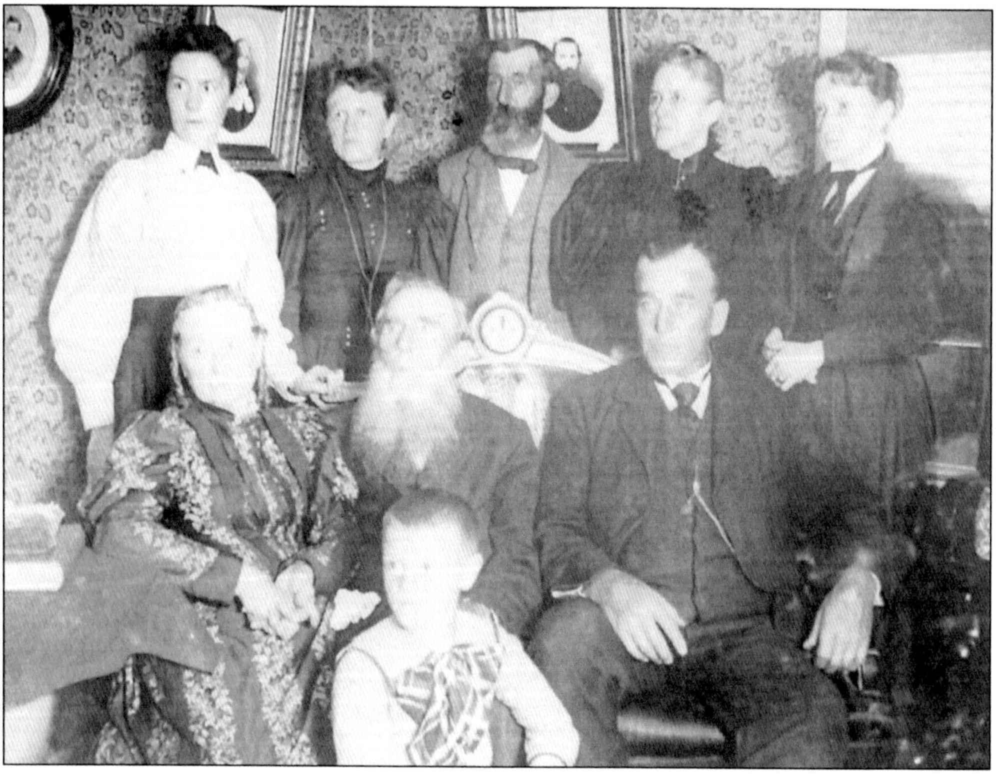

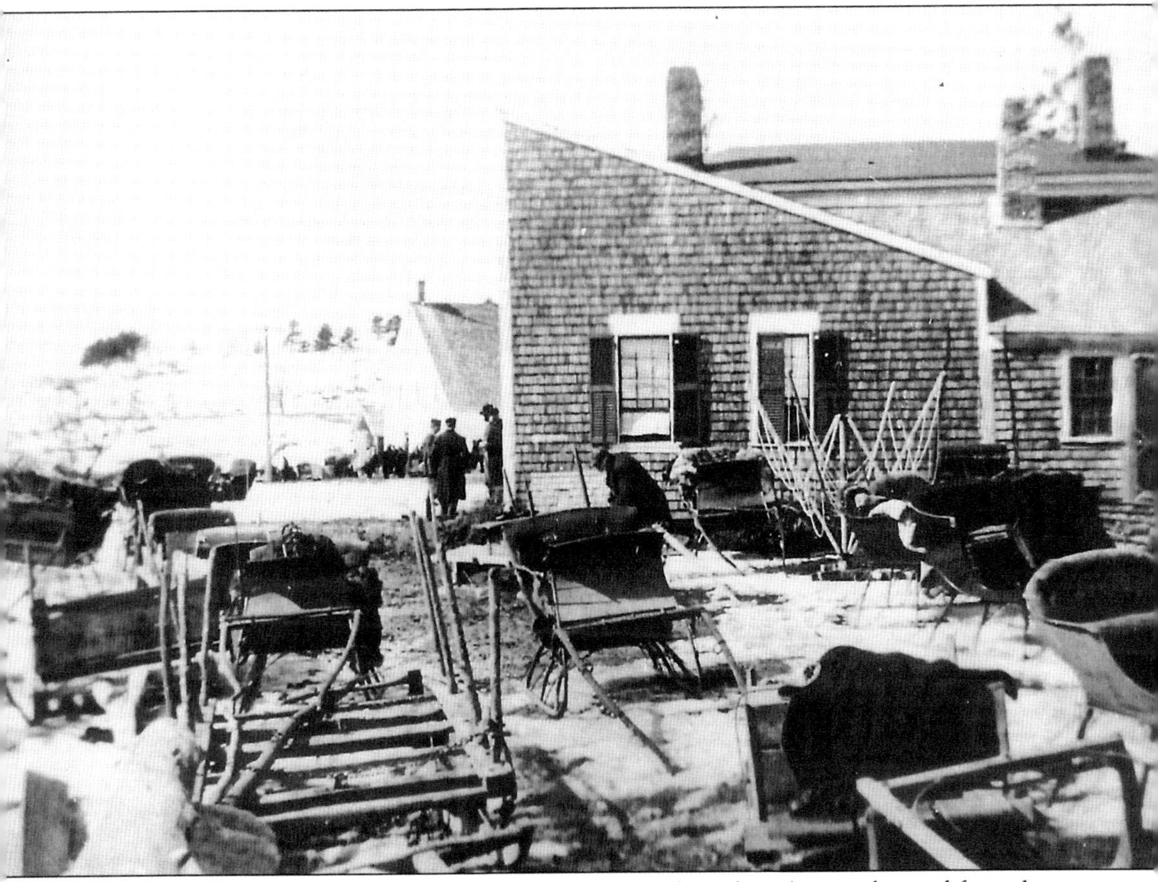

Judging from the number of sleighs parked at the Cunningham farm (across the road from the Town House), this town meeting in the 1920s was a well-attended event. When the town house parking area was full, Henry Cunningham allowed people to park their wagons and sleighs in his yard and to stable their horses in his barn. Since Jefferson did not began to plow its roads until 1932, most people used this method of transportation in the winter. The Jefferson Town House was built in 1869 and was last used for a town meeting in 1957. The building is now used by the Jefferson Historical Society. (Ralph Bond)

Opposite, top: In the winter, young people skated on the lake, skied on homemade skis, rode on "The Village Belle" bobsled down the hill through the village, and played basketball. This 1912/13 Jefferson High School team is made up of, from left to right: Harold Pitcher, ? Strout, Otto Turner, Ernest Bond, Earle Hodgkins, and Loren Sides. (Ralph Bond)

Opposite, bottom: Another winter activity was the singing school, taught for many years by Albert Richardson (man with the beard, seated). Meeting twice a week in the evening, members were taught concert singing and the rudiments of music for the sum of $2 for twenty-four lessons. On the last night of the school the group performed a free concert for village residents. (Ralph Bond)

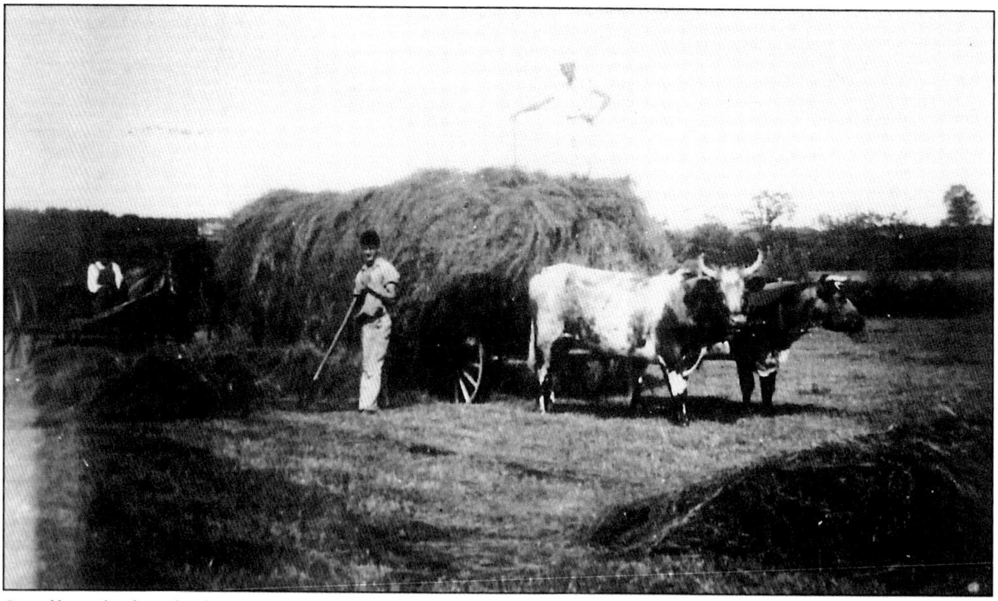

Small-scale family farming was the most common occupation around the head of the lake until the turn of the century, but by the mid-1900s several Jefferson families owned large successful farms and orchards. John R. MacDonald (center, shown haying with his oxen), farmed 85 acres of land near Clary Lake. Working with him are his father, John (left, on the hay rake), and his brother, Paul (now a retired district court judge). (Ralph Bond)

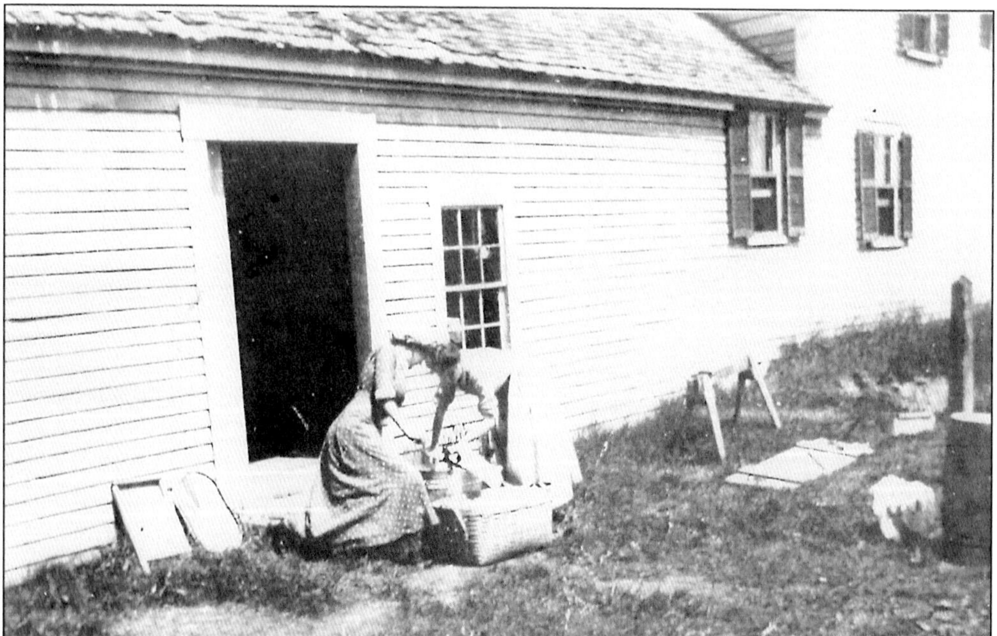

Women also did their share of work on the farm. Katie MacDonald and her sister, Florence MacMillan, are doing the weekly laundry on the steps of the MacDonald farm soon after the family bought the property in 1912. Using washboards and a hand wringer, and carrying the water from the well, the women worked long hours on washday. (Ralph Bond)

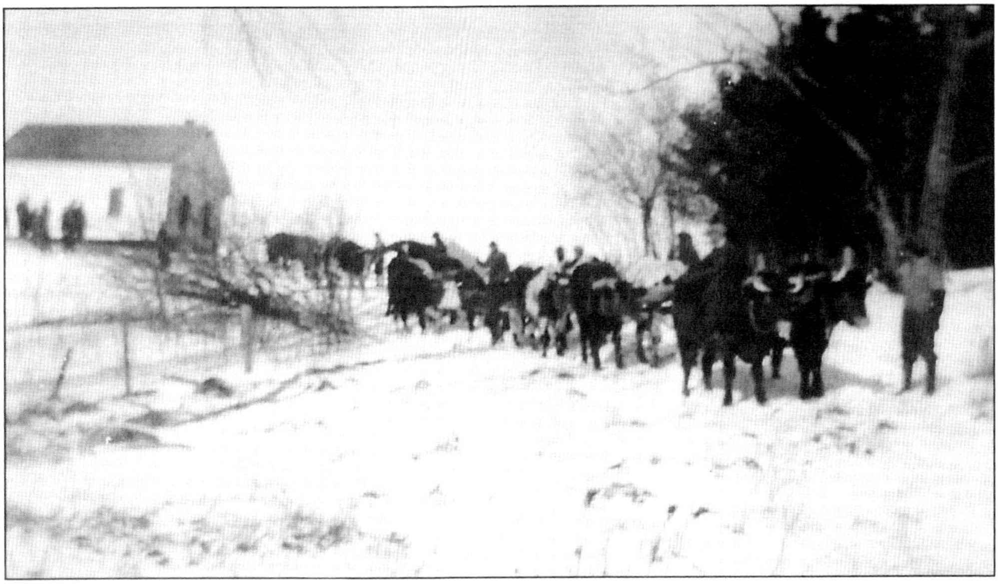

Henry Cunningham owned several teams of oxen which helped to move this house belonging to Roxie Benner in 1932. The house had to be moved onto the mill pond behind the Meserve Mill because it could not clear the mill's sawdust pipe which hung over the road. One of the skids broke and had to be replaced during the move, but it still took only two days to take the building to its present site on Route 126. (Ralph Bond)

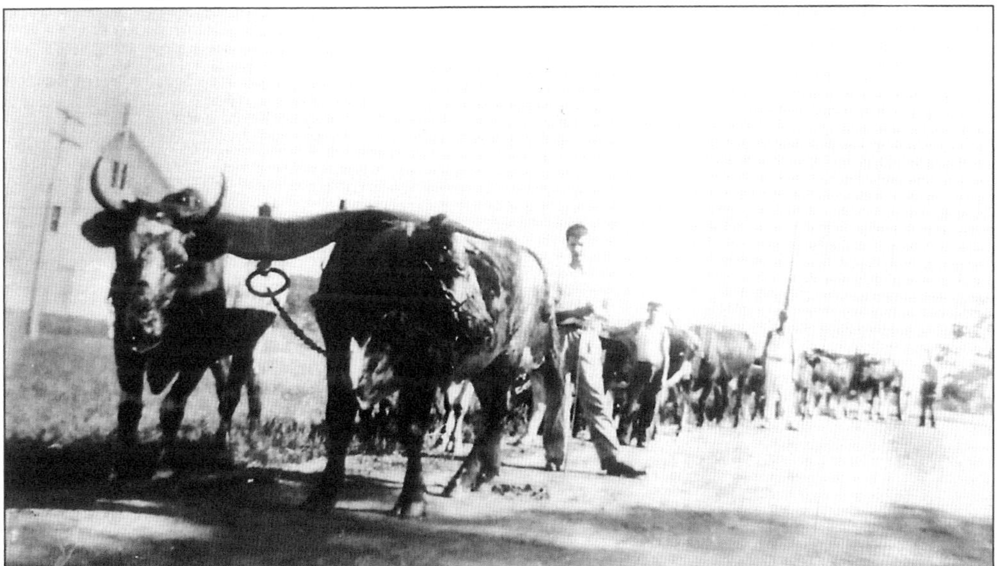

Every year Jefferson farmers drove their oxen to the Lincoln County Fair in Damariscotta. John MacDonald, Stuart Weatherhead, Walter Linscott, and John Weatherhead wait for more of Henry Cunningham's animals to join them as the group prepares to make the 14-mile trip down the Bunker Hill Road, c. 1937. The journey took four to six hours with two to three stops to water the animals at springs and brooks along the way. The route went past Lincoln Academy and through the Twin Villages, turning heads and inspiring local photographers. Once at the fairgrounds the cattle were shown in various judged events throughout the three-day fair. (Ralph Bond)

STATE OF MAINE.

IN THE YEAR OF OUR LORD ONE THOUSAND EIGHT HUNDRED AND SEVENTY-FOUR.

An Act to incorporate the Damariscotta Steamboat Company.

Be it enacted by the Senate and House of Representatives in Legislature assembled, as follows:

Section 1. H. K. Bond and C. M. Davis with their associates, are hereby incorporated a steamboat company by the name of the Damariscotta Steamboat Company, with a capital not to exceed three thousand dollars, for the purpose of navigating the Damariscotta lake, so called, by steam.

Section 2. Said corporation shall have all the rights and privileges usually conferred upon such corporations under the general laws of this state.

Section 3. The said corporation is hereby granted the right to navigate said lake for the period of fifteen years.

Section 4. This act shall take effect when approved.

IN HOUSE OF REPRESENTATIVES, February 26, 1874.

This bill having had three several readings, passed to be enacted.

W. W. Thomas Jr., *Speaker.*

In 1874, by an act of the Maine Legislature, the Damariscotta Steamboat Company was incorporated and granted the right to navigate the lake using steam-powered boats. The 53-ton *Queen of the Lake* was built in the same year, and the company transported passengers and freight from the head of the lake to Muscongus Bay, connecting with the Knox & Lincoln Railroad at the station near the Vannah farm. (Ralph Bond)

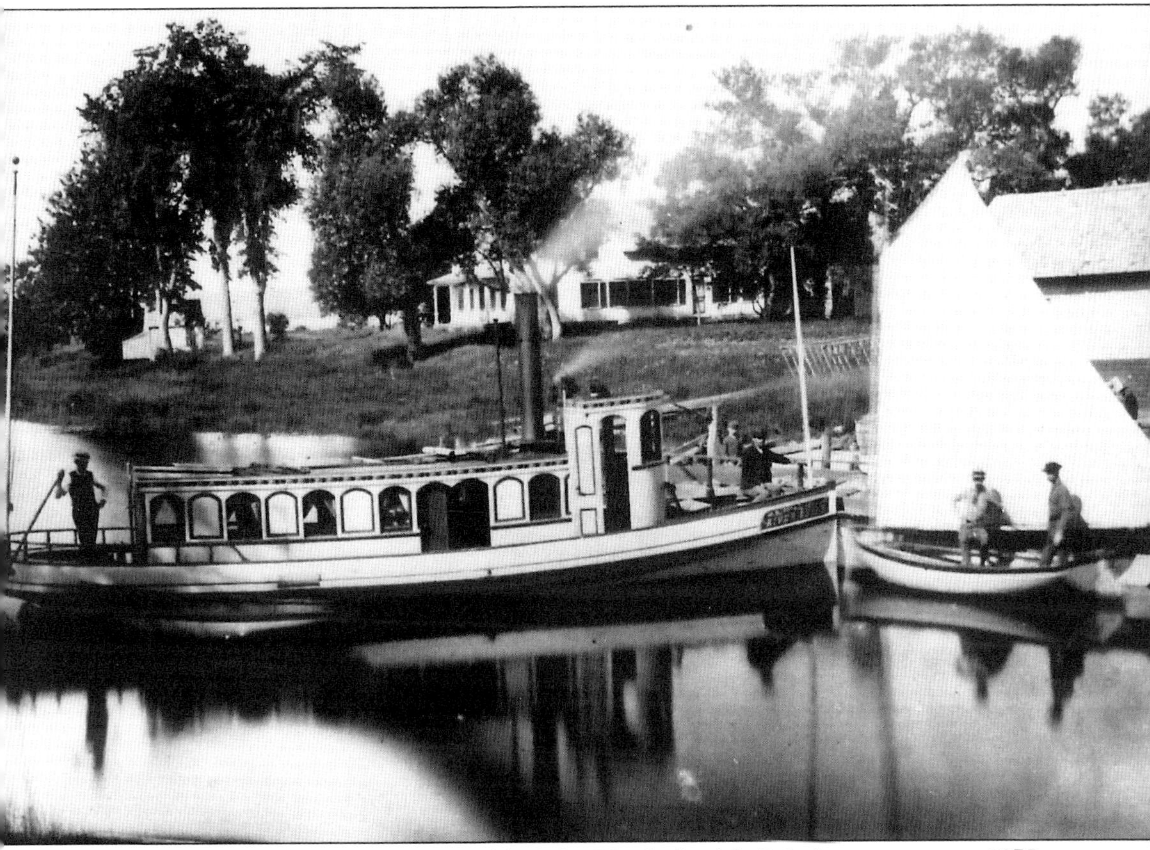

Two other steamers followed the *Queen of the Lake*. The *Lady of the Lake* began service in 1875, but was eventually moved to Great Salt Bay to take advantage of the coastal trade. The small, graceful *River Belle*, shown above at the dock on Davis Stream, was brought from Bangor in 1882 to provide transportation for guests at the hotel near the bridge. The little steamer spent only two years on the lake before also being moved to Great Salt Bay. (Ralph Bond)

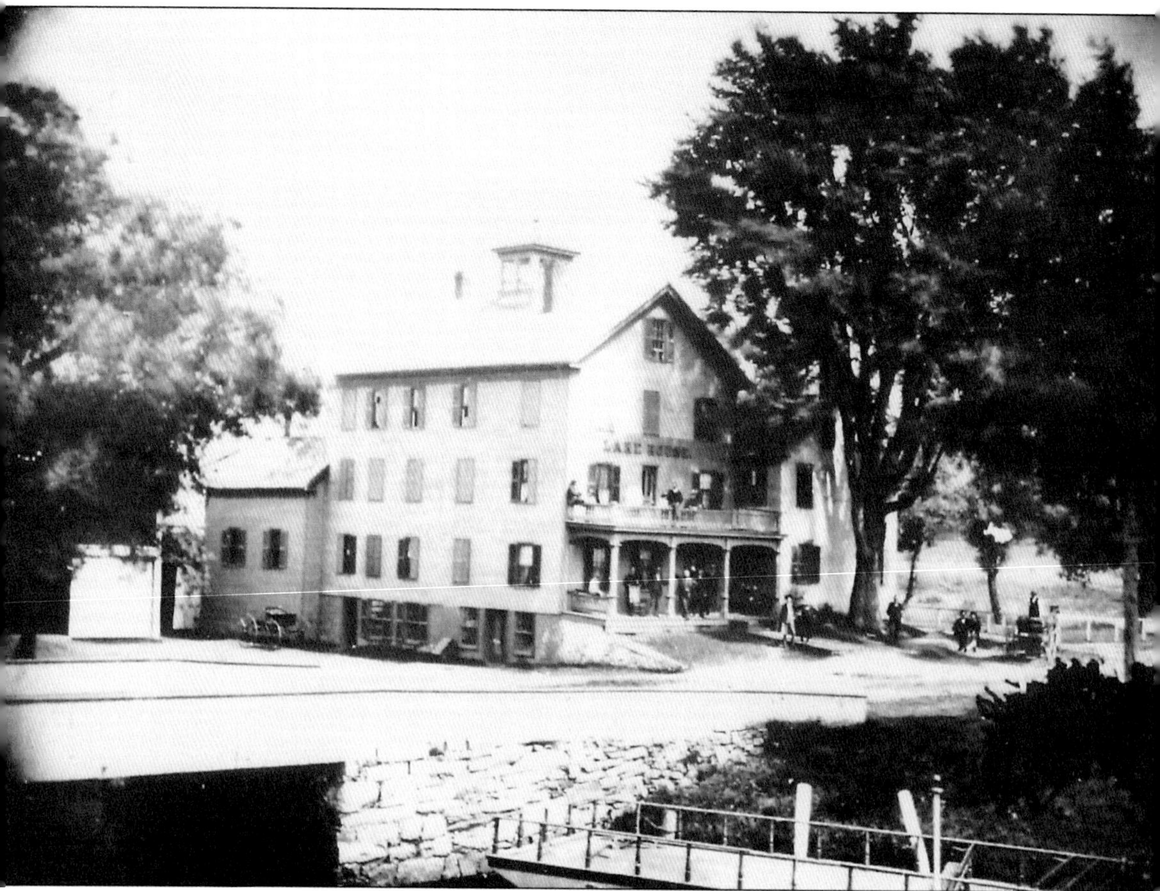

Mr. Brown's Lake House was actually an addition to Haskell's Tavern, originally built c. 1850. Guests at the hotel arrived via the Knox & Lincoln Railroad which made a stop at Muscongus Bay. They were then transported up the lake by a steamer. Note the barge in the foreground. This was used for carrying additional freight and occasionally passengers. The steamboats were also used for excursions, picnics, and for transportation to the religious camp meetings in the Glendon section of Nobleboro. (Ralph Bond)

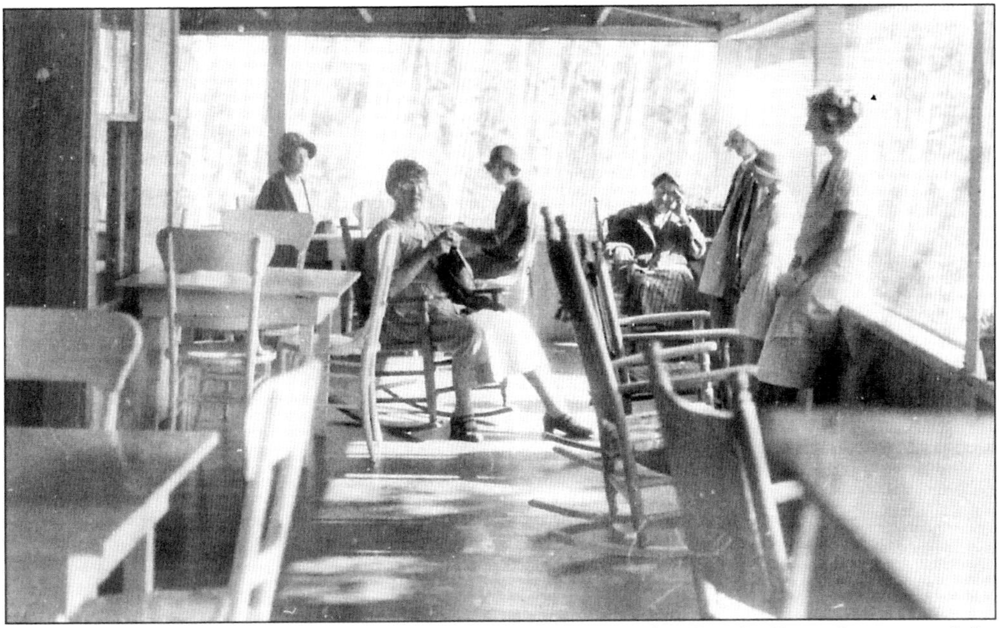

Another establishment catering to summer visitors was the Beach Farm Inn owned by George Kennedy. Guests at the inn relax on the sunny back porch as they enjoy the beauty of Damariscotta Lake in the 1930s. Mary Richardson, in the foreground, talks with Florence Kennedy, the owner's daughter, at the far right. (Ralph Bond)

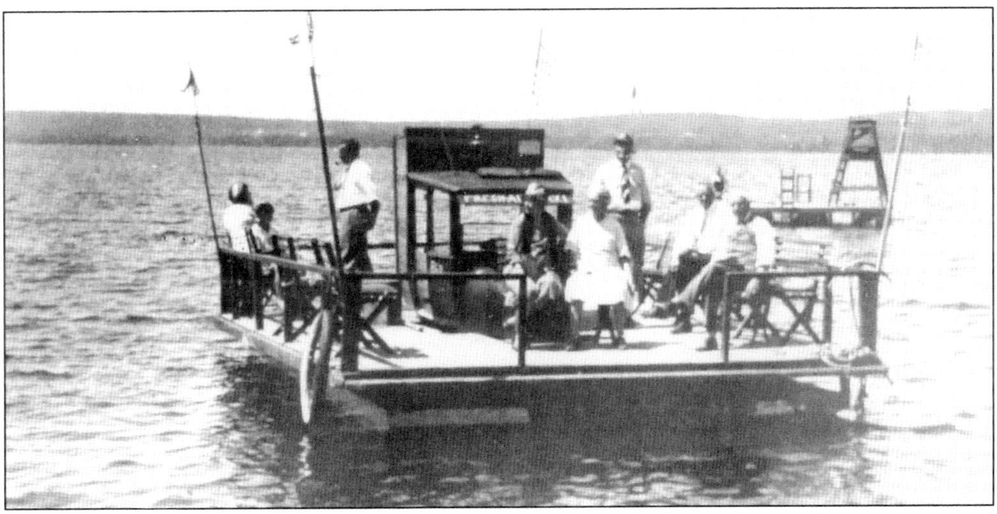

The "Fresh Air Taxi," an invention of George Kennedy (in the hat and striped tie), was created for the pleasure of his guests at the Beach Farm Inn and anyone else who dared to climb aboard. Fashioned from a pair of pontoons attached to a platform, and topped with the engine and cab of a Model T (shown in the center), the barge was often seen chugging through the waters at the head of the lake in the 1930s. (Ralph Bond)

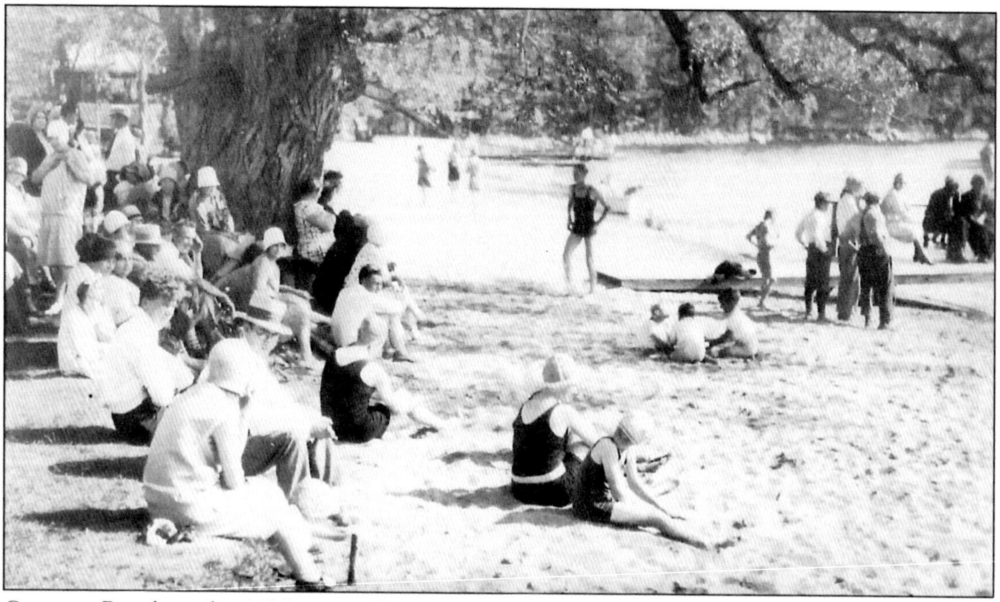

Crescent Beach in the 1920s was a favourite spot to cool off on a hot summer day. Swimming, boating, and picnicking under the old sycamore tree were activities that entertained generations of families who lived and vacationed near the head of the lake. (Ralph Bond)

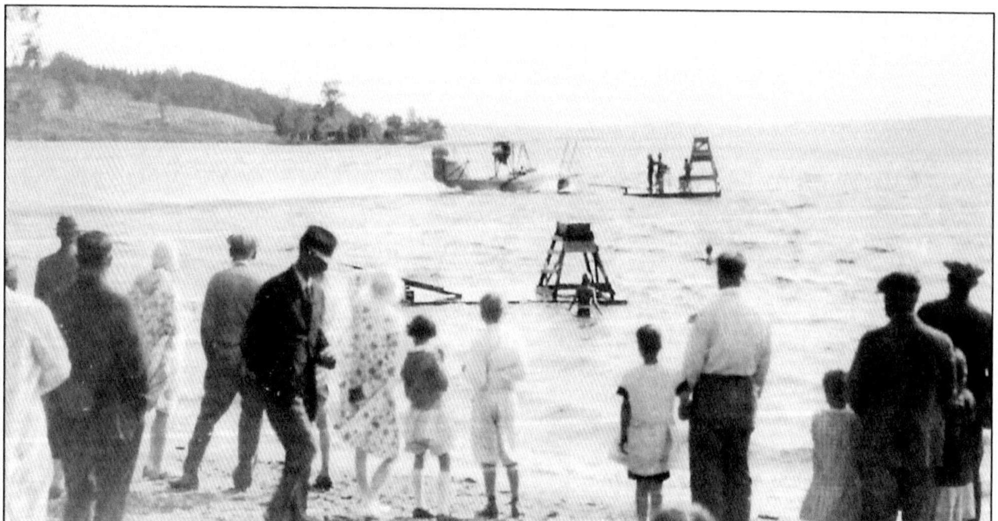

Seeing an airplane take off on the lake fascinated this beach crowd, *c.* 1930. Crescent Beach had been used by the public for many years and had passed through several owners before being sold to the State of Maine, which now operates it as Damariscotta Lake State Park. (Ralph Bond)

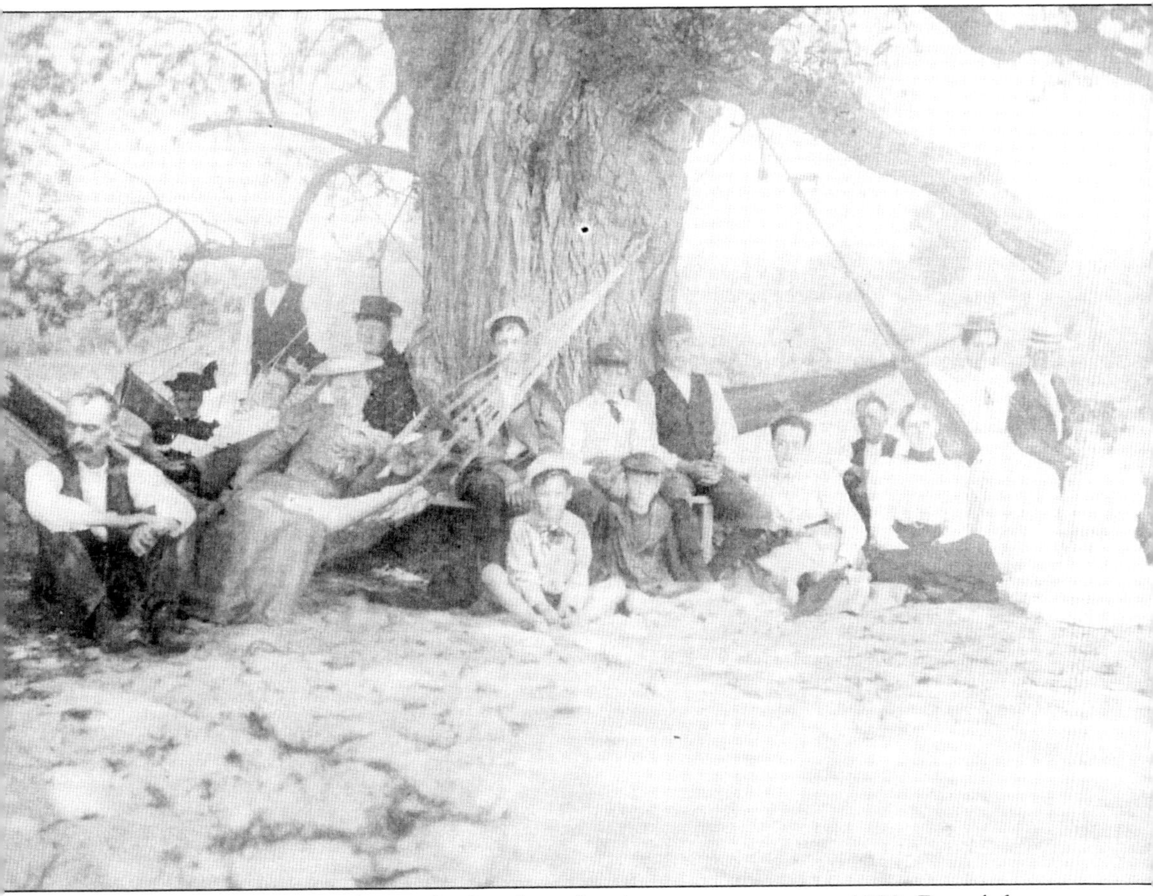

Local residents enjoying a day at the beach under the sycamore tree, c. 1900. From left to right are: Marden Johnson (who was the village blacksmith), Eva Bond, Clara Jackson, Herbert Bond, Emilie Richardson, Jennie Johnson, Ralph Jackson, Foster Jackson, Frank E. Richardson, Amanda Bond, Samuel J. Jackson, Emmy Sidelinger, Ina Avery, Samuel Bond, and unknown. The two young boys seated in front are Prescott Bond and Forrest Bond. (Ralph Bond)

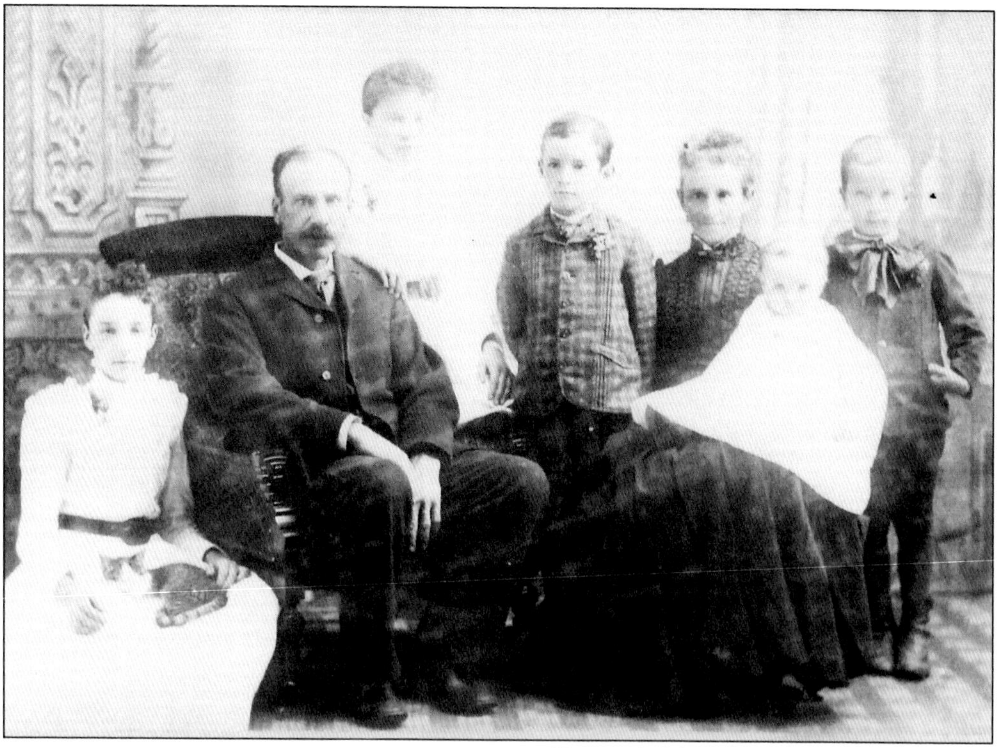

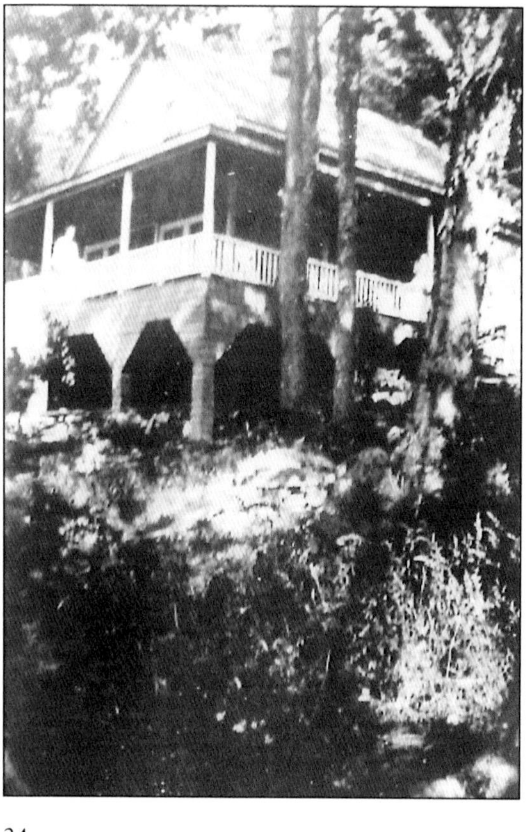

Descended from one of Jefferson's earliest settlers, the Bond family name is a familiar one in town. In this photograph taken in 1892 S. Herbert Bond and his wife, Eva, pose for a family portrait with their five children. From left to right are: Amanda, S. Herbert, Kate, Auraldo, Eva (holding Prescott), and Forrest. (Ralph Bond)

When Eva Bond had this cottage built at the head of the lake in 1912, she had no idea that it would be the harbinger of a new industry for the town. At a time when farms were being abandoned, mills shut down, and the population was declining, vacation cottages brought increasing activity and income to this part of the lake. (Ralph Bond)

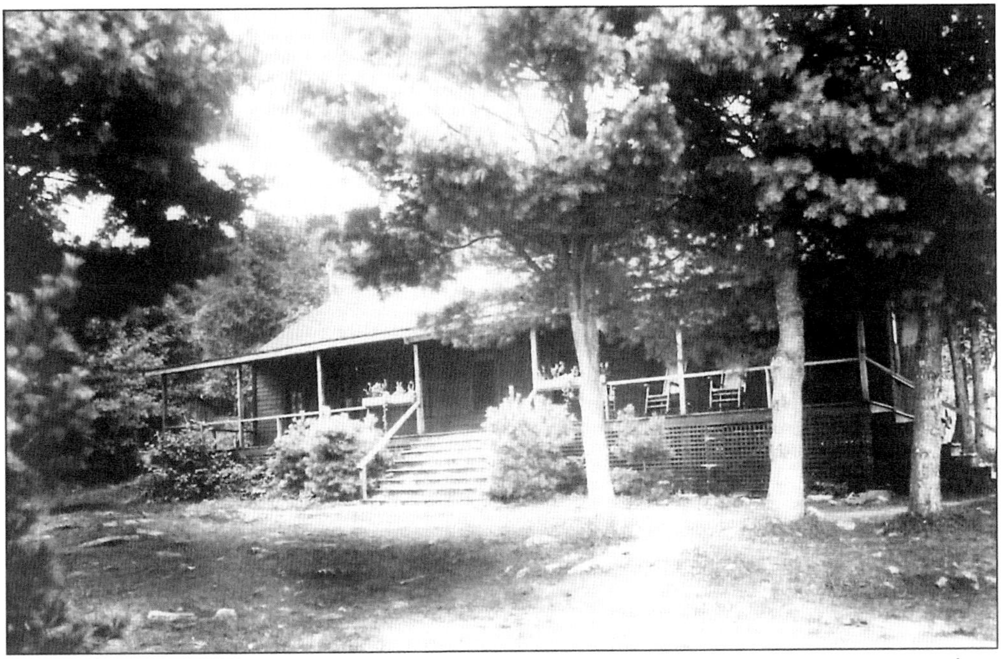

Sunset Lodge on the east shore was owned and operated by Chandler and Helen Stetson for a number of years after they purchased the property in 1928. They expanded the lodge and added several cabins to serve the large numbers of visitors who chose to spend some quiet days and nights along Damariscotta Lake.

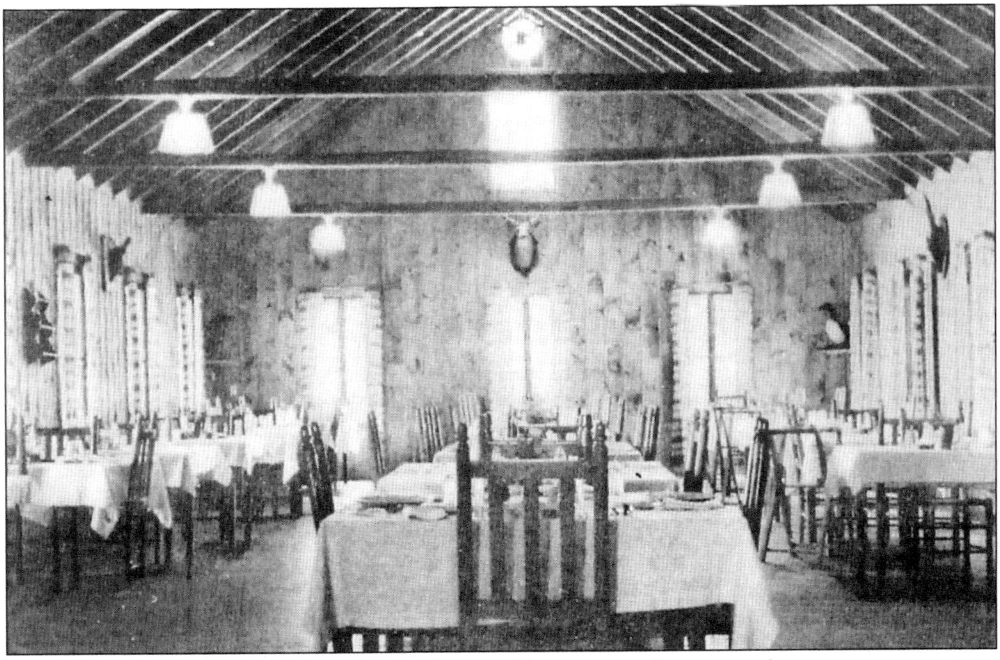

The rustic dining room at Sunset Lodge could accommodate several guests at one time. (Ralph Bond)

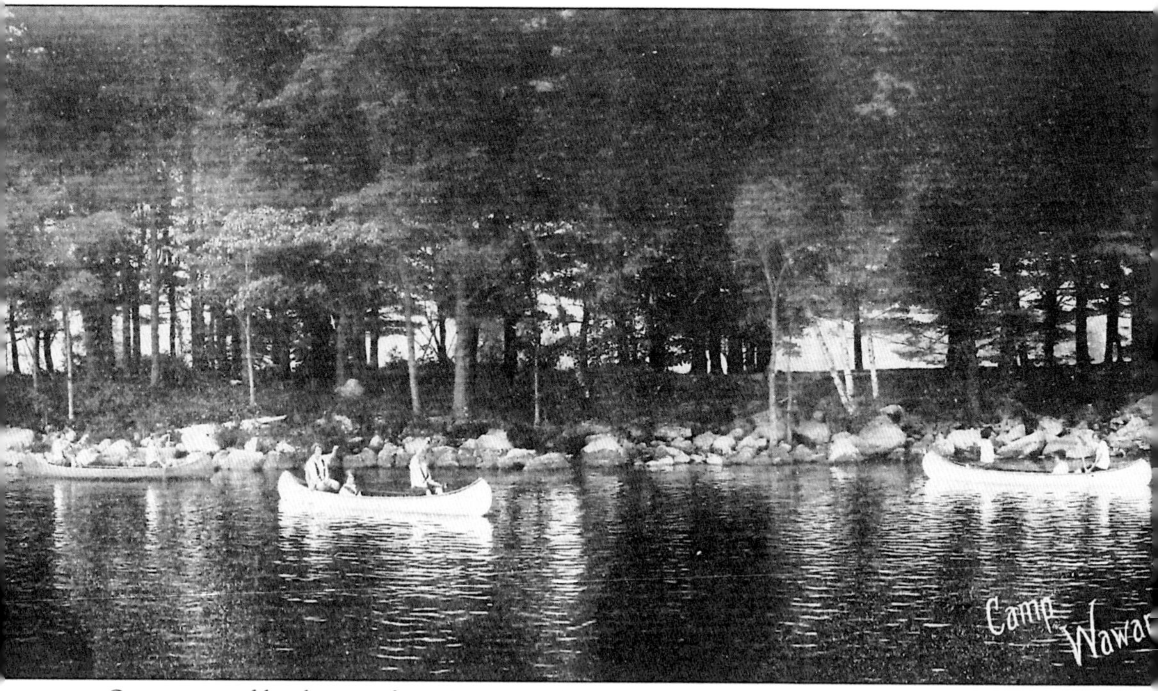

On a point of land across from Sunset Lodge on Damariscotta Lake's western shore, Delbert and Emma Andrews established one of the lake's best-known camps for young people. Camp Wawanock opened in 1922 for girls, and a year later Damariscotta Camp began its first season with the arrival of ten boys.

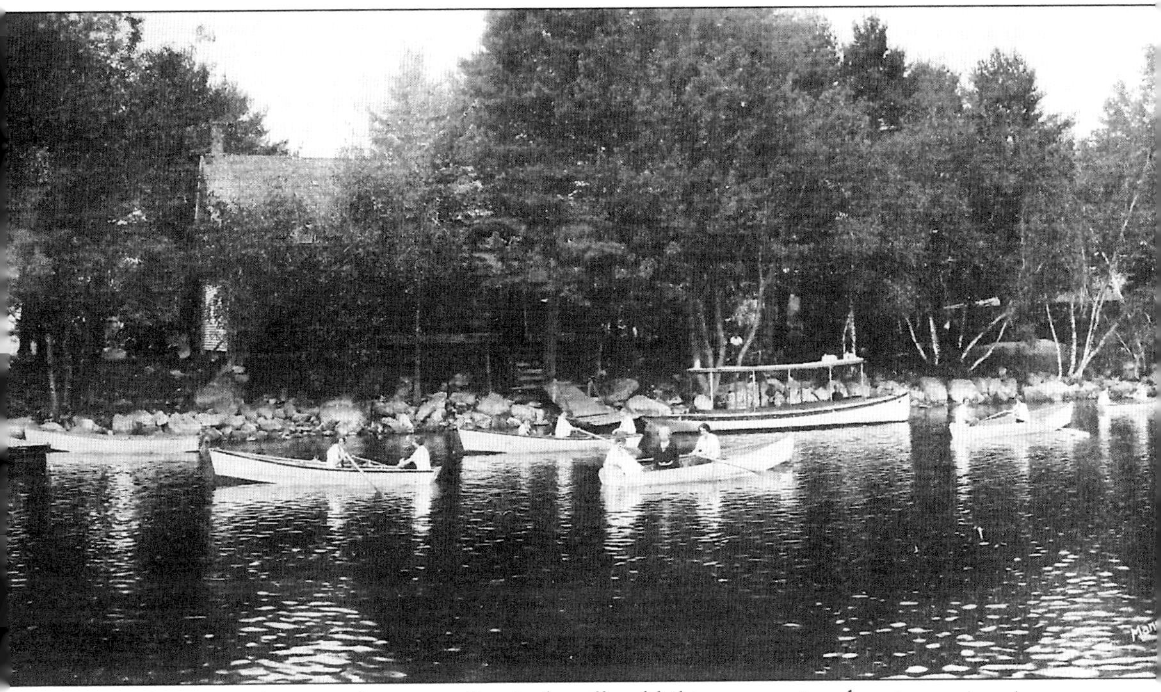

Wavus Camps, as they were known collectively, offered hiking, canoeing, boating, swimming, horseback riding, fishing, tennis, team sports, and crafts. The old Corner school was moved on the ice to serve as the camp kitchen and dining room. A main lodge, rustic cabins, tennis courts, and an outdoor chapel were also part of the accommodations. (Ralph Bond)

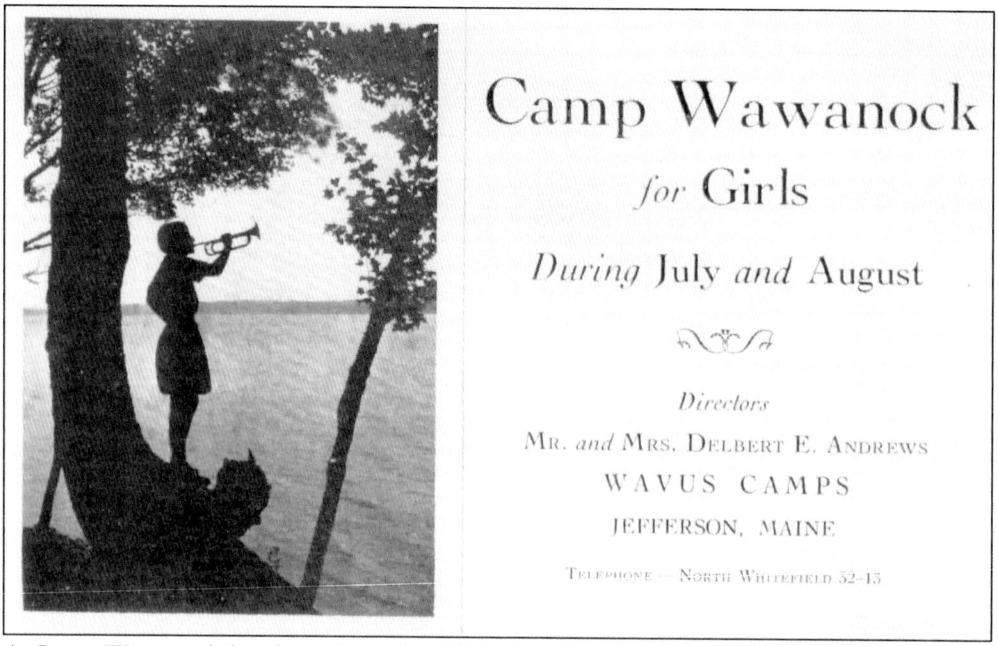
Camp Wawanock

for Girls

During July *and* August

Directors

Mr. *and* Mrs. Delbert E. Andrews

WAVUS CAMPS

JEFFERSON, MAINE

Telephone — North Whitefield 32-13

A Camp Wawanock brochure from the 1920s describes the summer program to prospective campers. After detailing a dozen activities designed to keep young people busy, the pamphlet hastens to add, "if there was nothing more to do than what is offered by this interesting old lake, with its hidden coves and mysterious inlets and tempting islands, the time would be freely occupied." Many a camper went home with new friends and wonderful memories of a summer spent on Damariscotta Lake. (Ralph Bond)

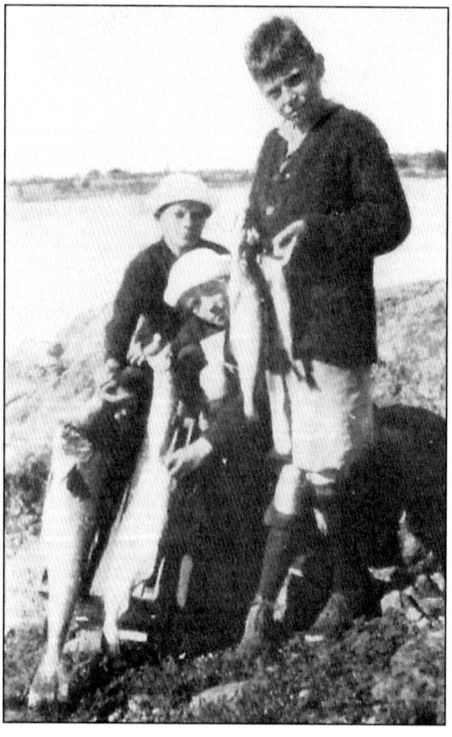

These boys from Damariscotta Camp proudly display the results of their very successful fishing trip. They often caught perch, black bass, and pickerel from the camp scow *Ke-ton-go* which was towed out to the fishing grounds off Wavus Point. The boys slept on the boat overnight and cast their lines over the side early in the morning for the best fishing of the day. (Ralph Bond)

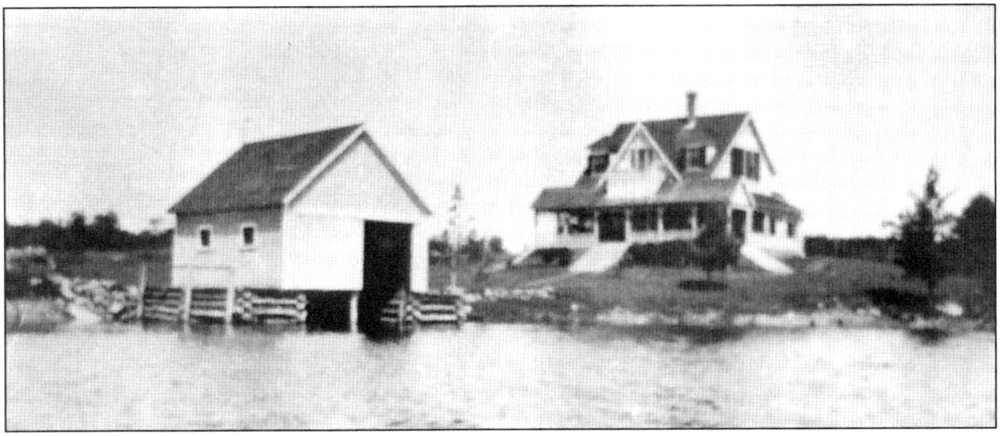

The Frank Pratt cottage at Weeks' Point (now known as Chimney Point) accepted summer guests around the turn of the century. It burned several years later and was replaced by another cottage which had a beautiful stone fireplace and chimney. After that cottage eventually burned, only the stonework remained; and when Bill Prizer bought the land in the 1950s for a boys camp, he built the lodge around the existing fireplace and chimney. Both the camp and the western shoreland at the Narrows have been known as Chimney Point ever since. (Arthur Jones)

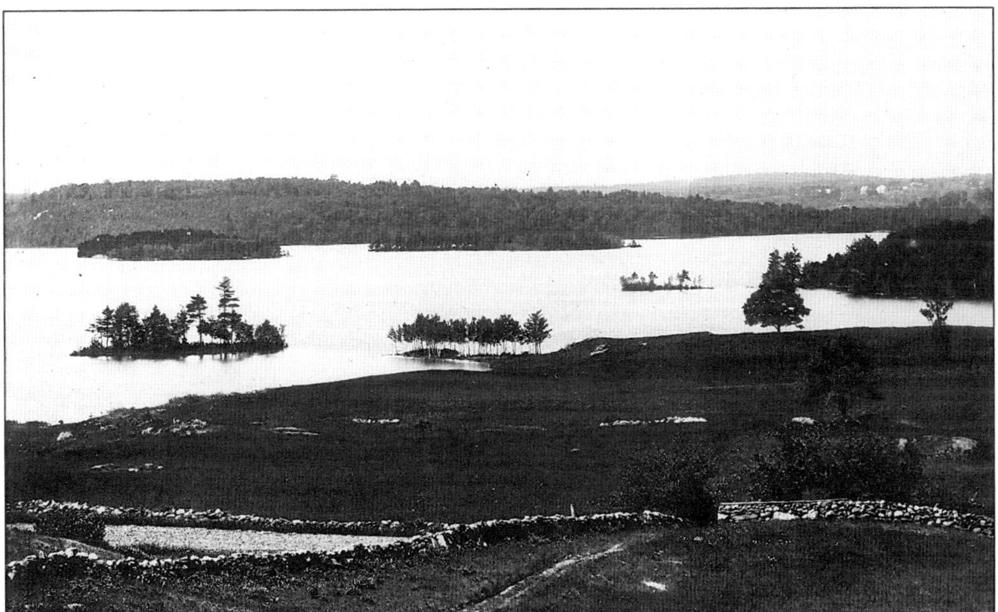

Moody's Cove in North Nobleboro with its adjacent fields and stone walls is reminiscent of a way of life that has all but disappeared on Damariscotta Lake. Family farms occupied most of the land along the shore at the turn of the century and much of this acreage was cleared to the waterline for hay and pasture. (Arthur Jones)

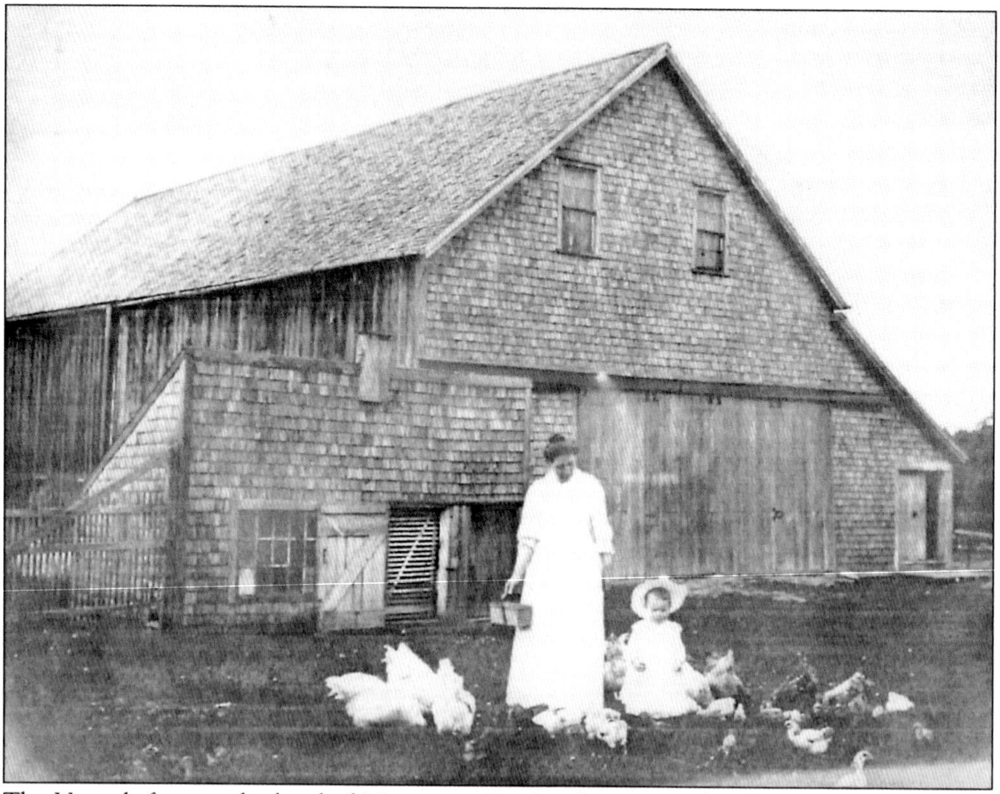

The Vannah farm at the head of Muscongus Bay has been owned and operated by the same family for five generations. Henrietta Vannah and her nephew, Hudson, feed a flock of chickens in front of the original barn in 1910. Three years later the barn burned to the ground after being struck by lightning. Fires have destroyed several farm buildings over the years in Nobleboro. Hudson Vannah recalls seeing eight fires burning at once from the hill behind his farm after an especially severe thunderstorm. (Hudson Vannah)

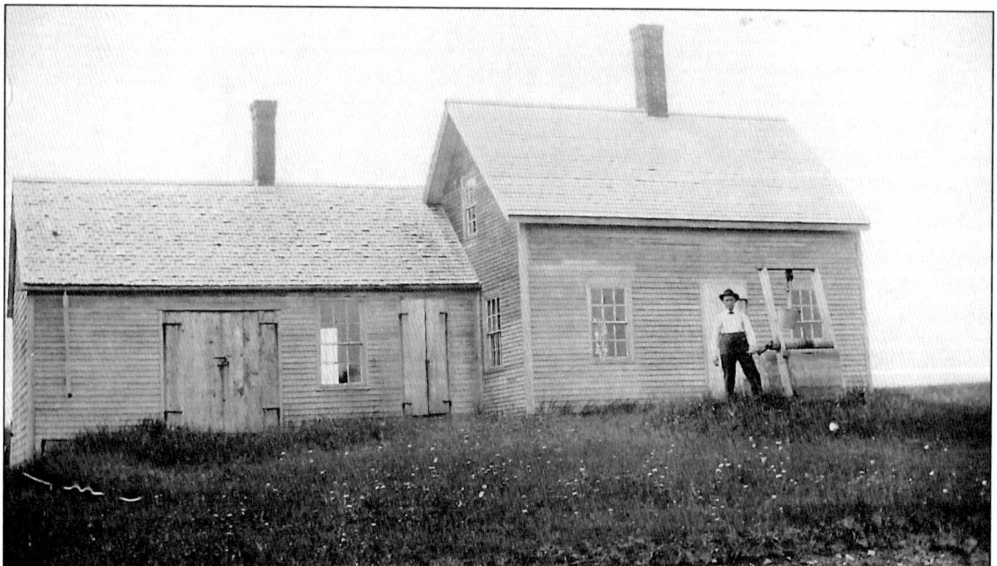

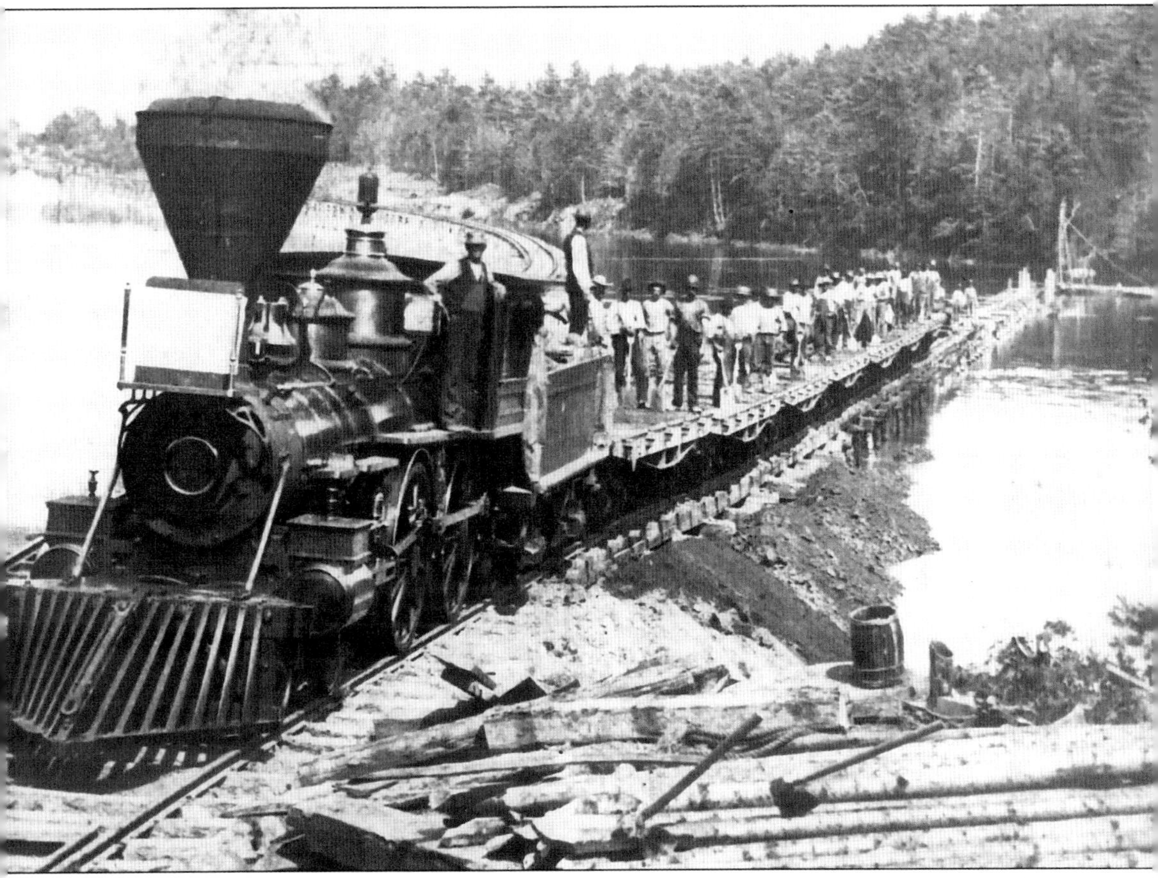

Construction workers labor on the extension of the Knox & Lincoln Railroad through the Great Heath at the head of Muscongus Bay, c. 1870. This was a particularly difficult section to build because of the swamp and numerous sinkholes. William Vannah had to rebuild at least one section of roadbed that had sunk overnight. The railway took several years to complete, but when it officially opened in 1871, it became a welcome link to the world beyond Lincoln County for local residents. It enabled farmers to send their produce to distant markets; it provided transportation to Boston for ice cut on the lake for a time in the nineteenth century; it enabled lumber milled in Jefferson and hauled down the lake on scows to be sent to Bath and beyond; and it brought passengers and vacationers to the little station where they could board a steamboat and be transported to various destinations on the lake. (Nobleboro Historical Society, Ivan Flye Collection)

Opposite, bottom: William Vannah (grandfather of Hudson Vannah) stands in front of his brother's house across the road from the Vannah farm. William was a versatile man who worked at a number of trades. In addition to being a farmer he built at least one of Nobleboro's one-room schoolhouses; he was captain of the *Queen of the Lake*, the steamboat running from Muscongus to Jefferson; and he built miles of right of way for the Knox & Lincoln Railroad which ran through his property. (Hudson Vannah)

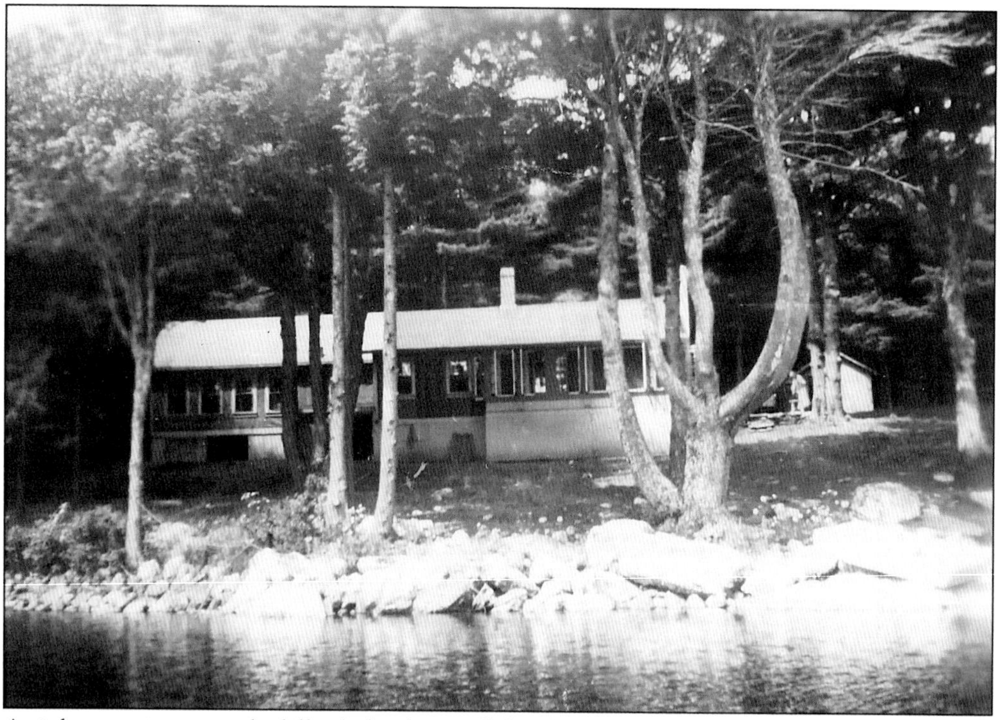

As it became increasingly difficult for the small family farms to succeed, many farmers sold their land, which had suddenly become more desirable for cottages. By the 1940s cottages and camps, such as this one owned by Ed and Inez Denny on the East Neck, became very popular. (Carolyn Reny)

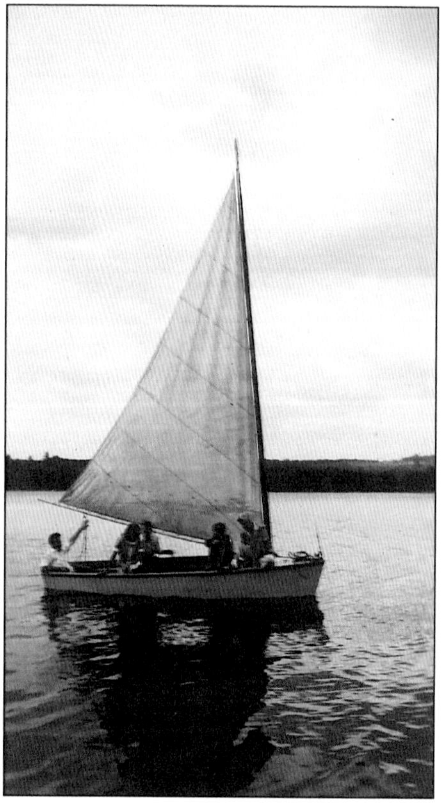

The various types of recreation possible on Damariscotta Lake created many fond memories for those who spent time there in the summer. Here, Ed Denny takes his daughter and a group of her college friends for a sail on Muscongus Bay, c. 1943. (Carolyn Reny)

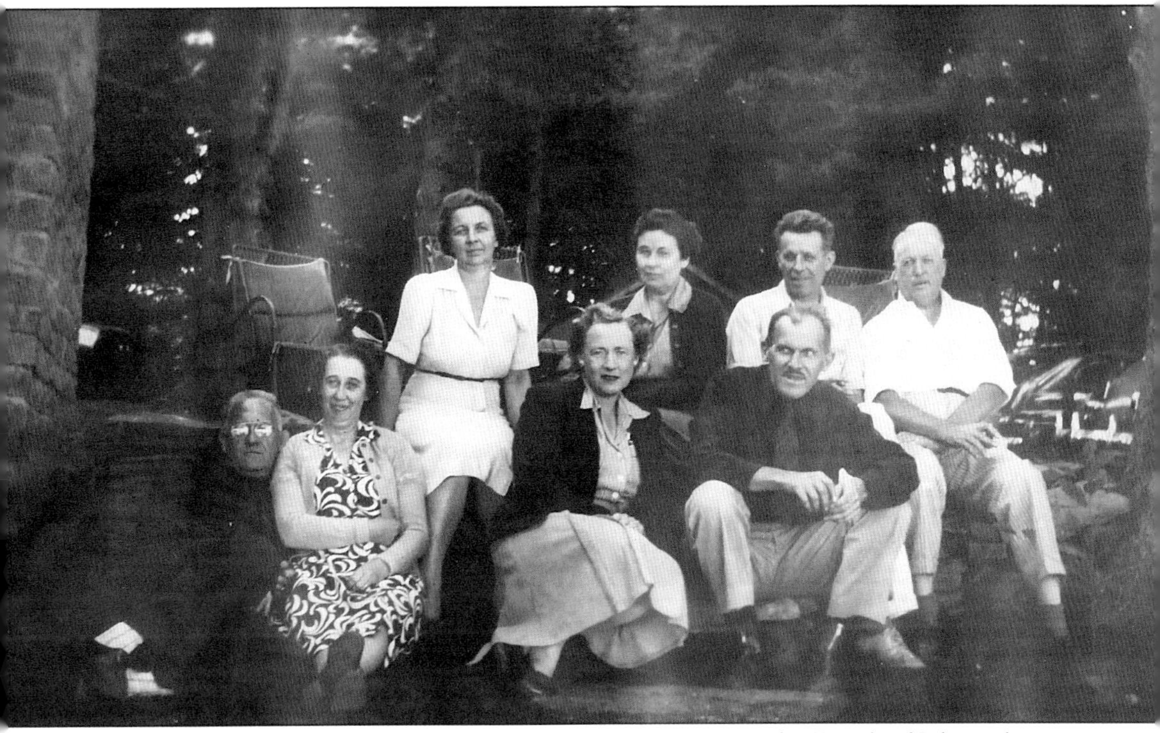

The Dennys often entertained family and friends at their cottage. The Fourth of July, with its traditional menu of salmon and fresh peas, was always enjoyed by their guests as Inez Denny was an especially good cook. This group of people from Newcastle and Damariscotta look comfortable after just such a meal. From left to right are: (front row) Linwood "Mutt" Pierce, Ella Pierce, Martha Griffin, and Maurice "Jake" Day; (back row) Gladys Page, Bea Day, Ed Denny, and Harold Page. (Carolyn Reny)

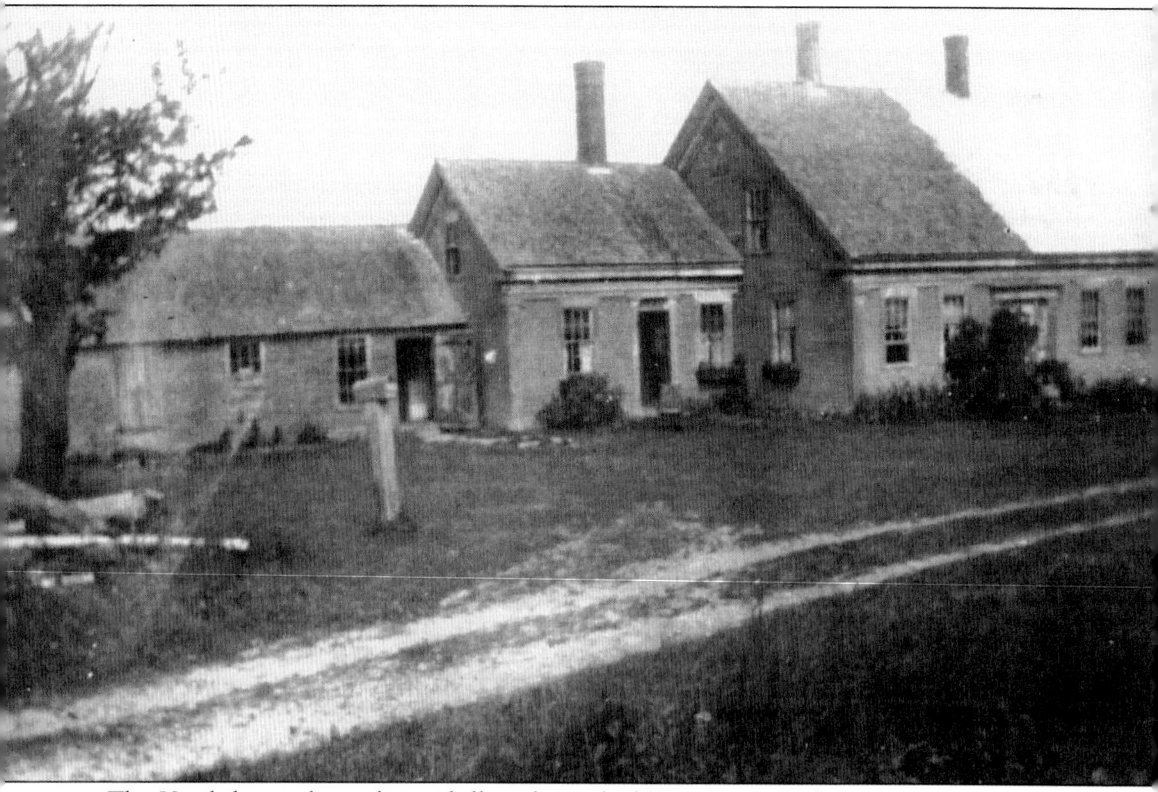

The Hatch house, located on a hill at the end of West Neck, had a view across the lake to Bunker Hill. It was inherited by two brothers whose families did not get along, so the house was completely separated through the center hall. Note that one brother has recently reshingled his half of the house. Purchased by the Kennedy family in the 1920s, the farmhouse and adjoining waterfront became Camp Kieve, a summer camp for boys. The farmhouse is still used for offices at Camp Kieve. (Arthur Jones)

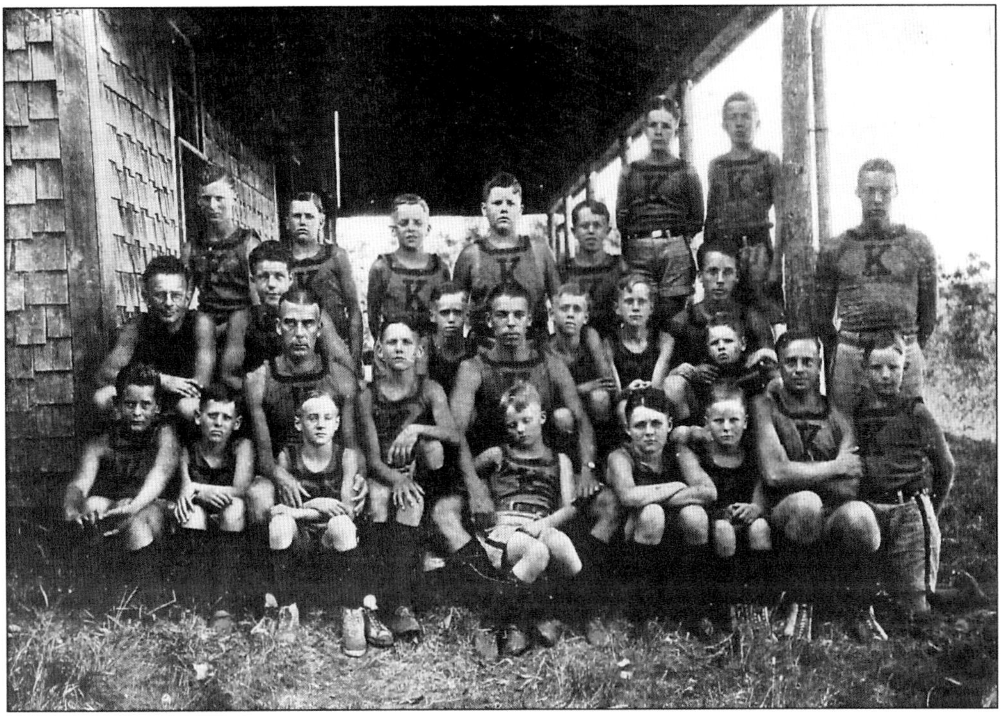

Campers and staff pose for a group photograph in 1926, the year Camp Kieve opened. Always maintaining high standards, the Kieve program emphasizes personal responsibility, cooperation, and healthy decision-making in the midst of summer-camp fun. (Camp Kieve)

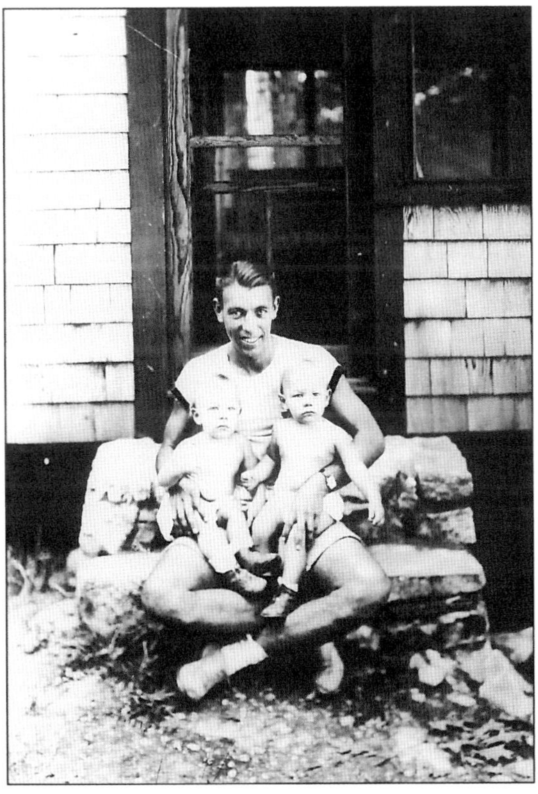

Camp Kieve's founder, Donald B. Kennedy, sits with his twin sons, Dick and Don, in front of one of the cabins in 1932. Dick served as Camp Kieve's director from 1959 to 1991, and has now turned over the day-to-day operations to his son Henry, while still maintaining an active role in the camp's innovative educational programs. (Camp Kieve)

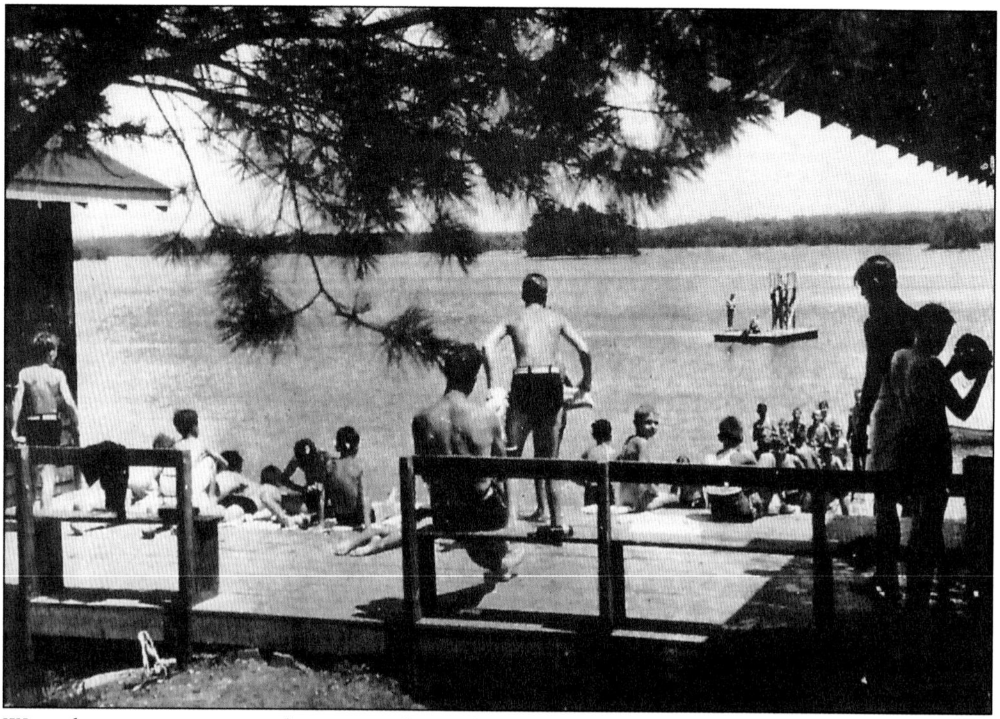

Waterfront activities are always popular with boys camping in Maine. Swimming, canoeing, sailing, and fishing occupy much of their time on hot days in July and August. This photograph was taken *c.* 1940. (Camp Kieve)

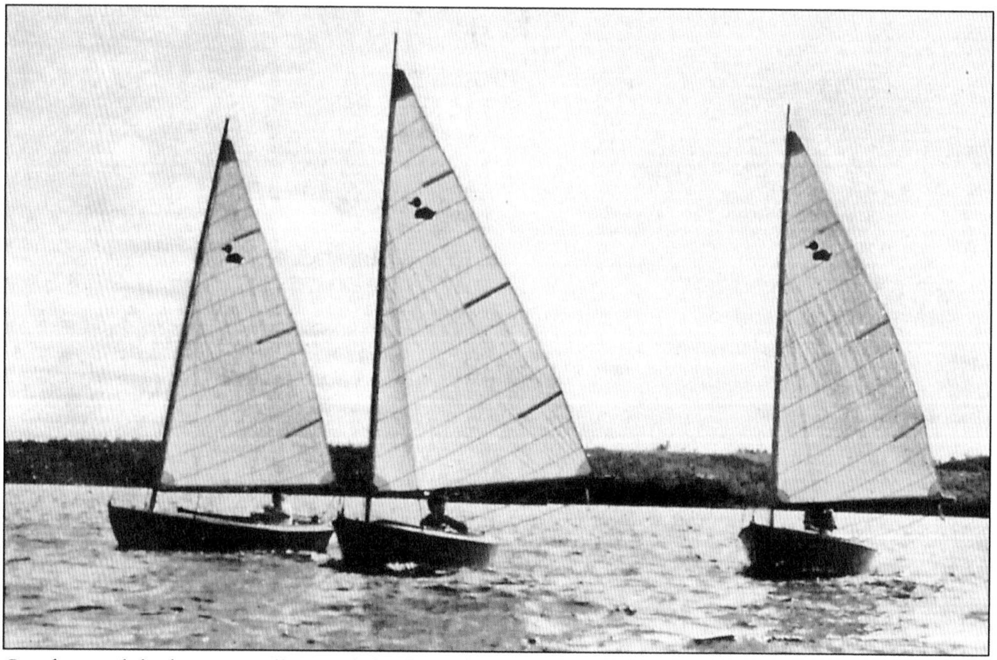

Catching a lake breeze, sailboats glide through the waters of Muscongus Bay as Kieve boys learn the fundamentals of sailing. These three Gosling boats were used constantly because they could be easily handled by beginners, according to the 1944 *Kieve Yearbook*. (Camp Kieve)

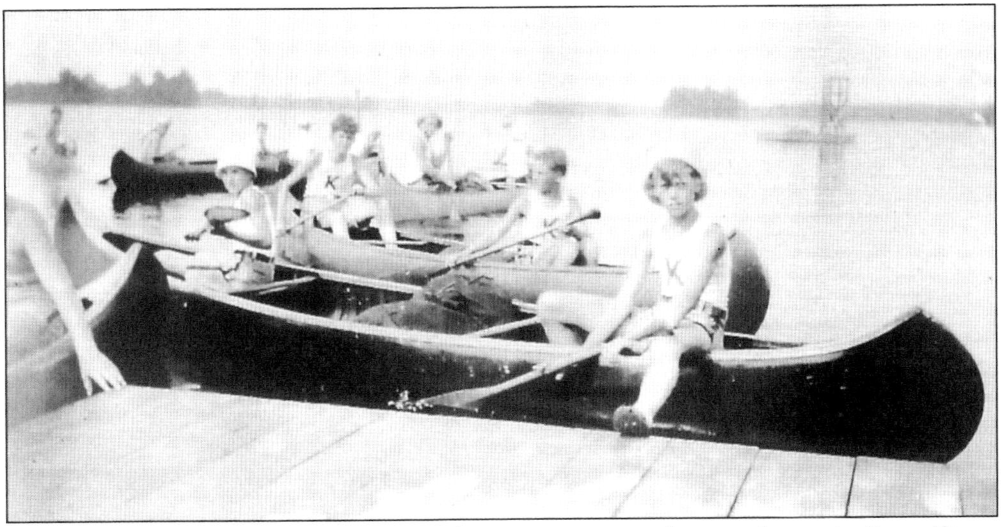

Canoe trips down the Damariscotta were always an important feature of a stay in Camp Kieve. With their gear carefully stowed, these boys prepare to embark on a voyage that will take them down the lake, through the portage at Damariscotta Mills, across Great Salt Bay (including a run through Johnny Orr), and down the river to an overnight encampment, perhaps at Fort Island at the Narrows in Boothbay. (Camp Kieve)

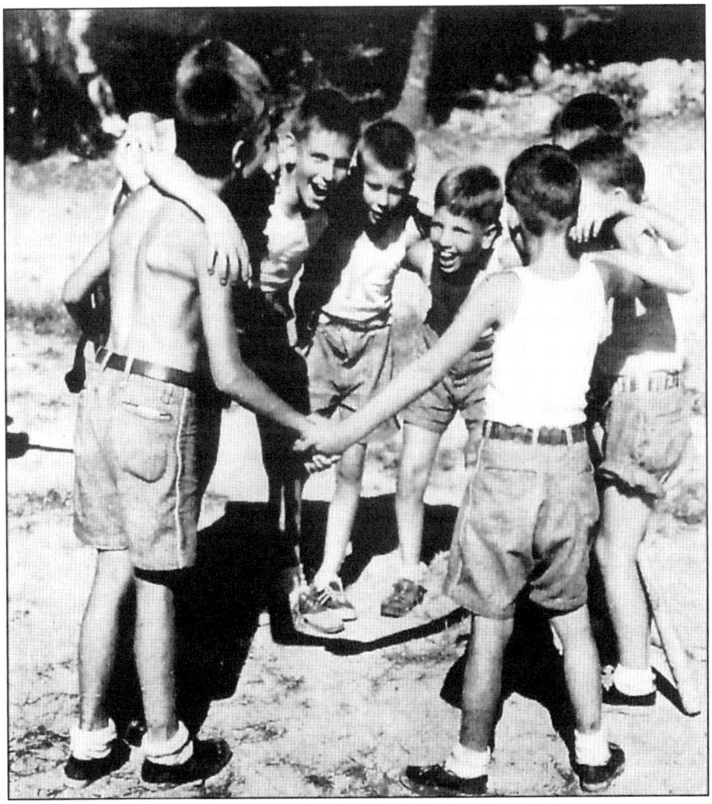

Baseball, tennis, archery, and crafts kept campers busy on shore. These happy teammates huddle en route to a win in the summer of 1944, the year there were no playoffs because of several days of rainy weather. (Camp Kieve)

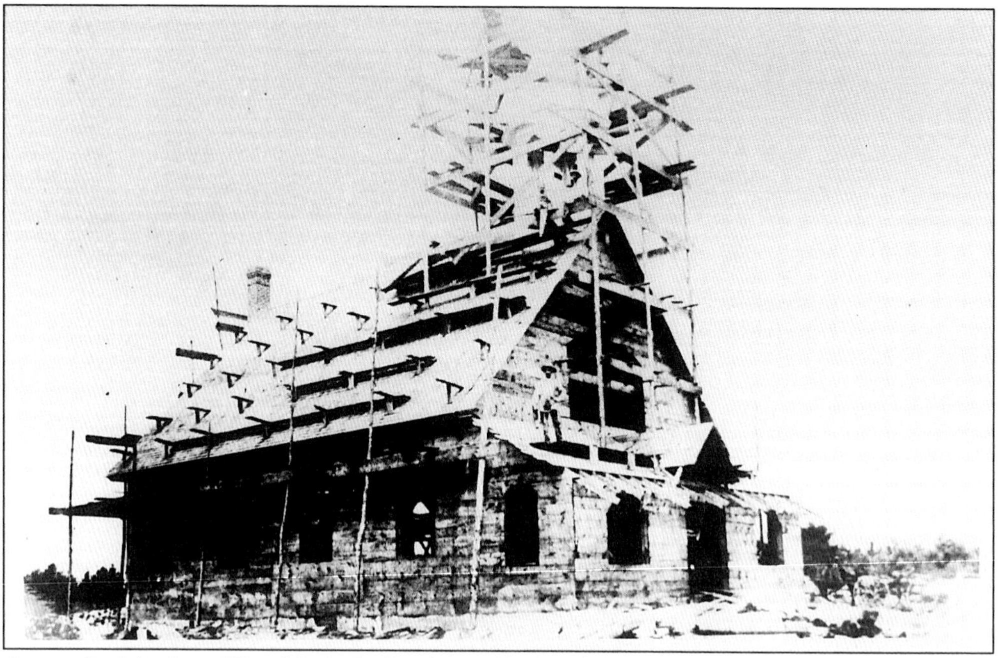

Across the lake from West Neck the Bunker Hill Church holds a commanding view of the lake at its mid-point. Being so far away from the Baptist Church in Jefferson, the people of Bunker Hill decided to build their own church, shown here under construction in 1889. Many of the materials were donated by parishioners, and the actual construction was done by Ben Ware and Will Vinal. Mr. Vinal is the man standing on the roof. (Nobleboro Historical Society, Ivan Flye Collection)

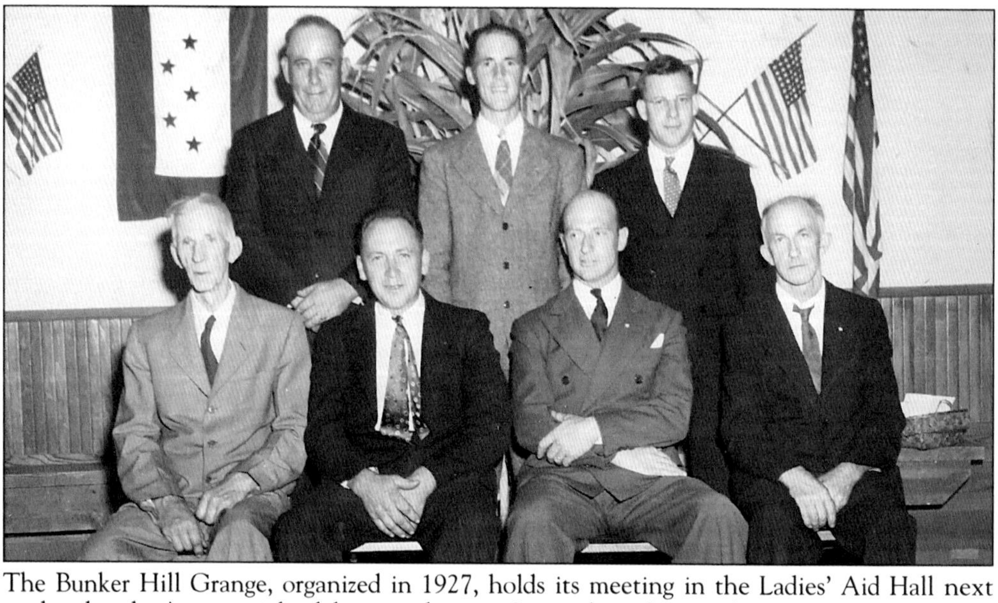

The Bunker Hill Grange, organized in 1927, holds its meeting in the Ladies' Aid Hall next to the church. At a special celebration there in September of 1948, the Grange paid a special tribute to its Past Masters. From left to right are: (back row) Clifton Hunt, Erland Johnston, and George Atkinson; (front row) Alden Hall, Eldon Hunt, William Carter, and Arthur Smith. (Beryl Hunt)

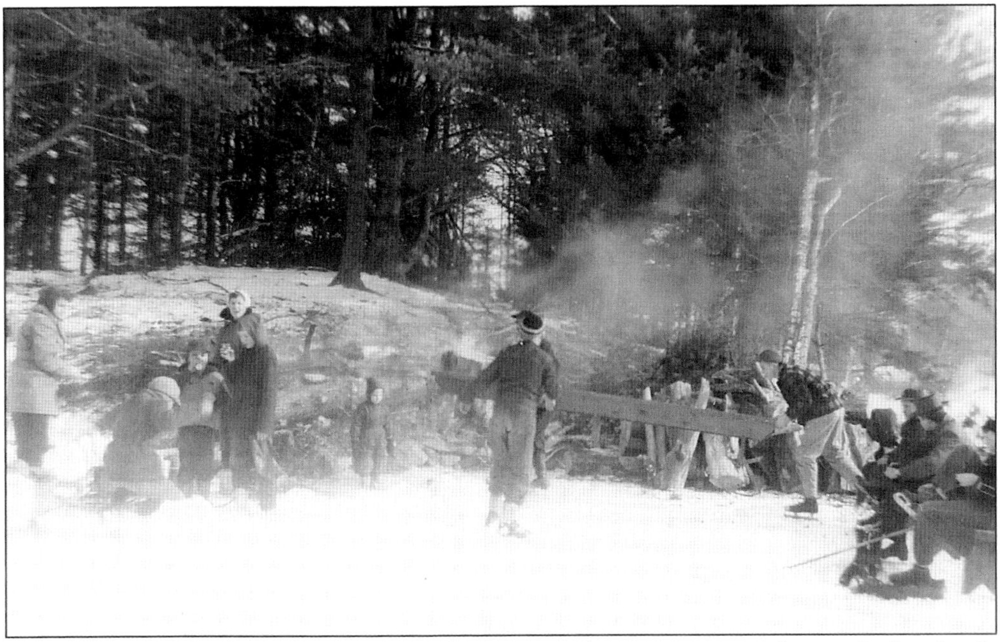

Throughout the years Bunker Hill Grange has sponsored suppers, picnics, fairs, and other family gatherings, such as this skating party on the lake, *c.* 1950. (Beryl Hunt)

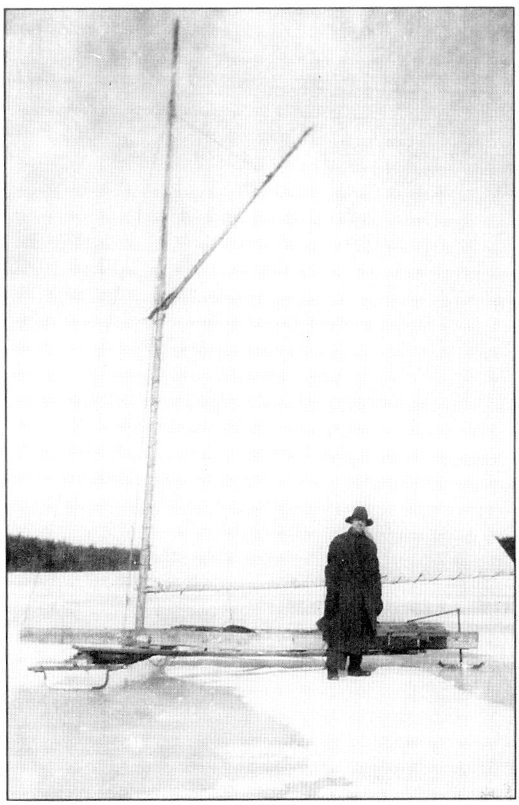

Although ice boating has never been as popular as some other winter sports, there have always been a few ice boats on the lake. Melrose Jones owned this one in 1921 and enjoyed the exhilarating ride up the lake from his home in Damariscotta Mills. (Arthur Jones)

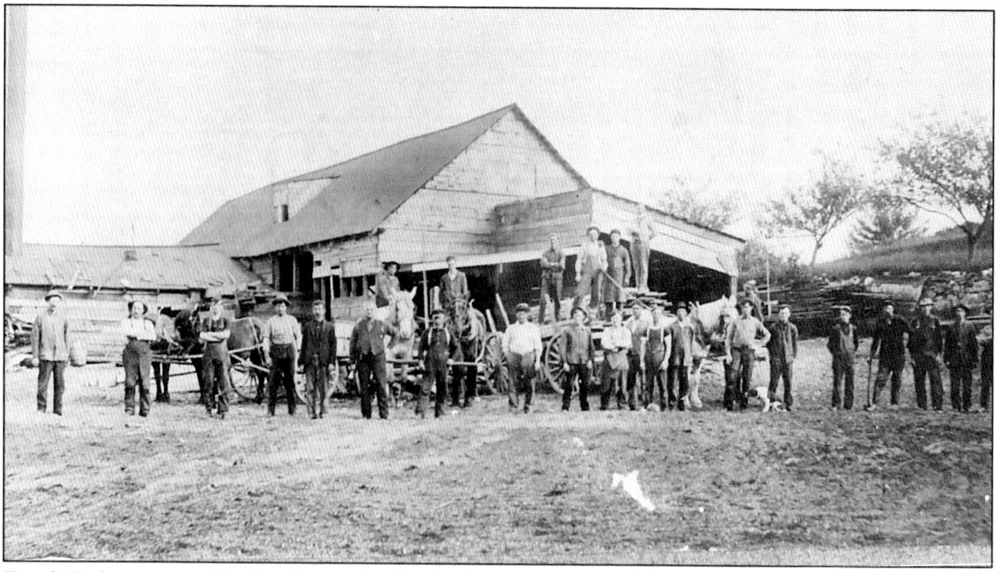

Frank Robinson and Perley Eaton built a steam-powered sawmill on a small cove on the lake's eastern shore (near the Wheeler home in Damariscotta Mills) soon after the turn of the century. During its operation the sawmill employed several men, but it closed in 1912 when lumber supplies began to diminish around the lake. It burned soon after. (Arthur Jones)

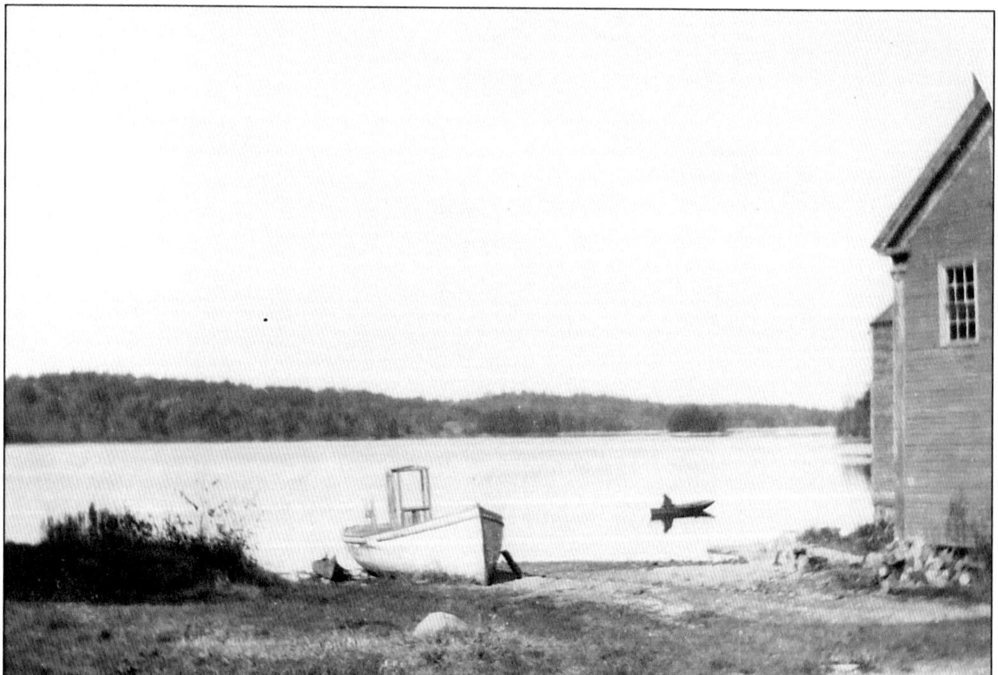

The hull of the steamer *Allison Reed* lies rotting on the beach at Damariscotta Mills in the 1920s. She was built by H. Glenwood Rollins and Adoniram Trask for hauling grain and other supplies from Haggett's Mill to farms around the lake. But when Haggett's Mill burned, business declined and her owners abandoned her on the shore. The steamer was eventually blown up on the beach, and the wreckage dragged out to deep water and sunk. (Arthur Jones)

Two

The Salt Bay

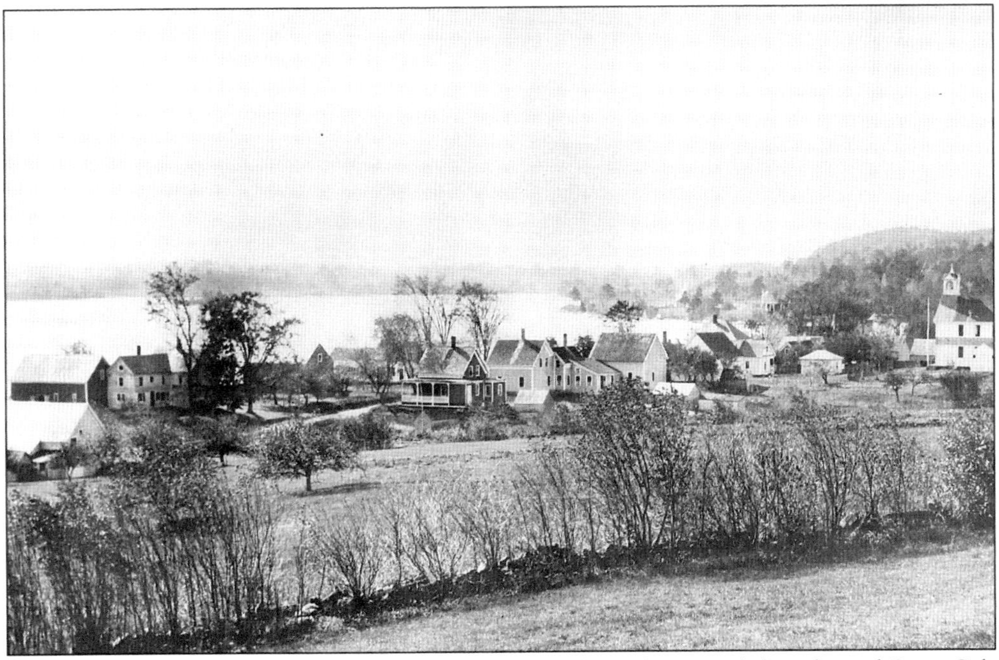

Houses in the village at Damariscotta Mills are tucked neatly around the edges of Great Salt Bay. The falls on the stream between the lake and the bay were an early source of water power, which drew settlers to the area in the eighteenth century. William Vaughan and his partner, James Noble, acquired a title to vast holdings of land along the Damariscotta River and Damariscotta Lake, as well as the rights to the water power at the freshwater falls. They built mills, and industry prospered; from those early times until the first two decades of the twentieth century, Damariscotta Mills bustled with industrial activity. (Arthur Jones)

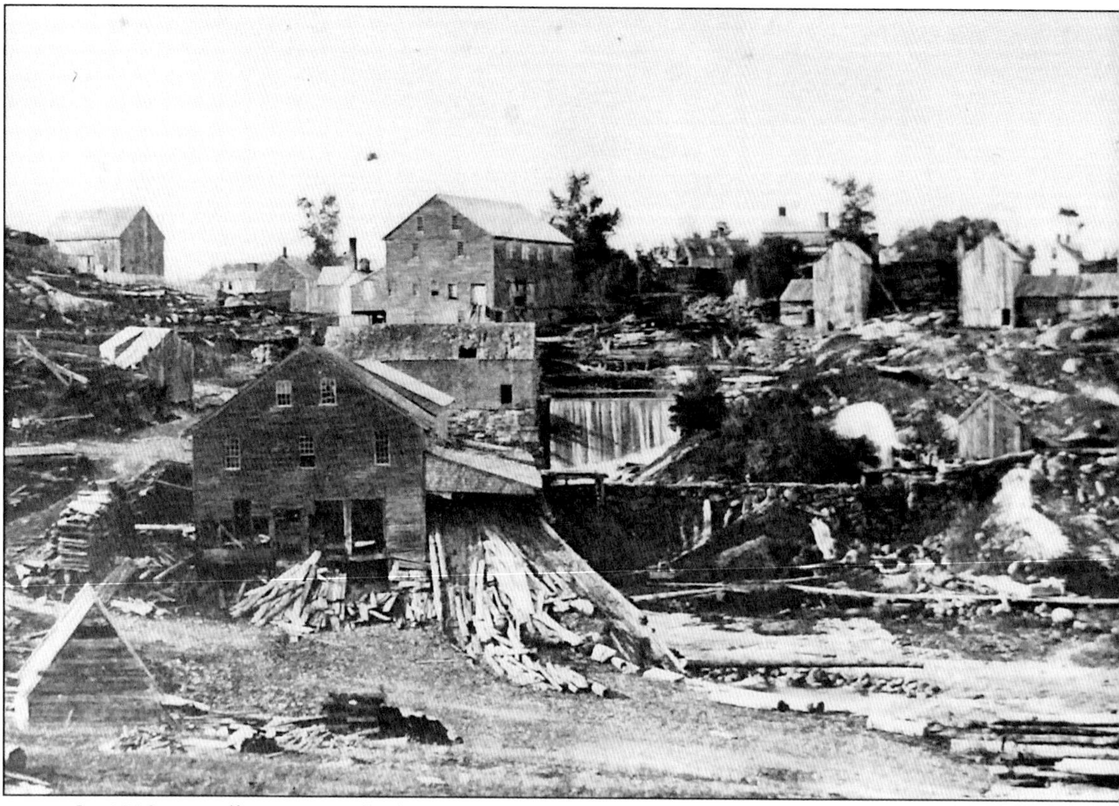

In 1883 sawmills, a grist mill, the Joseph Haines Match Factory (top center), and three drying and storage sheds dominated the landscape along the stream. Prior to the date this photograph was taken, a large sawmill and a foundry also occupied the site. Still earlier, at least seven shipyards, scattered around the salt bay, launched a variety of vessels, including several brigs, barks, and schooners. (Arthur Jones)

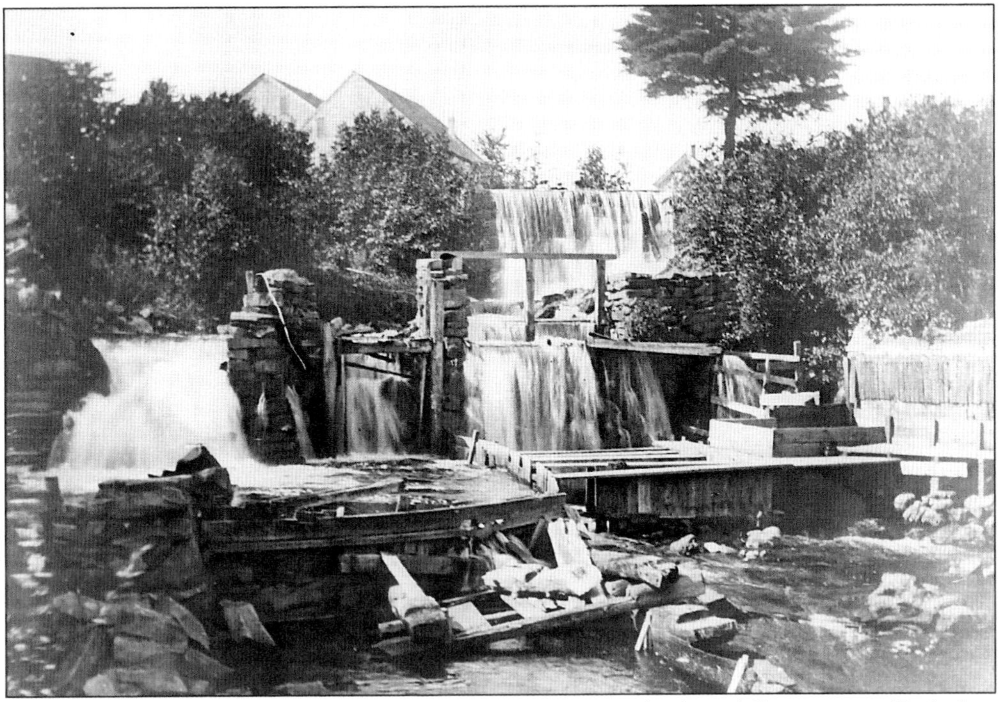

A close-up view of the falls shows a series of dams that were built at different times. Each dam provided water power for the saws and machinery of the various mills. The largest operation at this time (c. 1900) was the match factory shown at the top. (Nobleboro Historical Society, Ivan Flye Collection)

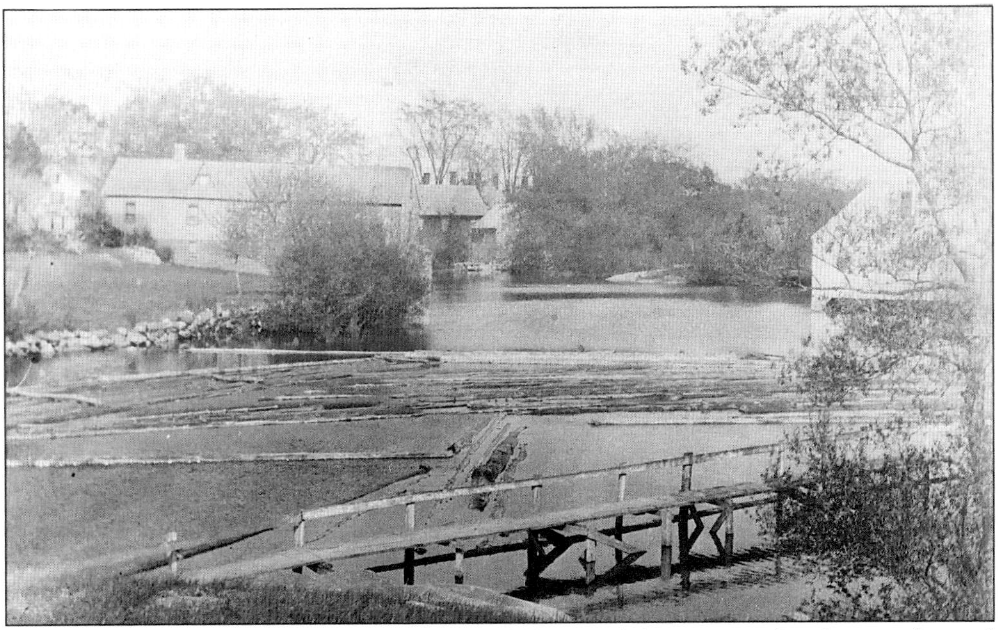

The mill pond above the first dam was used to hold logs until they were ready to be manufactured into lumber or match splints. The walkway in the foreground enabled men to push the logs along the pond to the mills below. (Arthur Jones)

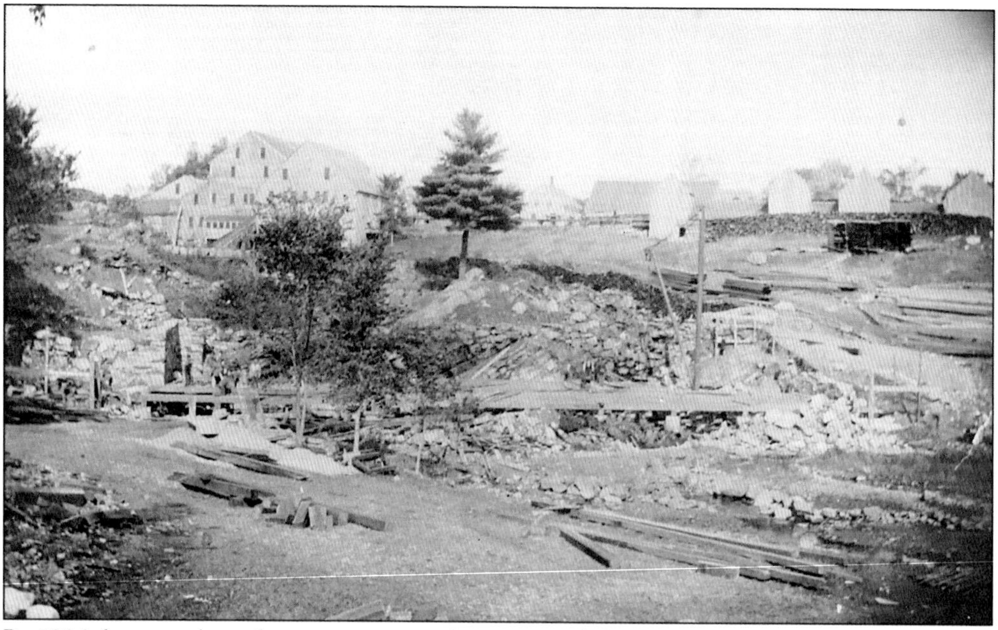

By 1906 the area along the stream was in the process of change. Much of the timber had been cut around the lake, and logs no longer floated in quantity to the mills below the dam. The match factory had been sold to the Centrifugal Leatherboard Company, which soon began construction of the large building just beginning to take shape in the center foreground of this photograph. (Arthur Jones)

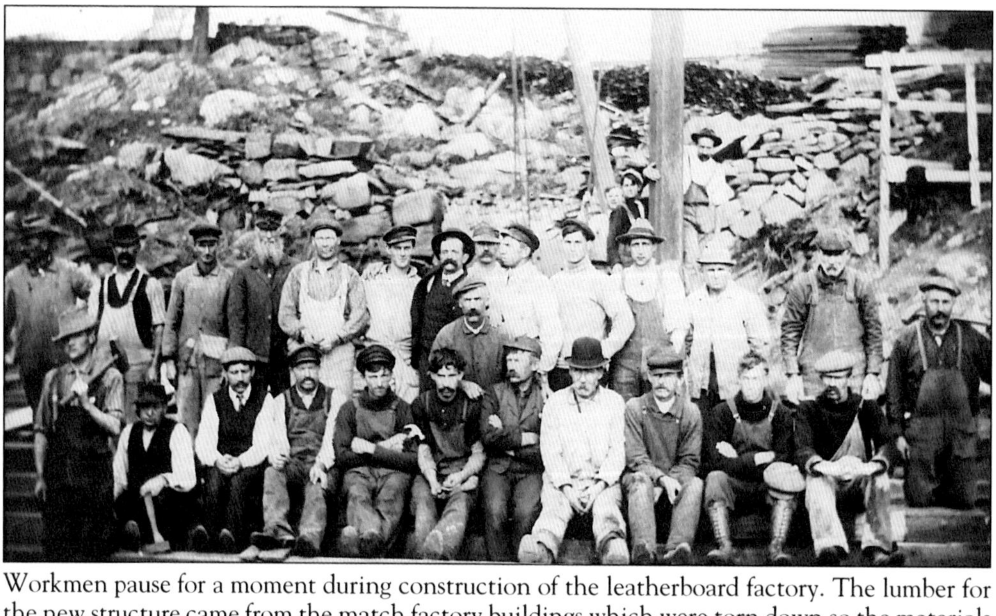

Workmen pause for a moment during construction of the leatherboard factory. The lumber for the new structure came from the match factory buildings which were torn down so the materials could be reused. The man in the center of the back row (with the mustache) is crew foreman William Hale. (Arthur Jones)

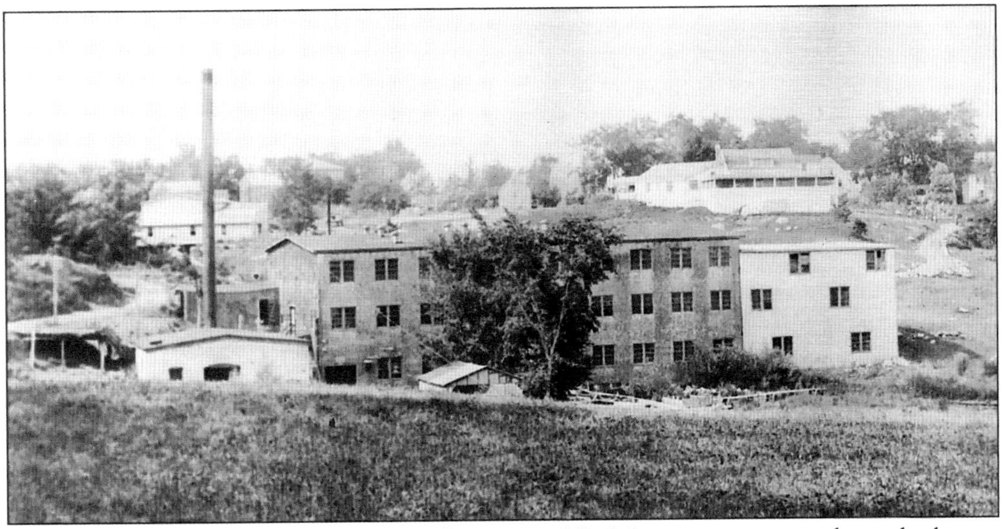

When the leatherboard factory was complete, it straddled the main stream and was the largest structure in the village. The boiler room is the building on the left with the tall chimney; the heel manufacturing portion of the company is the white addition to the right; and the home of plant superintendent Herman Castner can be seen at the top right. (Arthur Jones)

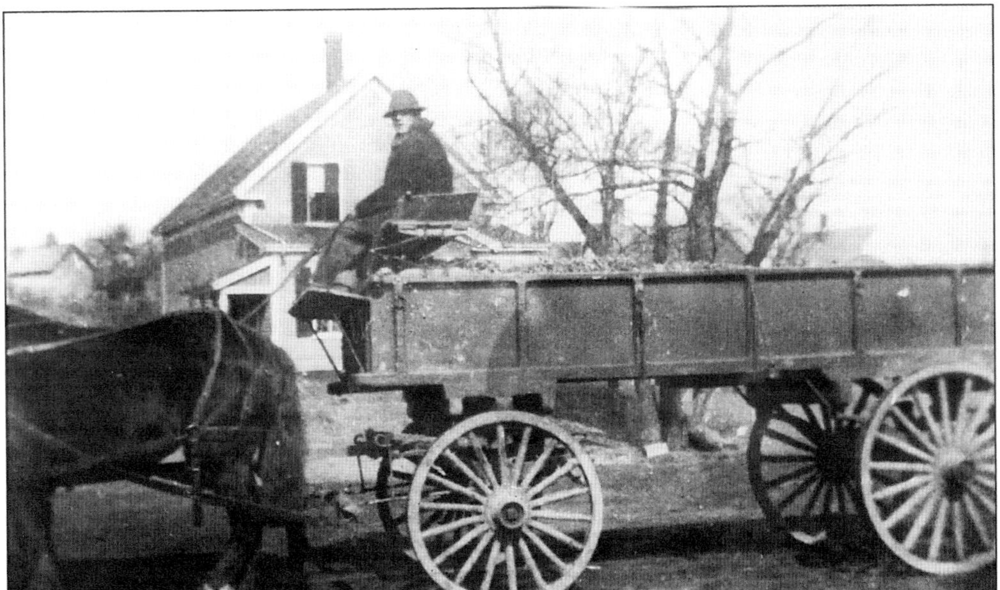

A workman hauls scrap leather from the railway station to the Centrifugal Leatherboard Company. The scraps were used to manufacture large sheets of leatherboard which were then shipped out to other manufacturers who turned them into useful products such as chair bottoms and the soles and heels for shoes. (Arthur Jones)

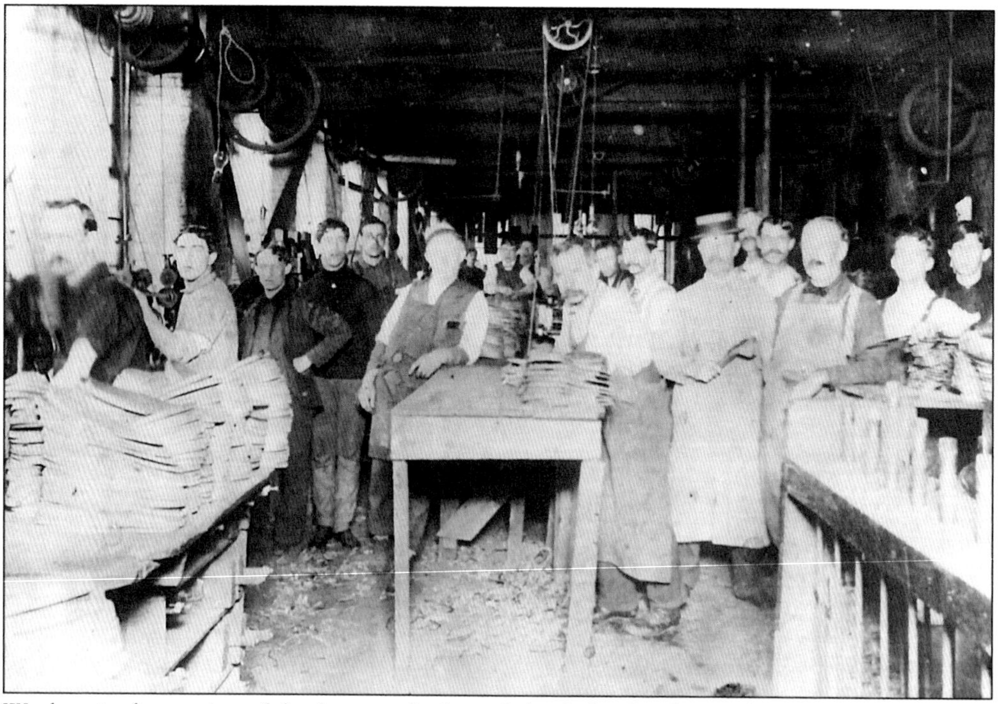

Workers in the portion of the factory which made heels for the shoe industry cut and shape the final product before it is shipped out. (Arthur Jones)

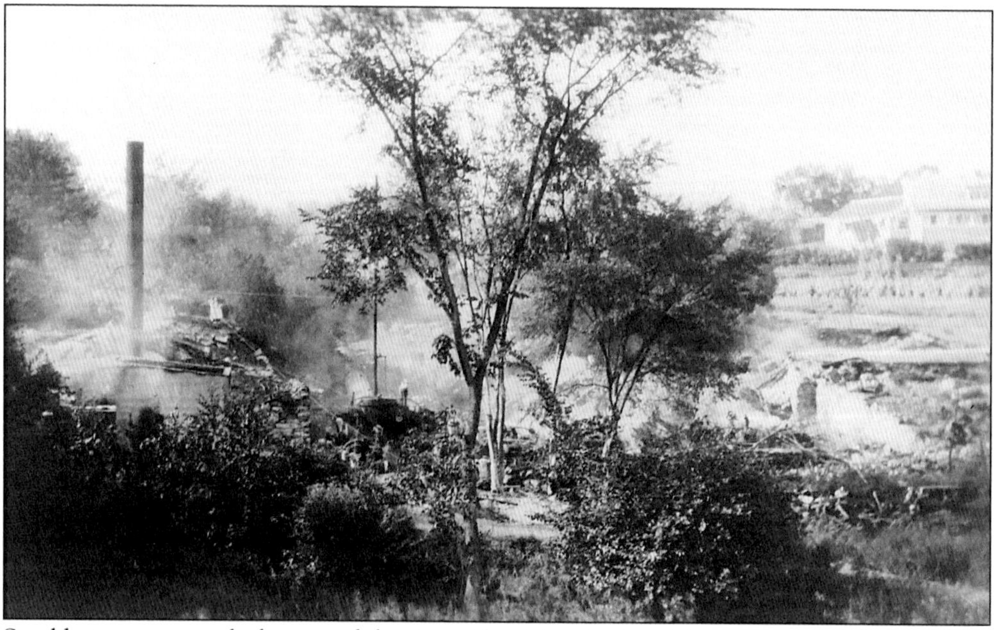

Smoldering ruins mark the site of the Centrifugal Leatherboard Company after a spectacular blaze destroyed the plant on August 22, 1921. The fire left the village of Damariscotta Mills without its major industry, and the loss was deeply felt. The company decided to relocate in Richmond, which meant that several workers and their families left the area and moved to that town. (Arthur Jones)

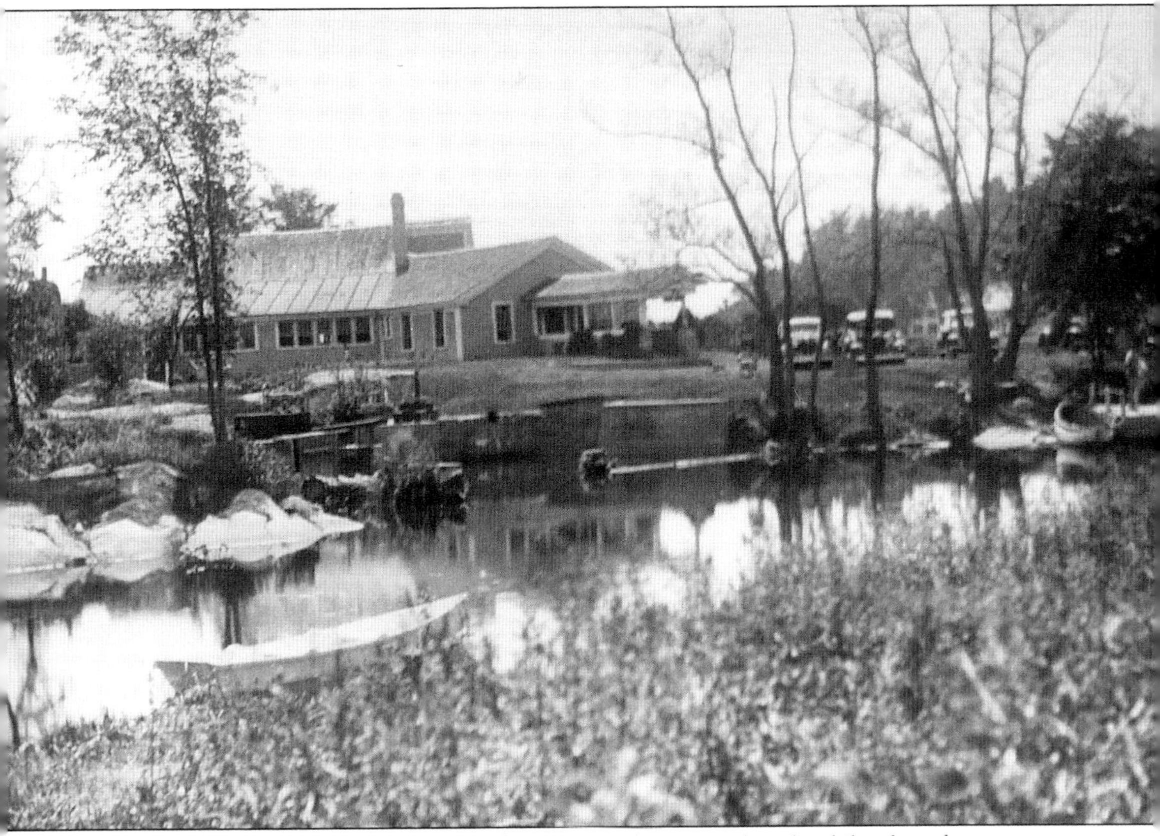

Plant superintendent Herman Castner built a spacious home on the island dividing the eastern and western streams. The bungalow, with its stables and outbuildings, had a commanding view of the village and bay and reflected the prosperity and stability of Damariscotta Mills' largest employer. After the fire the Castners left, and the home and leatherboard property came under the ownership of Central Maine Power Company. Central Maine Power rented the house to company officials and to Major Howard, who, during 1937/38, operated it as the Stella Maris Dude Ranch. Several years later the power company decided it had no further use for the buildings and tore them down. (Arthur Jones)

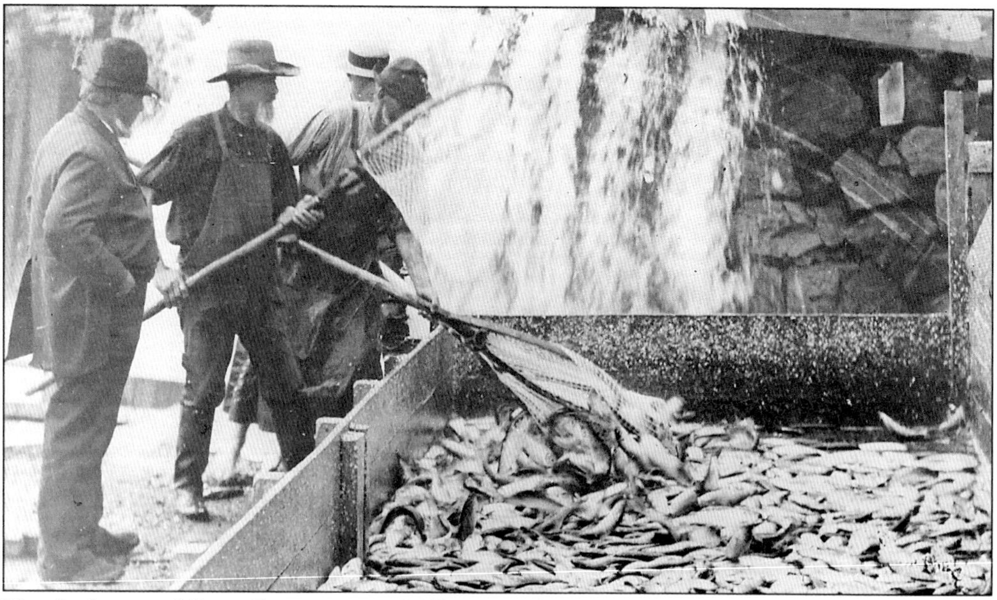

The freshwater falls at Damariscotta Mills were also important for the annual alewives run. Alewives return in the spring, fighting their way up the stream to lay their eggs. Usually the fish were smoked in smokehouses next to the stream, and they were an important food source a century ago. In 1890 men hand-dipped the fish into storage bins using large dip nets. Many years later Nelson Hancock designed mechanical dippers which made the harvest less labor intensive. (Arthur Jones)

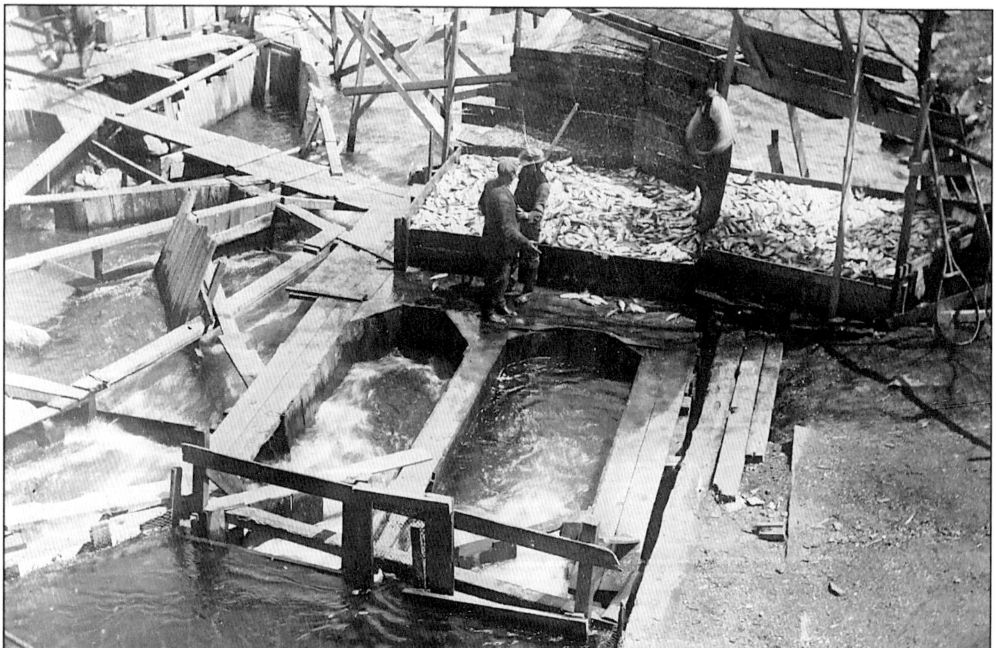

A larger view of the alewives operation shows the dipping tanks and the storage bins full of fish. A condition of the fishery lease required that widows and needy persons be given two bushels of alewives free each season, a law that is still in effect. (Arthur Jones)

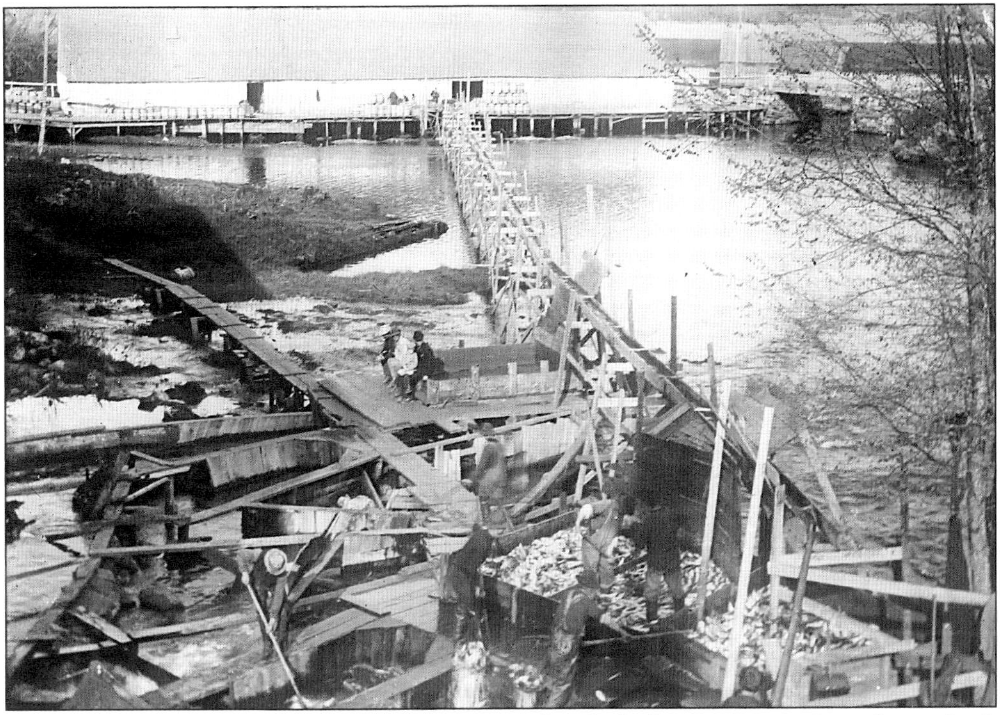

When the bins were full, the alewives were scooped with shallow nets into a long sluice which carried them to a large storage shed at the end of the stream. Until 1946, the alewives not sold locally for smoking were packed and stored as soon as they were caught. (Arthur Jones)

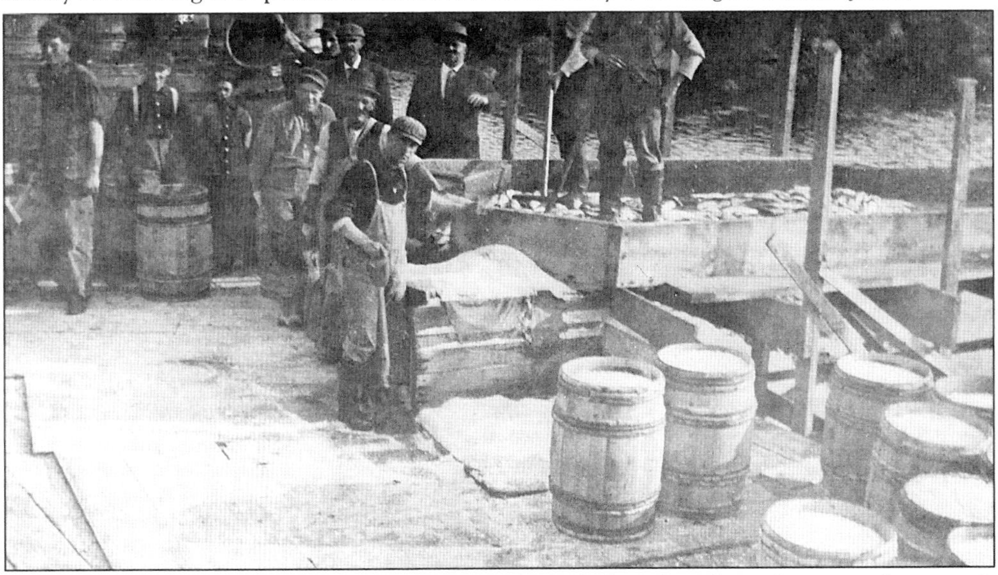

After reaching the storage shed the fish were packed whole in barrels in alternating layers with salt and left for three weeks. At the end of that period they were unpacked, washed, repacked, and marked for shipment. Many years ago alewives found ready markets in the West Indies, and more than a century ago sea captains purchased them as food for their crews. In more recent years, as demand for human consumption decreased, they have been processed as fish meal and used for lobster bait. (Arthur Jones)

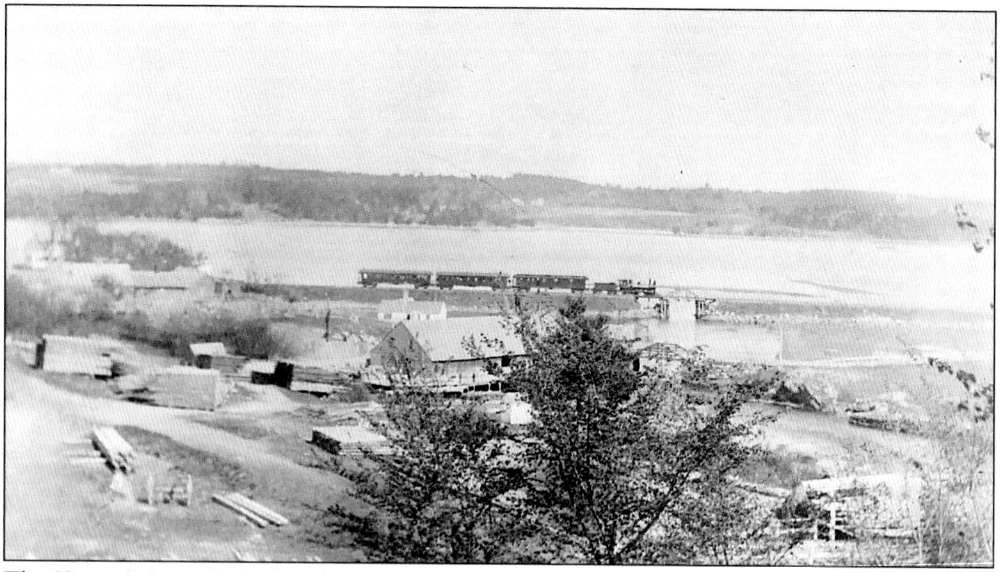

The Knox & Lincoln Railroad passed along the edge of the salt bay between Newcastle and Nobleboro. The line was merged with Maine Central Railroad in 1901, and at that time the railroad made four eastbound and westbound passenger trips daily, except on Sundays. (Arthur Jones)

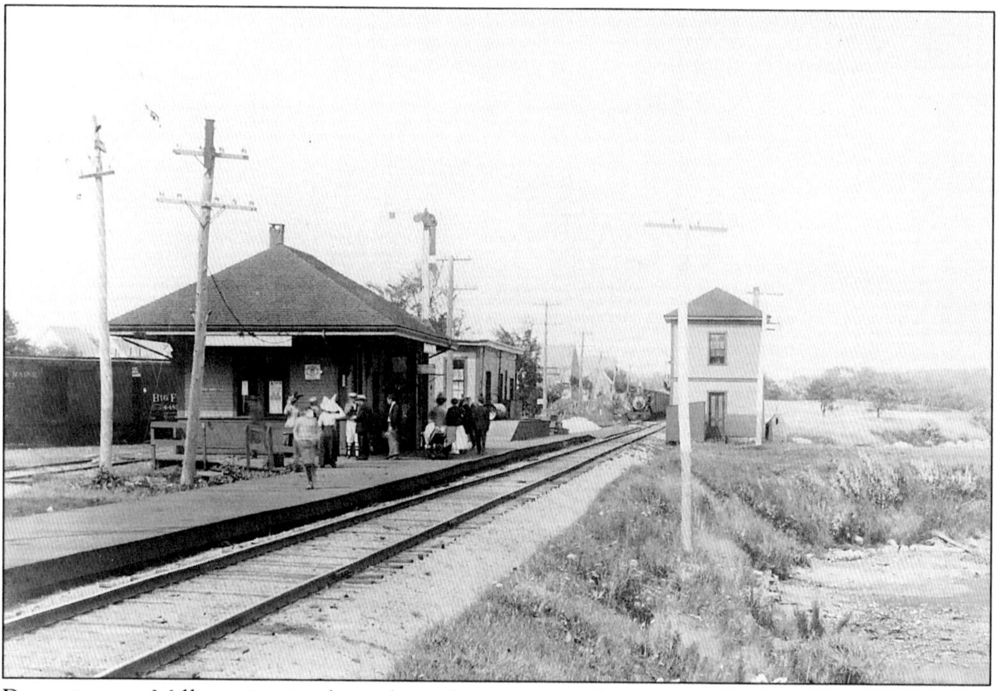

Damariscotta Mills maintained a telegraph station and was a regular stop on the railroad schedule. Here, passengers await the train just coming into view, *c.* 1910. In the early years of the railroad steam engines required large quantities of wood to fire their boilers. Hundreds of cords of wood were cut and floated down the lake to Damariscotta Mills and Muscongus Bay for this purpose, creating jobs for many area residents. (Arthur Jones)

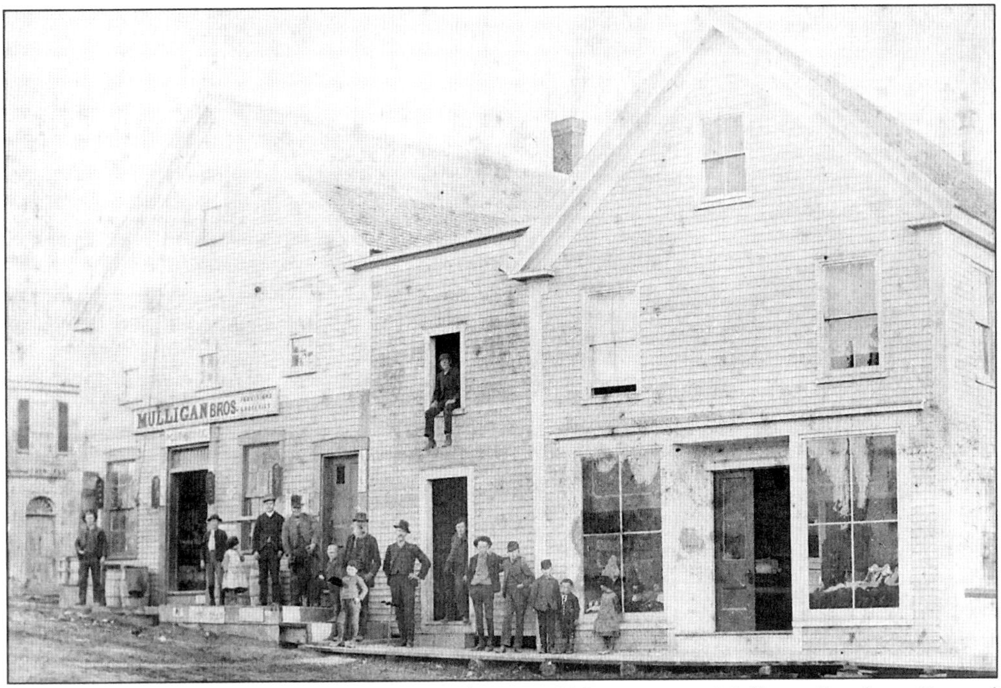

James and John Mulligan formed a partnership in 1885 to operate Mulligan Brothers General Variety Store in the village. The building also included a post office with John Mulligan serving as postmaster. This structure burned in April 1890, but the Mulligan brothers set up another store just west of the bridge at the end of the lake, where Hollis Nelson's welding shop was located for a number of years. (Arthur Jones)

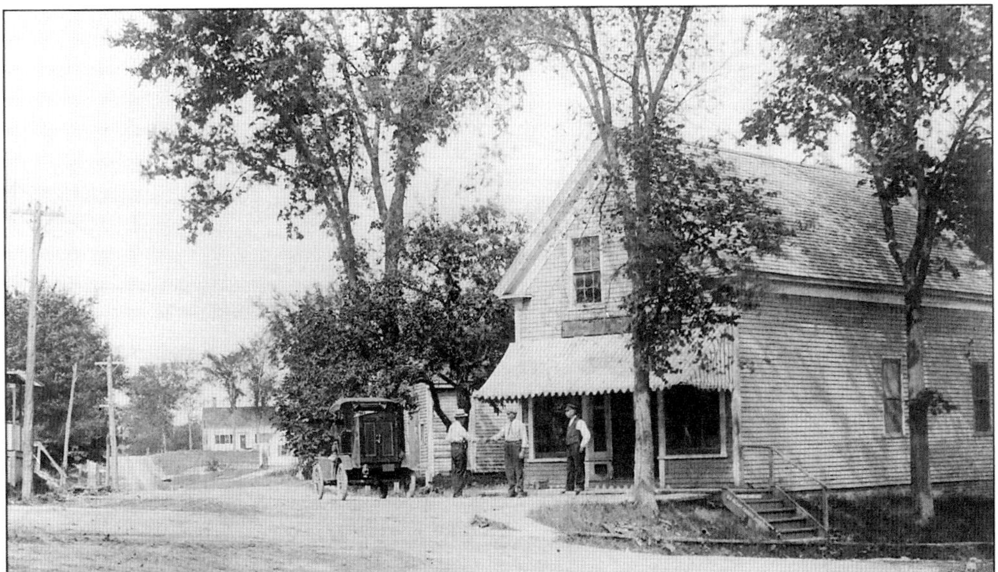

After the Mulligan Brothers' store burned, the post office was moved to the corner of Bayview Road and the road to the railroad station. Ruel York was postmaster when this picture was taken in 1912. He and his wife, Vida—who assumed the responsibilities when her husband died—served the town for twenty-two years. (Arthur Jones)

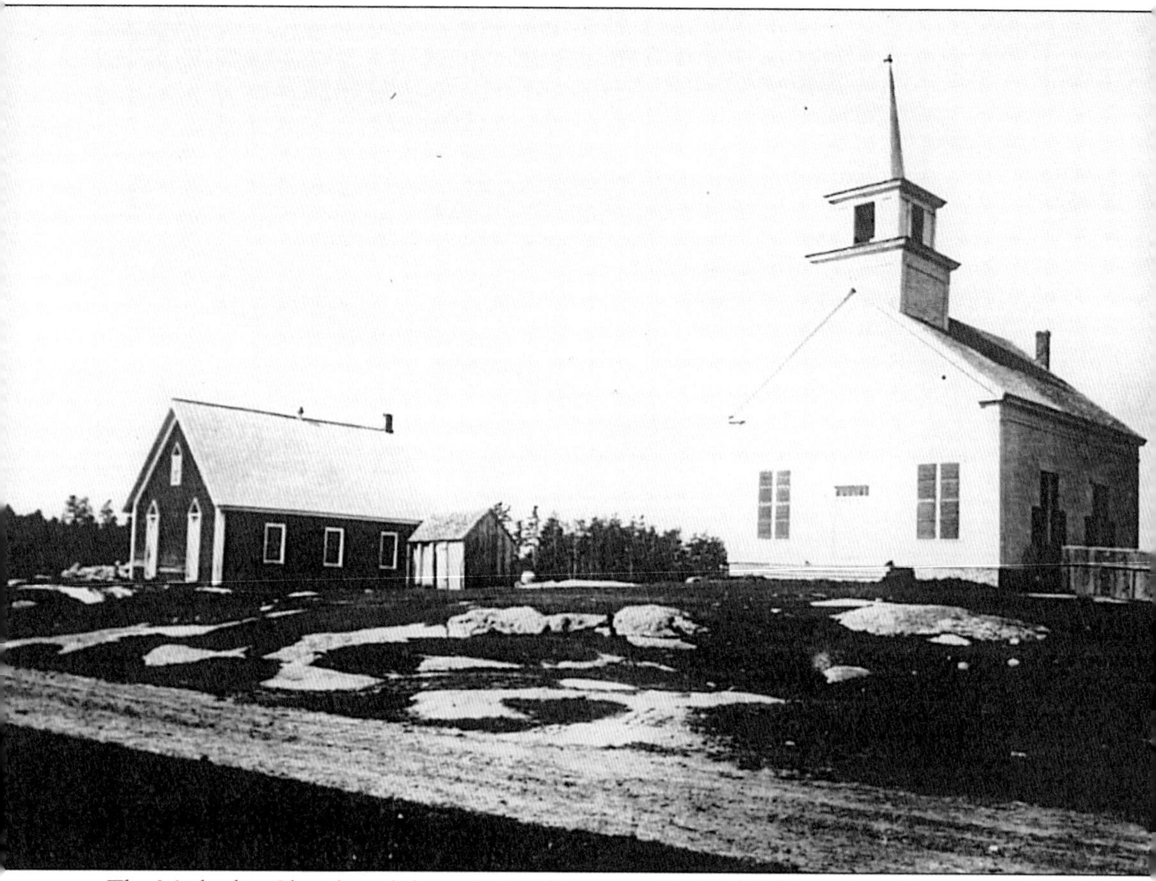

The Methodist Church and the red schoolhouse on Borland Hill stand starkly against the sky in 1886. The church was built in the 1850s on land bought from Samuel Borland for $100. A few years later declining membership and dwindling finances forced the church to at first share a minister with a nearby congregation, and then to hold summer services only. Finally in 1955 the church was sold and it is now a private residence. The school was later moved into the village and used as a store before it eventually burned. (Arthur Jones)

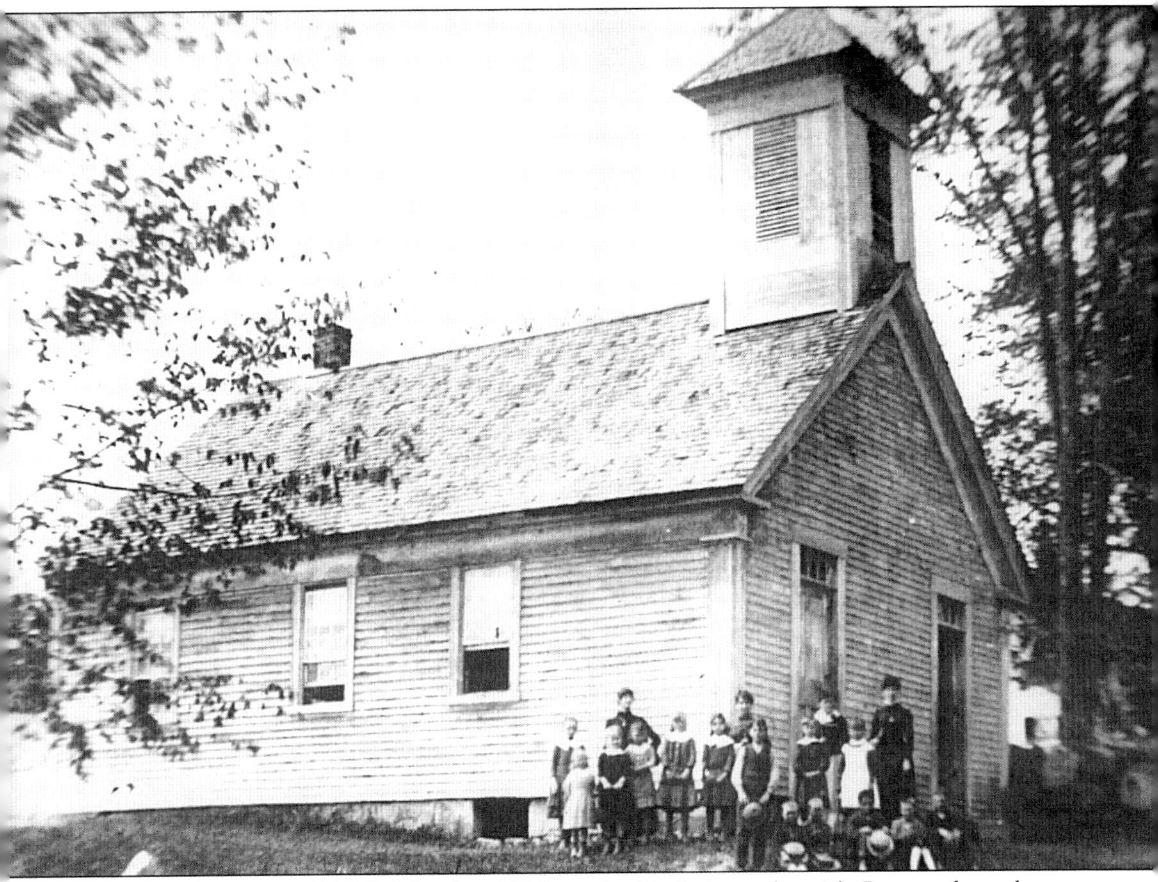

Students at the Kavanagh Hill School in 1885 stand with their teacher, Ida Benner, for a class portrait. This was one of several one-room neighborhood schools which operated during the nineteenth century; because of declining enrolments a few years later, many were forced to close. When the Kavanagh Hill School closed in 1927, the building was torn down, and the land reverted to St. Patrick's Rectory. The students in the picture are: Annie McCurdy, Ella Sidelinger, Mabel Eastmans, Mamie Sidelinger, Maude Austin, Mamie Webster, Josephine Hopkins, Frank Webster, Jennie Webster, Abbie Boyd, Lizzie Clark, Dora Rollins, Otis Morgan, Glen Rollins, Horace Jones, Charlie Morgan, and Joe Jones. (Arthur Jones)

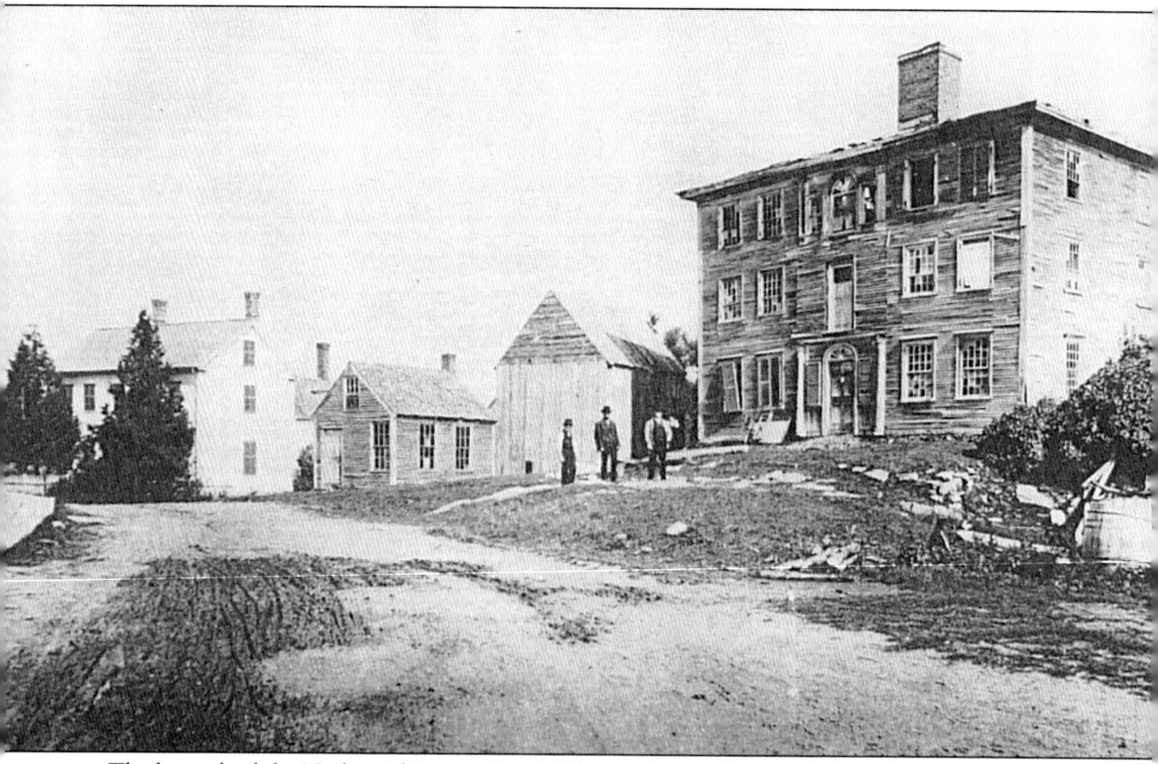

The house built by Nathaniel Bryant II in 1801 was about to be torn down when this photograph was taken in 1887. Owned and occupied by the shipbuilder and his wife, who had eighteen children, the house was known as "the beehive." A story passed down through generations contends that Mrs. Bryant, in order to accommodate her large family, had the third floor added while her husband was away on business. The house on the left belonged to Carleton Jones, with Peter Jones' shoe shop located between the two homesteads. The men are identified as W. Colson, John Eastman, and Ed. Mulligan. (Arthur Jones)

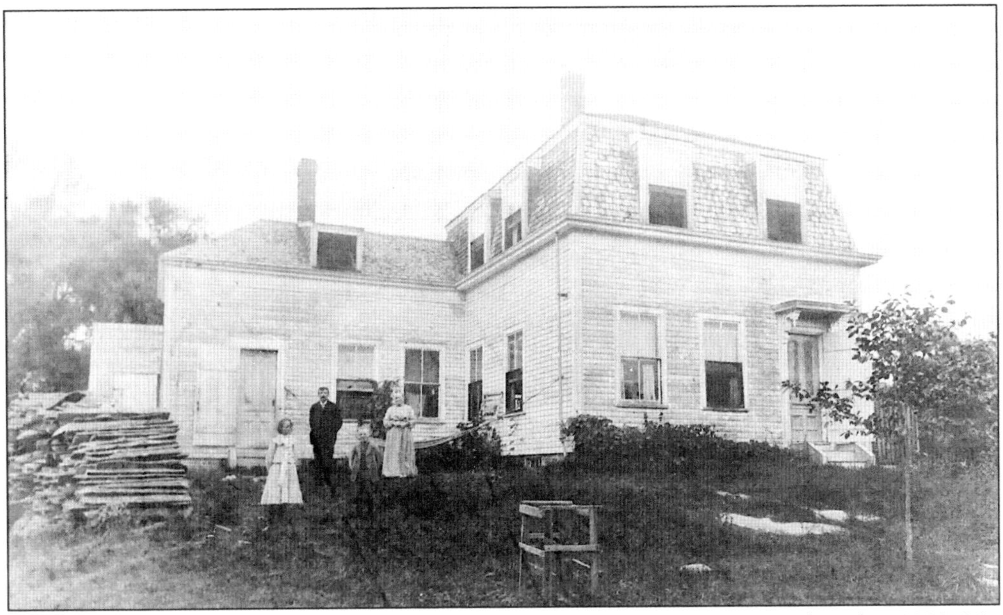

Elijah Jones bought the Bryant property and built this home with a mansard roof in 1890. Mr. Jones and his wife, Susie, and their children Anastasia (Tasie) and Melrose stand outside their new home c. 1902. This house still stands on the road between the lake and the mill pond. (Arthur Jones)

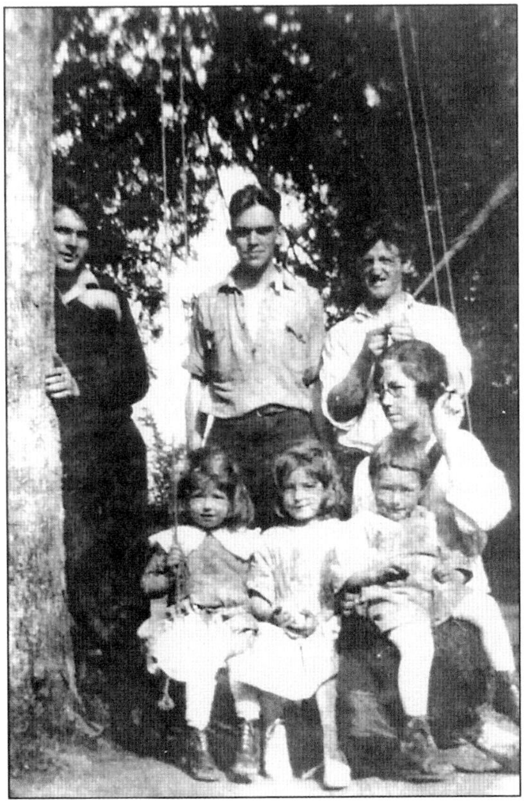

Melrose Jones, who lived all his life in the Mills, is photographed with his wife, Eola (Jackson) Jones, their three children, Ruth, Mellicent, and Arthur, and friends Bill and James Mulligan in 1921. (Arthur Jones)

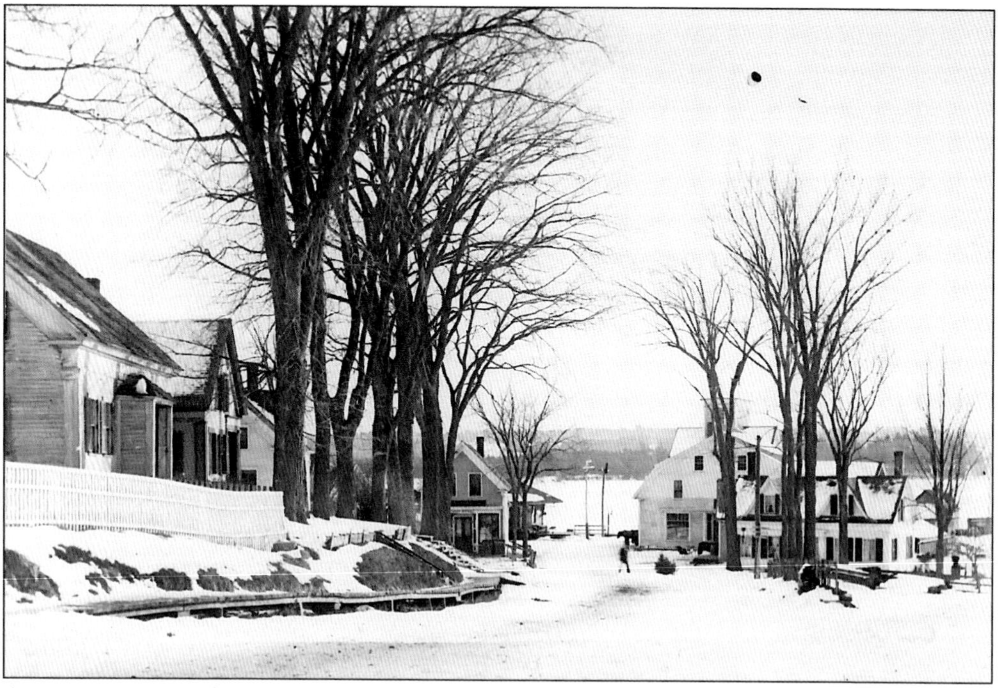

A winter scene in the village looking toward the bay shows the number of stately elms that lined the streets, c. 1920. Joe Bryant, a Mills resident and an amateur photographer, took this photograph and many others around the town and along the river. Fortunately his glass negatives of 1911/12 have been found and preserved. Several of his photographs are included in this book. (Bryant photograph, courtesy Arthur Jones)

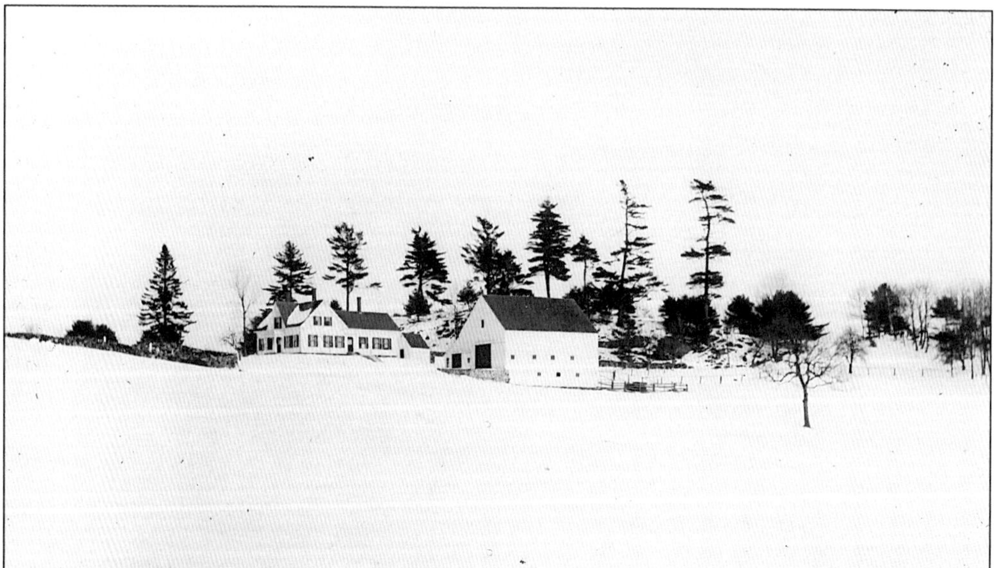

The Bryant farm overlooks the water from its vantage point on Oak Hill at the head of the bay. Raising chickens and dairy cows in the 1940s, the Bryants continued to farm until the mid-1960s. The farm was eventually sold to the Wriggins family. (Bryant photograph, courtesy Arthur Jones)

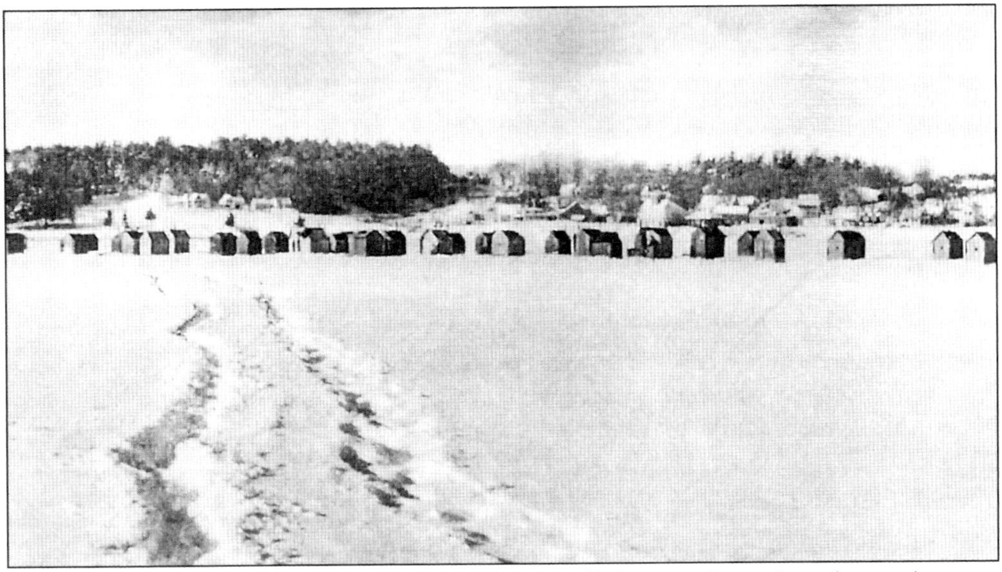

This winter scene of smelt shanties on Great Salt Bay really has not changed much over the years. Fishermen still move their huts onto the ice as soon as it is thick enough, and brave the cold to catch the small silvery fish. In the last decades of the nineteenth century large quantities of eels were also caught along the bay. In 1878 Joseph Sidelinger reported one of the largest one-day catches: 400 pounds. At that time fishermen were paid 9¢ a pound for eels. (Ralph Bond)

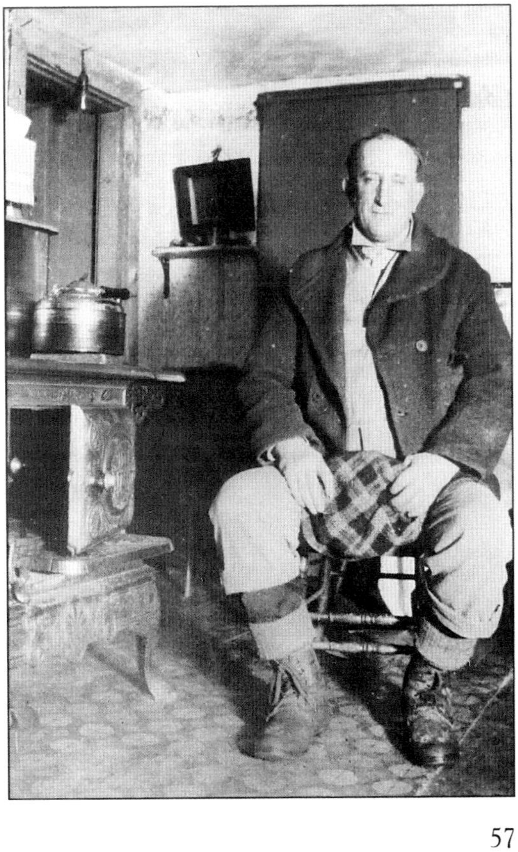

Sam Rankins is welcomed into the kitchen of the Carleton Jones house to be warmed by the cookstove on a cold winter day, c. 1916. Mr. Rankins, a practical joker and a "character" to those who knew him, managed the J.B. Ham grain mill in the village and was a Nobleboro selectman in 1933. (Arthur Jones)

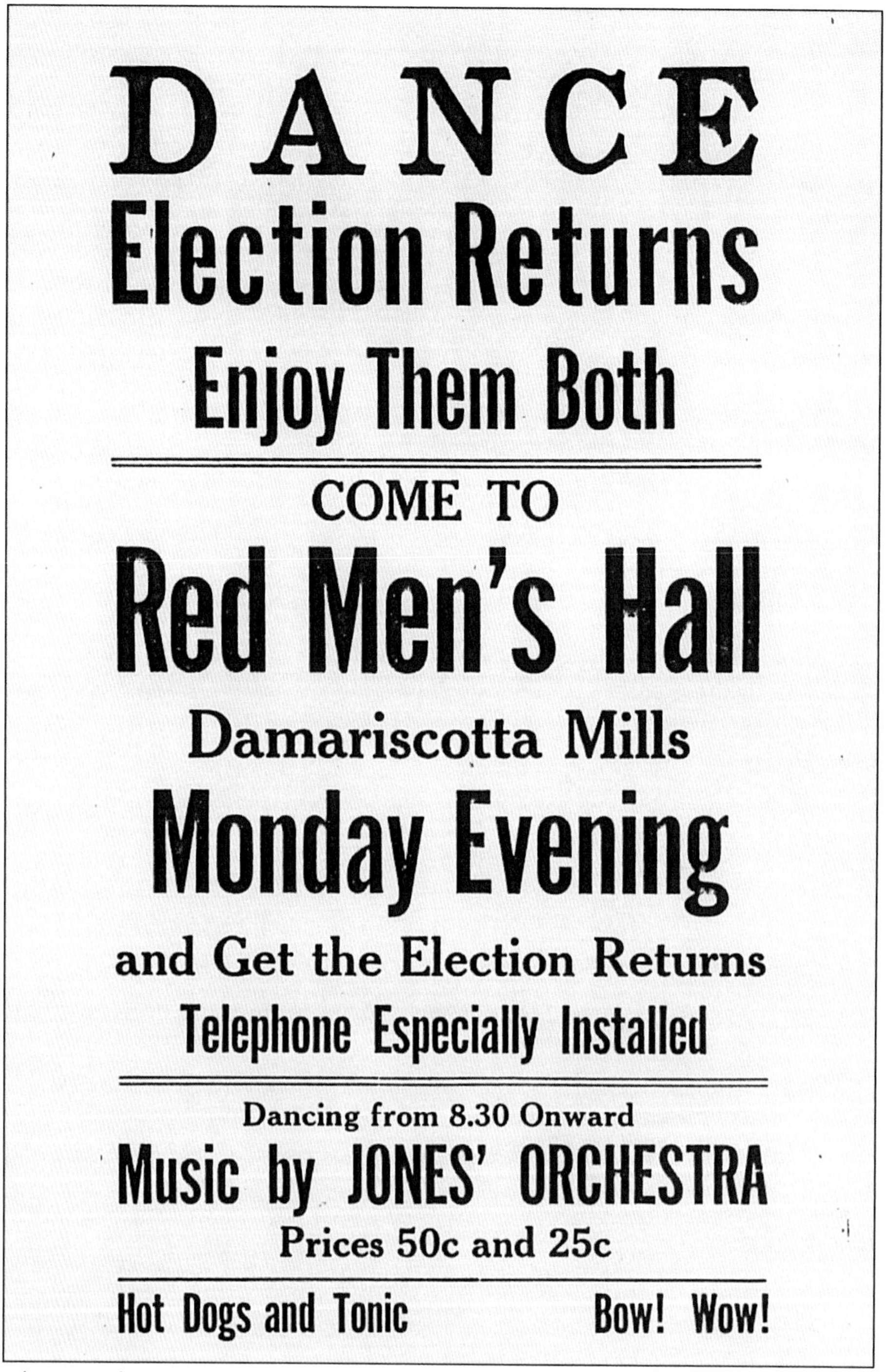
DANCE

Election Returns

Enjoy Them Both

COME TO

Red Men's Hall

Damariscotta Mills

Monday Evening

and Get the Election Returns

Telephone Especially Installed

Dancing from 8.30 Onward

Music by JONES' ORCHESTRA

Prices 50c and 25c

Hot Dogs and Tonic Bow! Wow!

The election of 1924 prompted the Red Men, a local fraternal and social organization, to sponsor a dance at its meeting hall in the building formerly occupied by Mulligan Brothers General Variety Store (until recently the Hollis Nelson welding shop). This group frequently held dances for entertainment and fund-raising until difficult economic times in the 1930s made it impossible for the group to meet expenses on the building. (Arthur Jones)

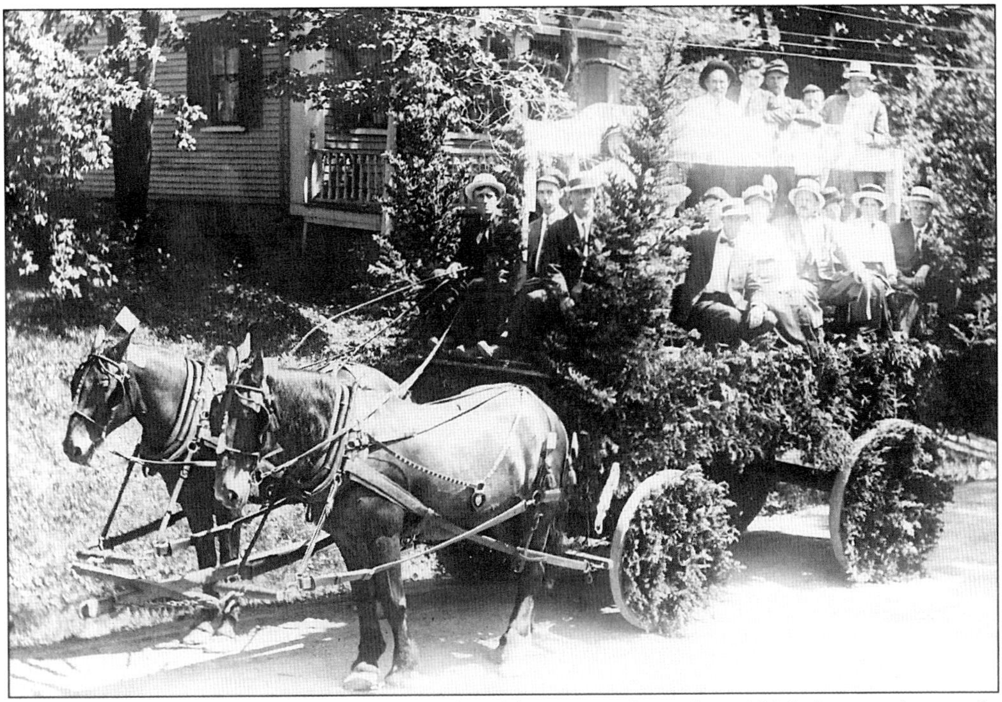

The Red Men also sponsored a Fourth of July celebration and parade in 1916. Among the people on this decorated float are: James Dalton and Henry Tomlinson (drivers), Tasie (Jones) Dalton, Will Hale, Lester Plummer, Melrose Jones, Mr. and Mrs. Fred Dyer, and Mr. and Mrs. Almore Vannah. (Arthur Jones)

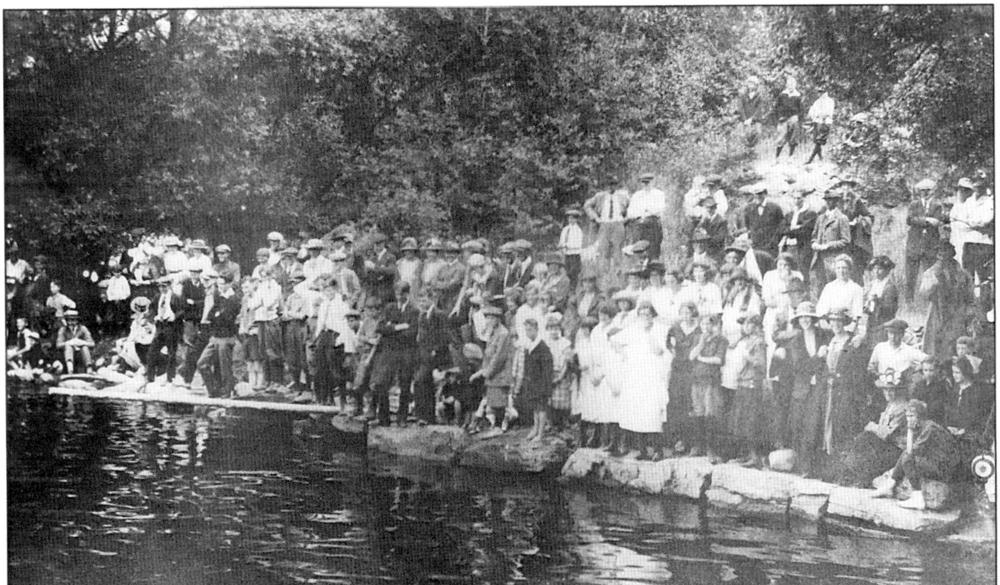

A crowd gathered during the 1916 Fourth of July celebration to witness several events at the shore of the lake. The greased log in the water had a one dollar bill nailed to one end, and the delighted crowd watched as village boys tried to reach the money without falling off and getting wet. (Arthur Jones)

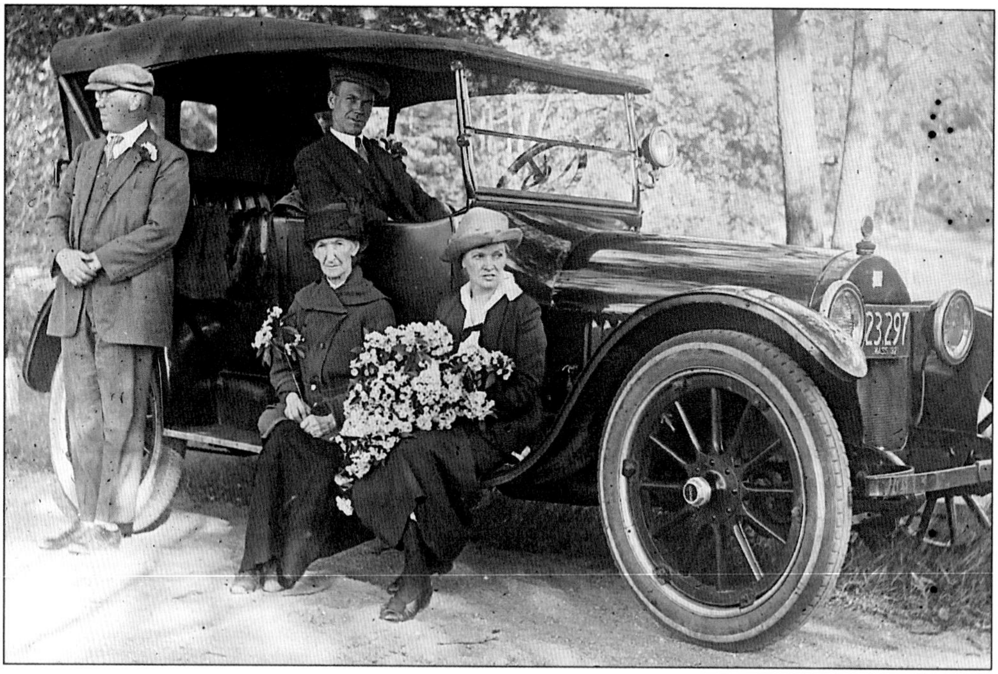

Joe Bryant (seated in the car) and his family strike a pose in their new Buick. Will Bryant is standing to the left. His mother, Sophia, and his sister, Elizabeth, sit on the running board. (Bryant photograph, courtesy Arthur Jones)

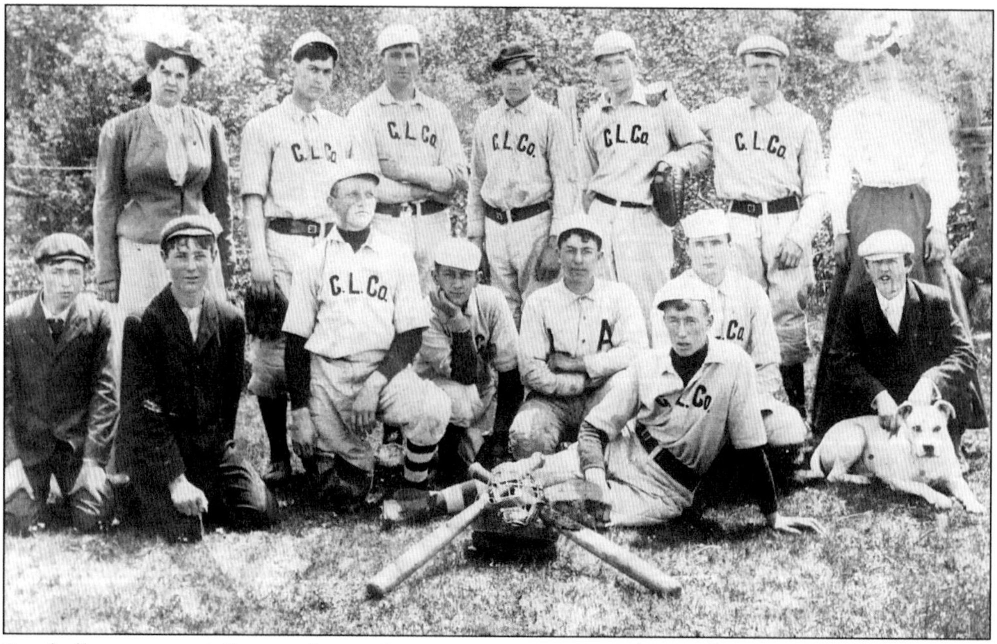

Baseball was especially popular and very competitive in the mid-coast area c. 1920, with Damariscotta Mills and the Centrifugal Leatherboard Company both fielding teams. Some members of the factory team were: (in front) Arthur Rice; (front row) Edgar Witham/third from the left, Harold Wiswell/sixth, and Melrose Jones/seventh; (back row) Flossie Rankins, Russell Newcomb, Harold Clark/fifth from the left, and Arthur Witham/sixth. (Arthur Jones)

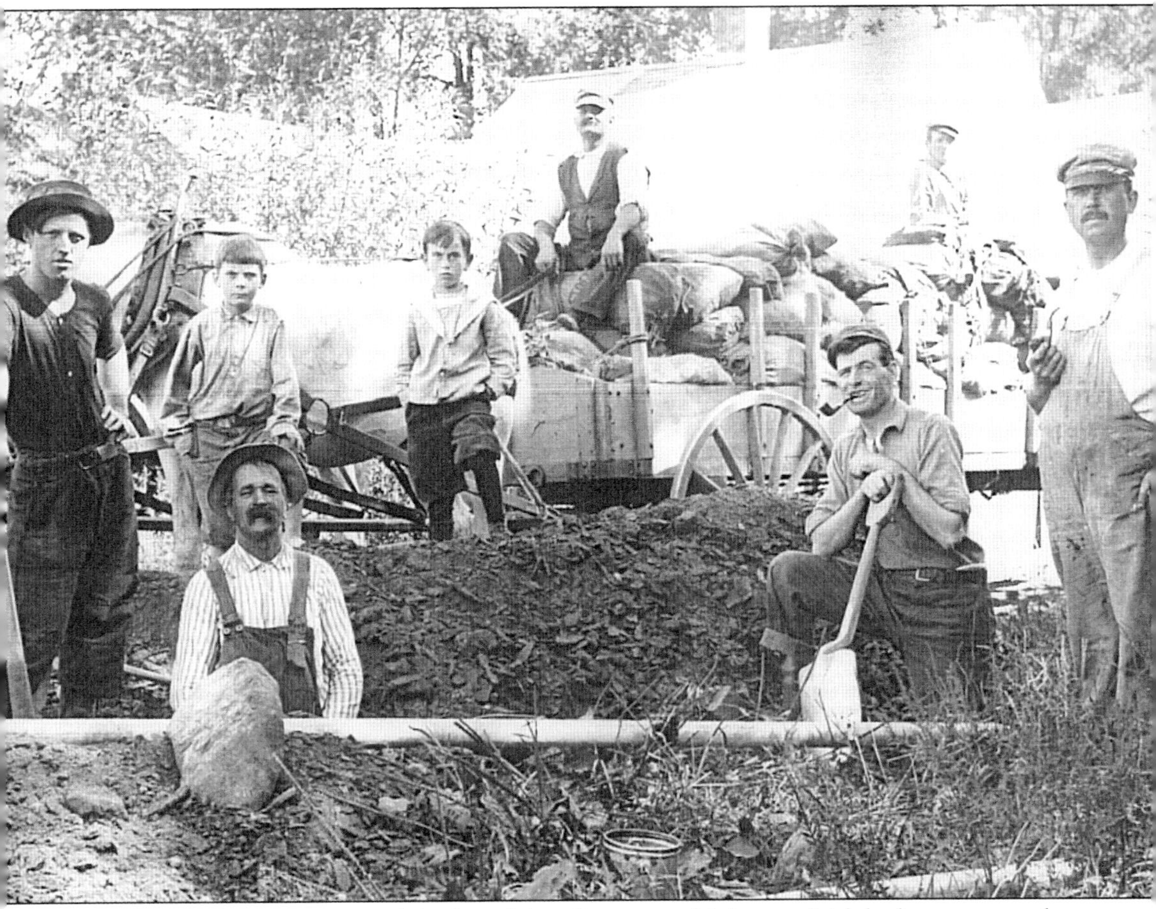

Brad White had a watering trough built on Main Street near his home which he later presented to the town. This group of public-spirited citizens, with the help of some interested bystanders, makes repairs on the pipes to the watering trough in 1911. From left to right are: Melrose Jones, boys William Mulligan and Donald Weston, Will Hale (in front of boys), George Tomlinson, Eddie Bouchey, Glen Rollins, and Maurice Tomlinson. (Arthur Jones)

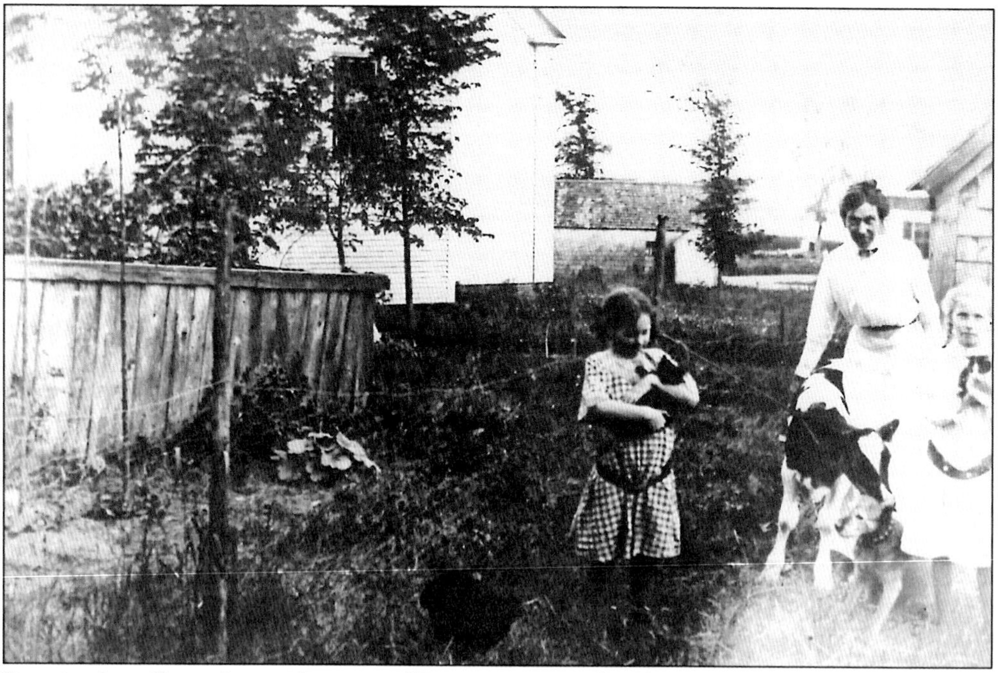

Even in the village, the rural nature of Damariscotta Mills allowed most families to have farm animals. With Blanche Bryant's guidance these little girls enjoy the animals in her backyard behind the Baptist Church. Lillian Boynton and Margaret Simpson cuddle the kittens. (Lillian Hale)

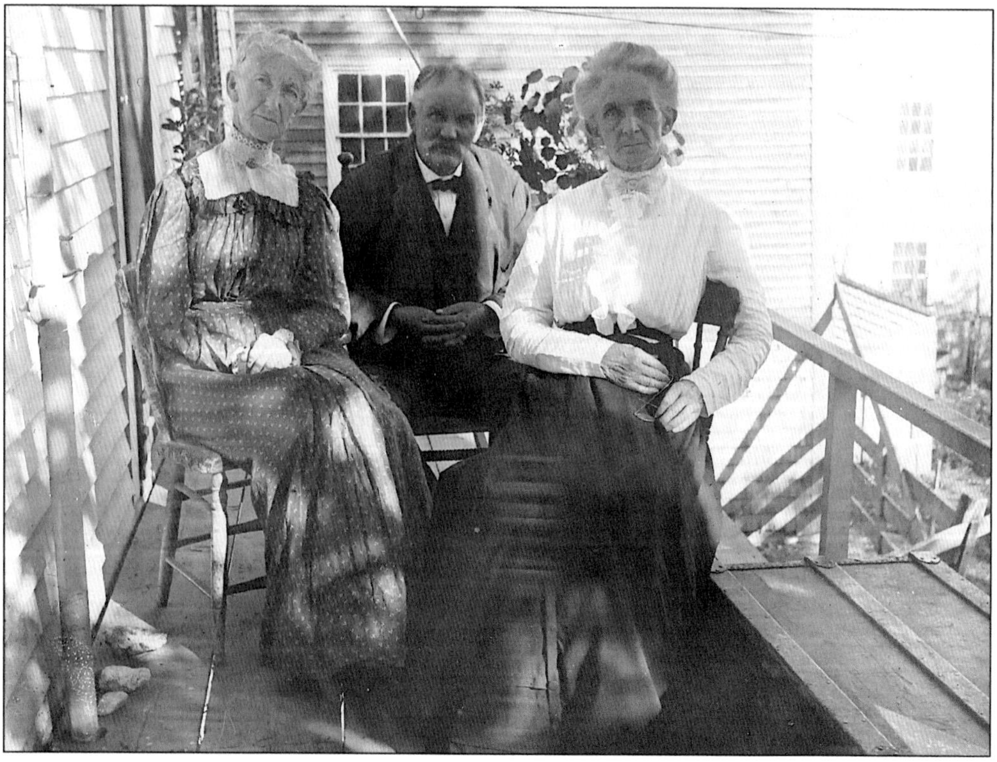

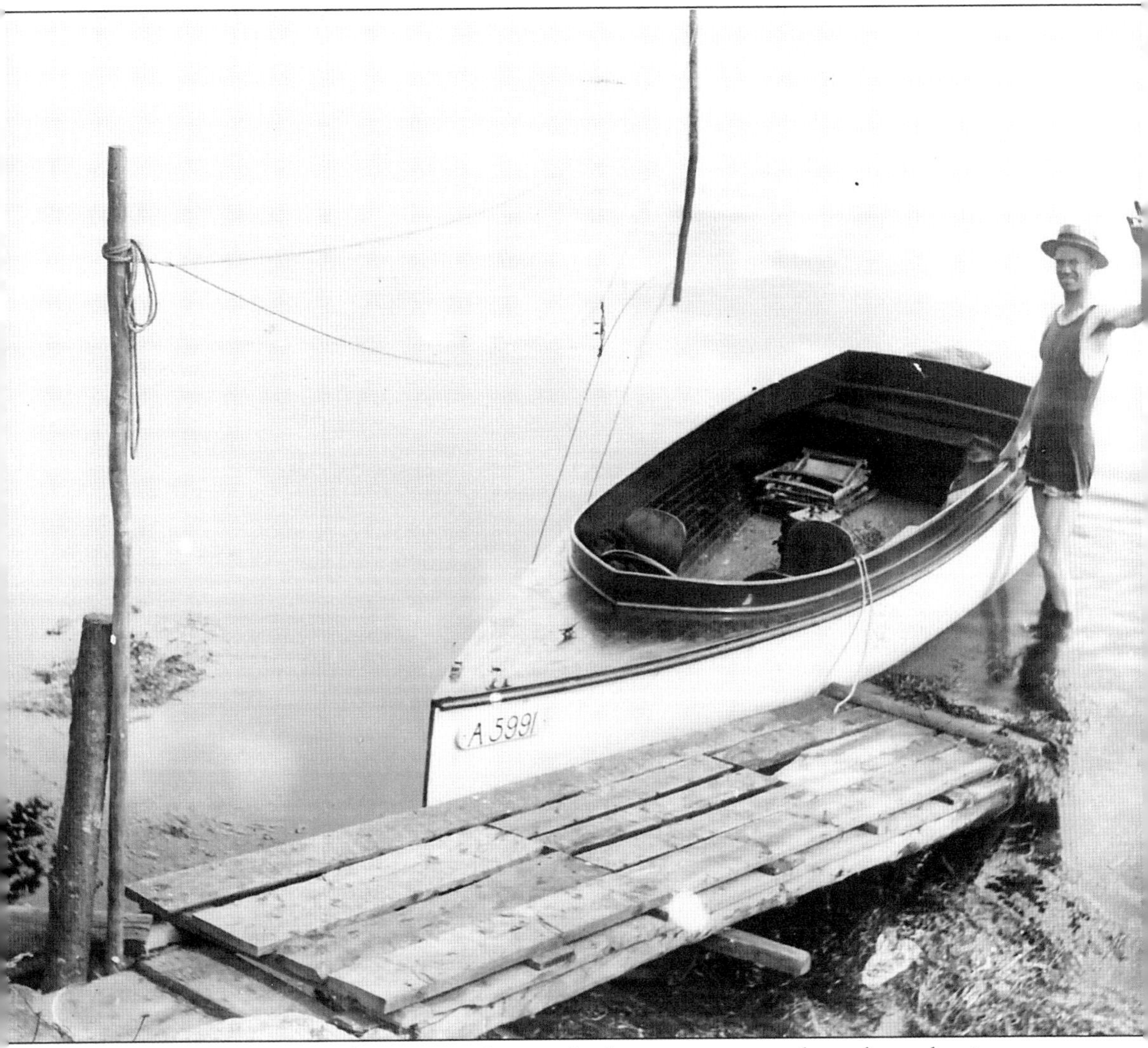

Joe Bryant and his boat, *Sally*, seem ready to embark on a voyage, perhaps down the river to South Bristol, a popular destination for Mr. Bryant and his friends. The *Sally* was a familiar sight on the river, and many of her excursions were recorded on film, detailing the picnics and pleasures of boating on the Damariscotta in the 1920s. Joe Bryant knew the river well, and was sometimes asked to guide a marine law enforcement boat through the difficult Johnny Orr into the salt bay. It was illegal to set gill nets above the bridge in Damariscotta during the annual alewives run. But poaching did occur, so officials sometimes sent a boat to the bay for two or three weeks in May as a deterrent. (Bryant photograph, courtesy Arthur Jones)

Opposite, bottom: In the quiet of a summer afternoon Sophia (Smithwick) and Ephraim Bryant enjoy a visit with an unidentified woman (right) on the back porch of their home in Damariscotta Mills. (Bryant photograph, courtesy Arthur Jones)

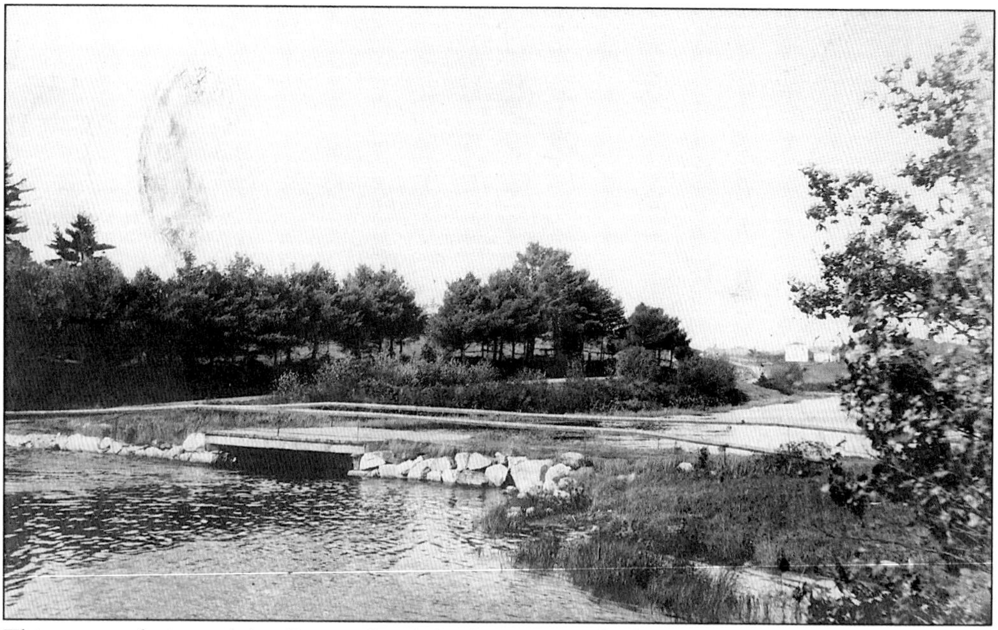

This postcard view of the Oyster Creek bridge, postmarked 1905, reveals the natural beauty surrounding the salt bay. Just visible on the right is the Coombs house, one of the oldest in Nobleboro, which was moved from its original site at Harrington Corner by several teams of oxen. (Arthur Jones)

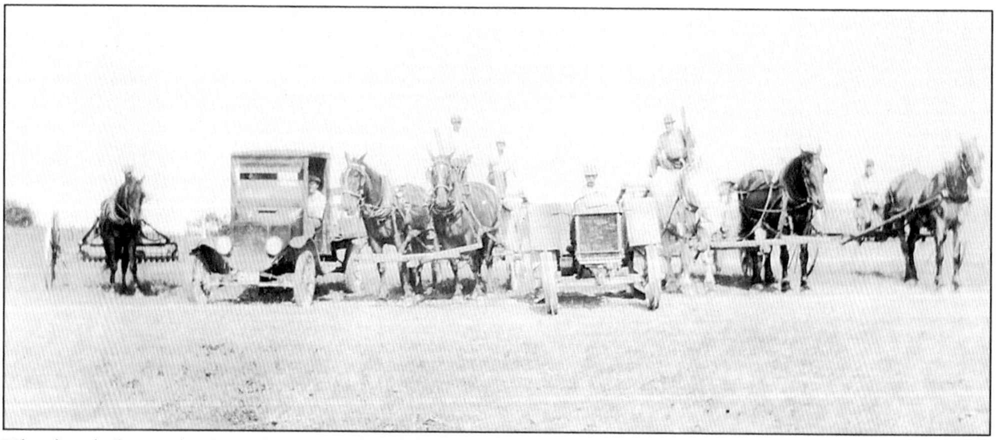

The land along the bay shore south of Oyster Creek in Damariscotta was owned for a number of years by Edward W. Freeman who started Round Top Farms. Haying the farm's rolling fields c. 1922 is this Round Top crew. Note that the men are using an iron-wheeled tractor in addition to their teams of horses. The property is now owned by the Damariscotta River Association, which has its offices in the farmhouse once occupied by George Pitcher, a teamster at Round Top Farms. (Carolyn Reny)

Three

The River

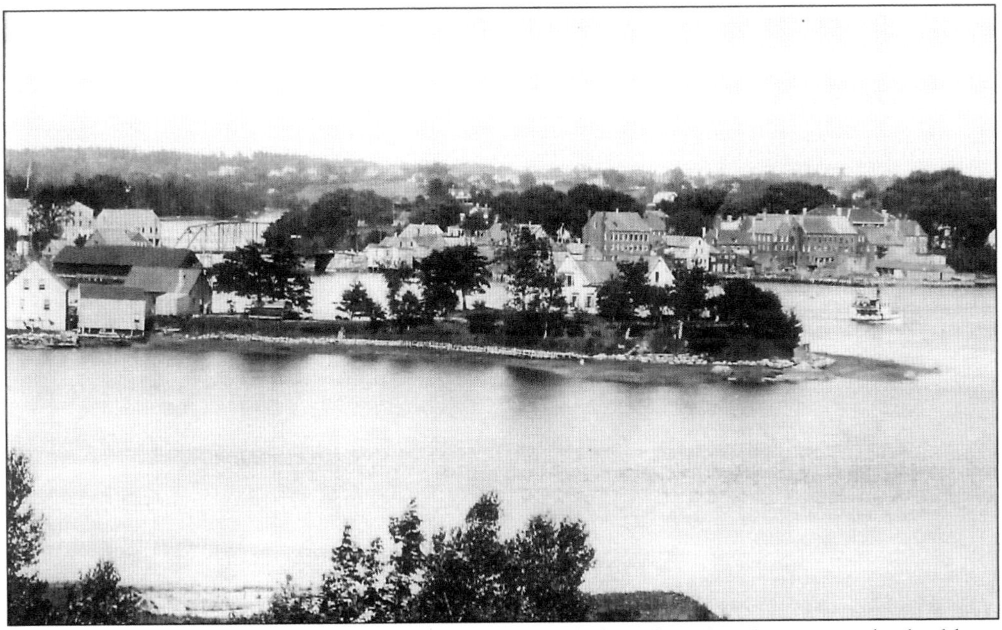

The early history of Newcastle and Damariscotta includes a lengthy chapter on shipbuilding. The tremendous forests of oak and pine along the river attracted skilled men who built hundreds of sloops, schooners, barks, brigs, and full-rigged ships. This portion of the river developed around the shipbuilding and brickmaking industries, turning the area at "The Bridge" into one of considerable activity during the mid-nineteenth century. Day, Stetson, Bryant, Metcalf, and Norris are among the names associated with shipbuilding along the river and salt bay, and whose fortunes are reflected in many of the large commercial buildings in the Twin Villages. (Norman Kelsey)

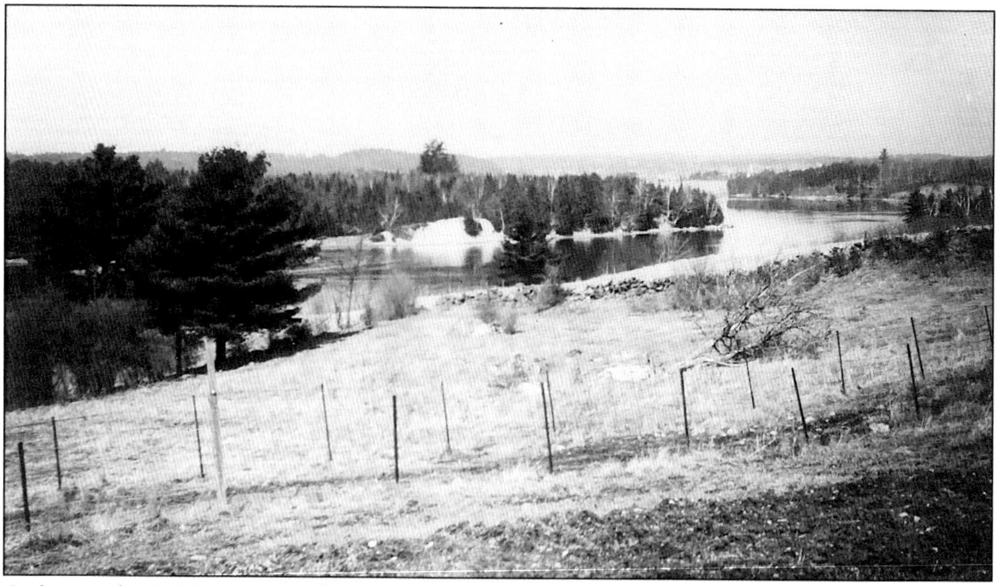

As late as the 1880s mounds of shells several feet high could still be seen on both shores of the river just as it narrows from the salt bay. These shell middens were evidence of the plentiful supply of food that the Damariscotta provided Native Peoples in their seasonal migration to the coast. The shells on the western shore, as seen from the fields at Round Top c. 1920, were never destroyed, largely due to the efforts of the Glidden family (and later the Hart family) who owned the land and wanted them preserved. (Carolyn Reny)

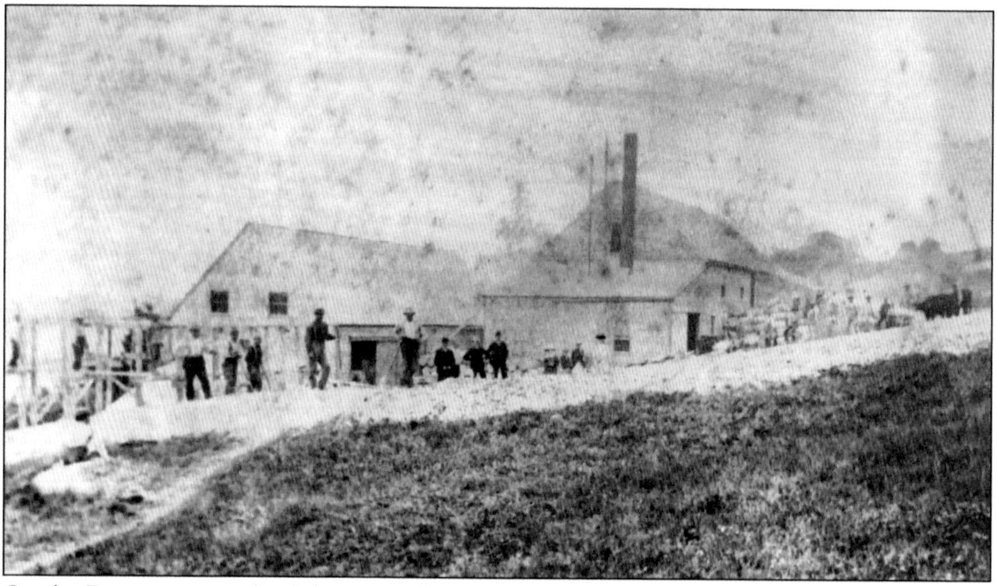

On the Damariscotta side of the river a Boston company built a factory in 1886 which ground up the shells for use in fertilizers and poultry food. Workmen removed shells from the large "Whaleback Mound" which was said to be 341 feet long and from 4 to 20 feet deep. The enterprise was short-lived, but not before hundreds of tons of shells had been removed from the riverbank. E.C. Holmes revived the plant in 1891 shortly before the buildings burned in November of that year. The shell middens were placed on the National Register of Historic Places in 1969 and are now protected. (Nobleboro Historical Society, Ivan Flye Collection)

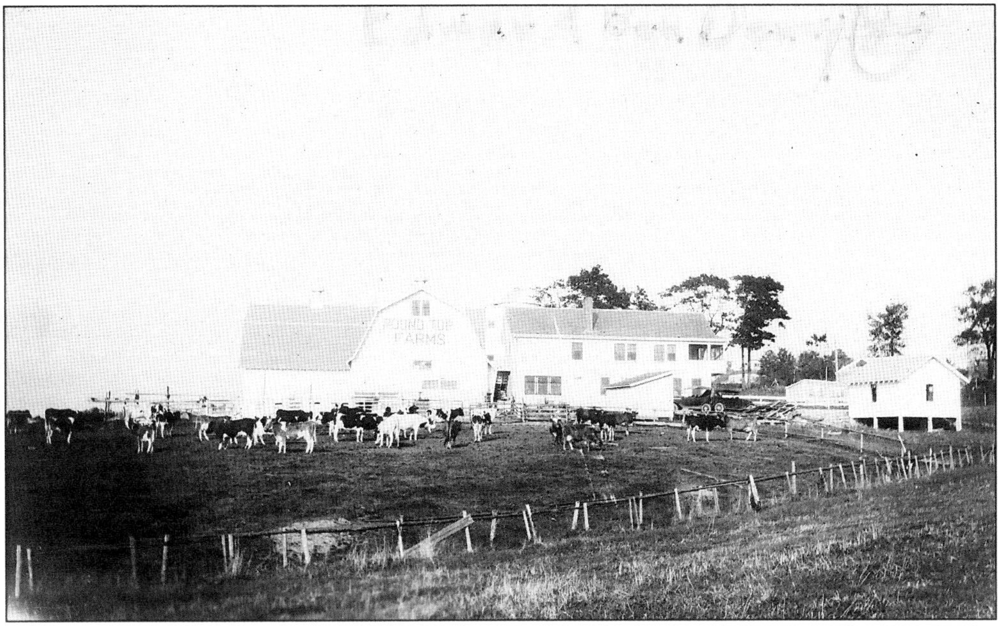

The Round Top Farms barn and dairy as the buildings looked in the 1920s. The farm had a large herd of Holstein and Guernsey cattle, a dairy processing plant, an ice cream business, an apple orchard, and haying and logging operations. It had several year-round employees with additional help hired during the busy summer months. The farm was managed for Mr. Freeman at that time by Edward Denny who lived with his family in the house which is now used for the offices and galleries of Round Top Center for the Arts. The barn has been converted into a performing arts center. (Carolyn Reny)

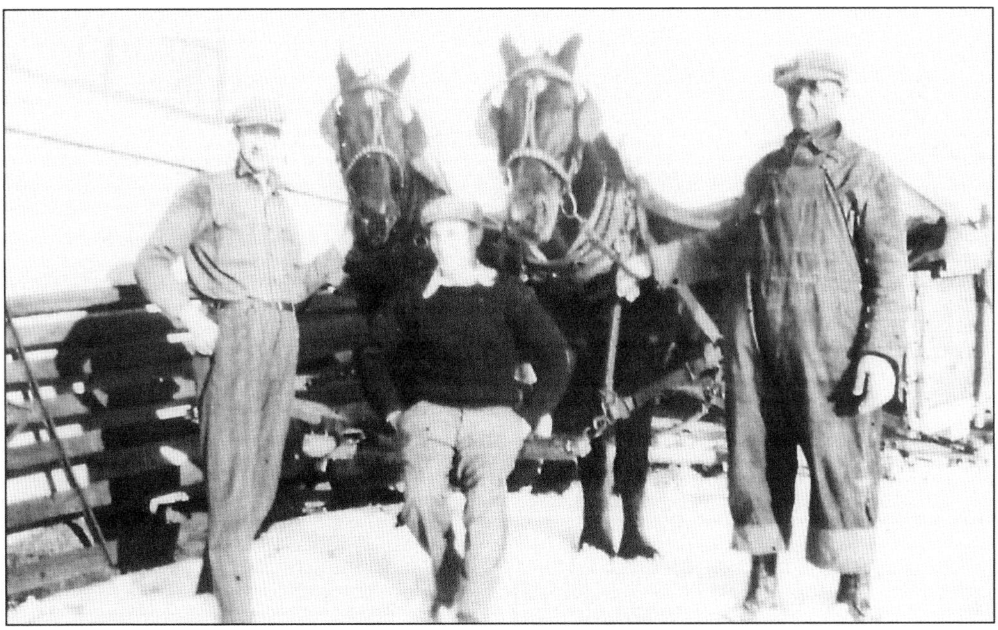

Winfield Cooper (a Round Top herdsman) and George Pitcher (a teamster) flank an unidentified man and one of the farm's teams of horses during a winter logging operation. (Marjorie Dodge)

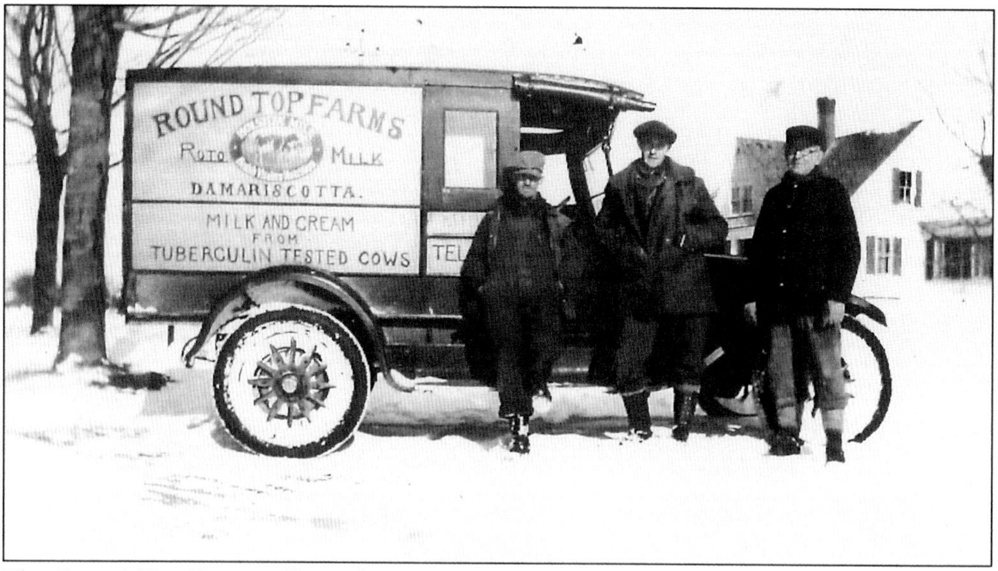

This Round Top Farms milk truck appears to have plowed through a few snowdrifts on the way to its customers. Home-delivered milk products in returnable glass containers characterized the dairy business in the 1920s and '30s. Winfield Cooper is the man in the center. (Marjorie Dodge)

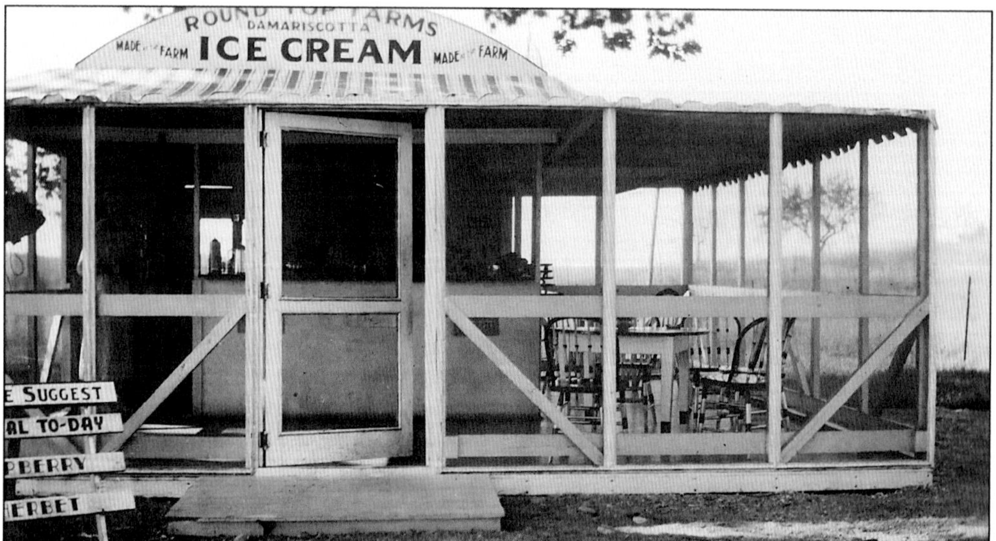

The first Round Top ice cream stand was portable. These screens were made in sections and put in place every summer when the stand opened for business. The ice cream business was started by Mr. Denny, who made the first product himself. (Carolyn Reny)

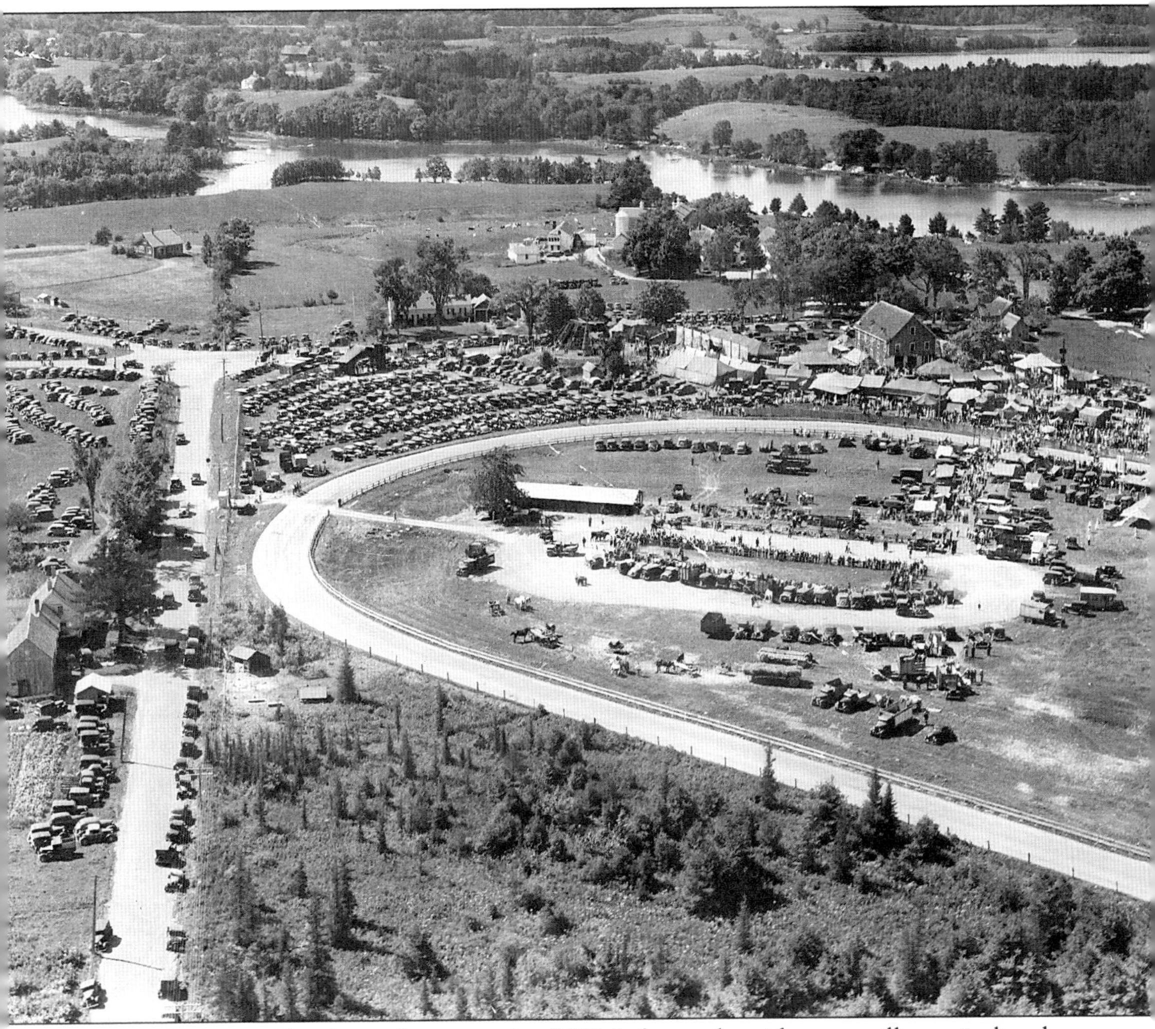

The Lincoln County Fair drew a large crowd, *c.* 1935. It featured a midway as well as agricultural events and exhibits. The race track, reported to be one of the finest in the state, encircles the field used for ox-pulling. Farmers from all over the county brought their animals to this annual event (see page 17). The fair operated until the mid-1940s, and after closing for two years due to financial problems, reopened for one last season in 1947. This photograph is an excellent view of the section of river between the salt bay and the bridge linking the Twin Villages. Round Top Farms is located in the upper center between the fairgrounds and the river, with the shell heaps and a few Glidden Street houses just visible on the Newcastle shore. (Carolyn Reny)

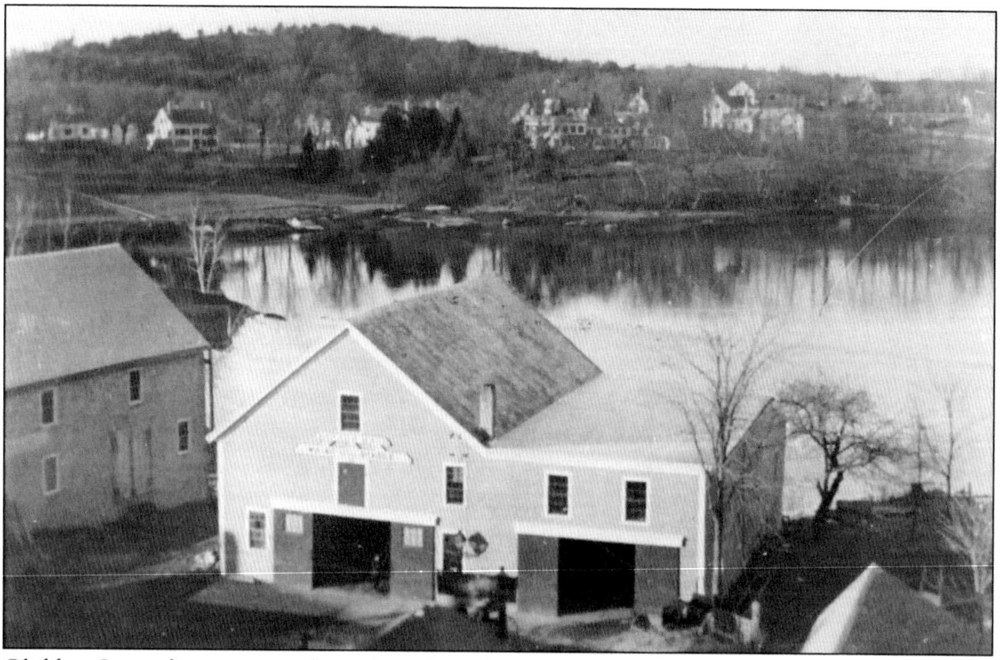

Glidden Street houses are reflected in the calm water of the river just before it flows under the bridge. The building in the foreground was the barn and stable for the Maine Hotel which was located in the Day Block on Main Street. "Stylish Rigs and Good Horses" became the advertising slogan for the stables which sat on the site now occupied by the Elm Street Plaza. (Nobleboro Historical Society, Ivan Flye Collection)

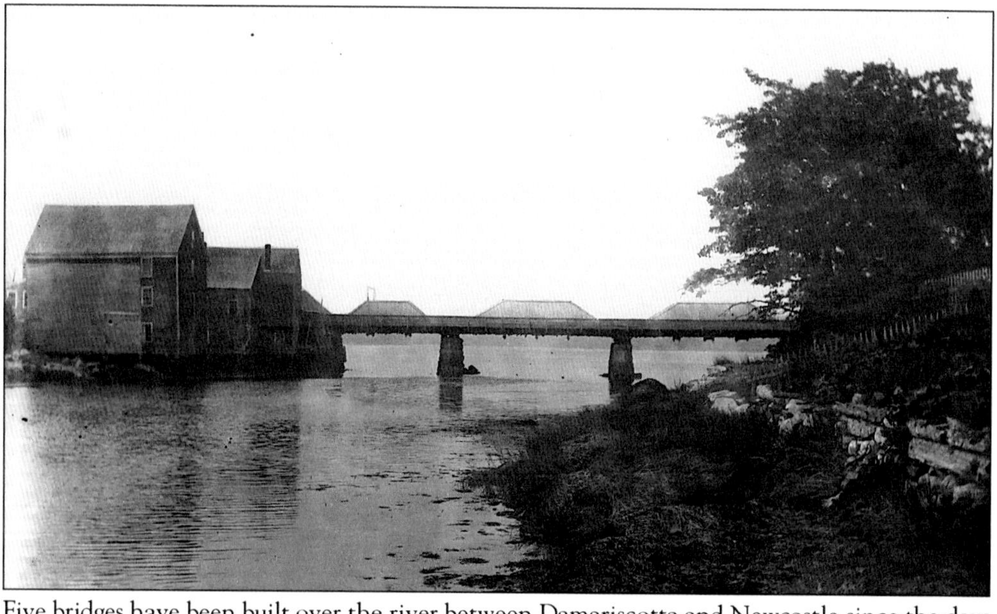

Five bridges have been built over the river between Damariscotta and Newcastle since the days of Mr. Trumbull's eighteenth-century ferry. This three-span wooden bridge, photographed from the Glidden Street shore, was built in 1888 and remained in place until the Merrill buildings, on the left, burned in 1905. The Damariscotta end of the bridge caught fire in that blaze and it had to be replaced, this time with an iron bridge. (Mac Blanchard)

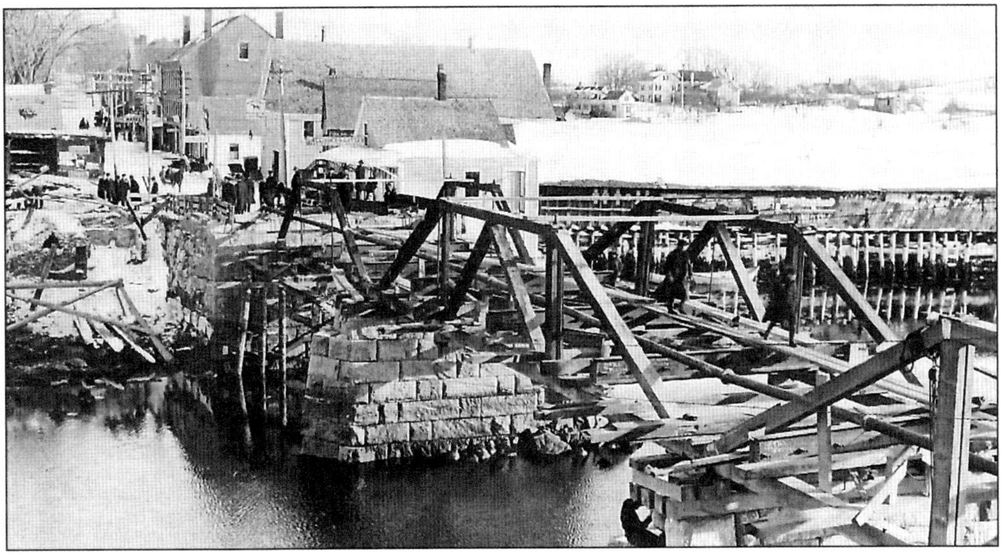

Shortly after the 1905 fire onlookers came to view the scorched timbers of the bridge as it was being demolished. Foot traffic only was allowed at this critical phase of reconstruction, forcing vehicular traffic around the salt bay through Damariscotta Mills. The cost of the new iron bridge was $9000, which included the removal of the two granite piers. Newcastle and Damariscotta shared the cost. (Marjorie Dodge)

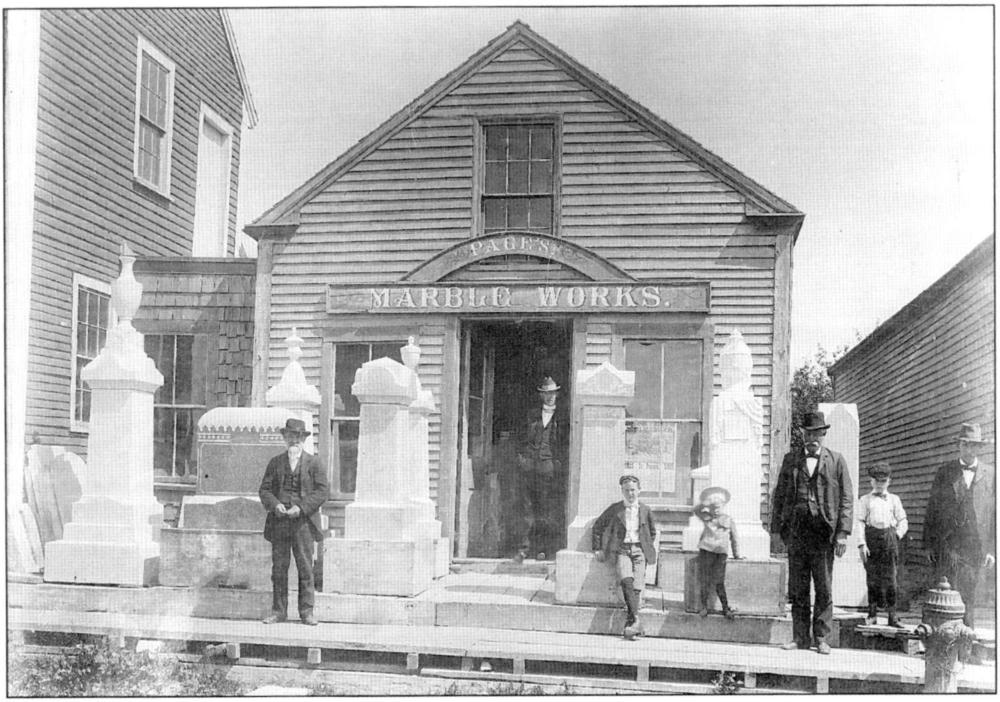

Close to the bridge but escaping serious damage in the fire was Page's Marble and Granite Works, a business started in 1879 by Marius Page. This photograph, taken c. 1900, shows the elaborately carved stones displayed for sale outside the shop. From left to right are: unknown, Harry Dow (in doorway), Harold O. Page, Otis S. Page, Marius H. Page, B. Taylor, and Herbert Dow. (David Page)

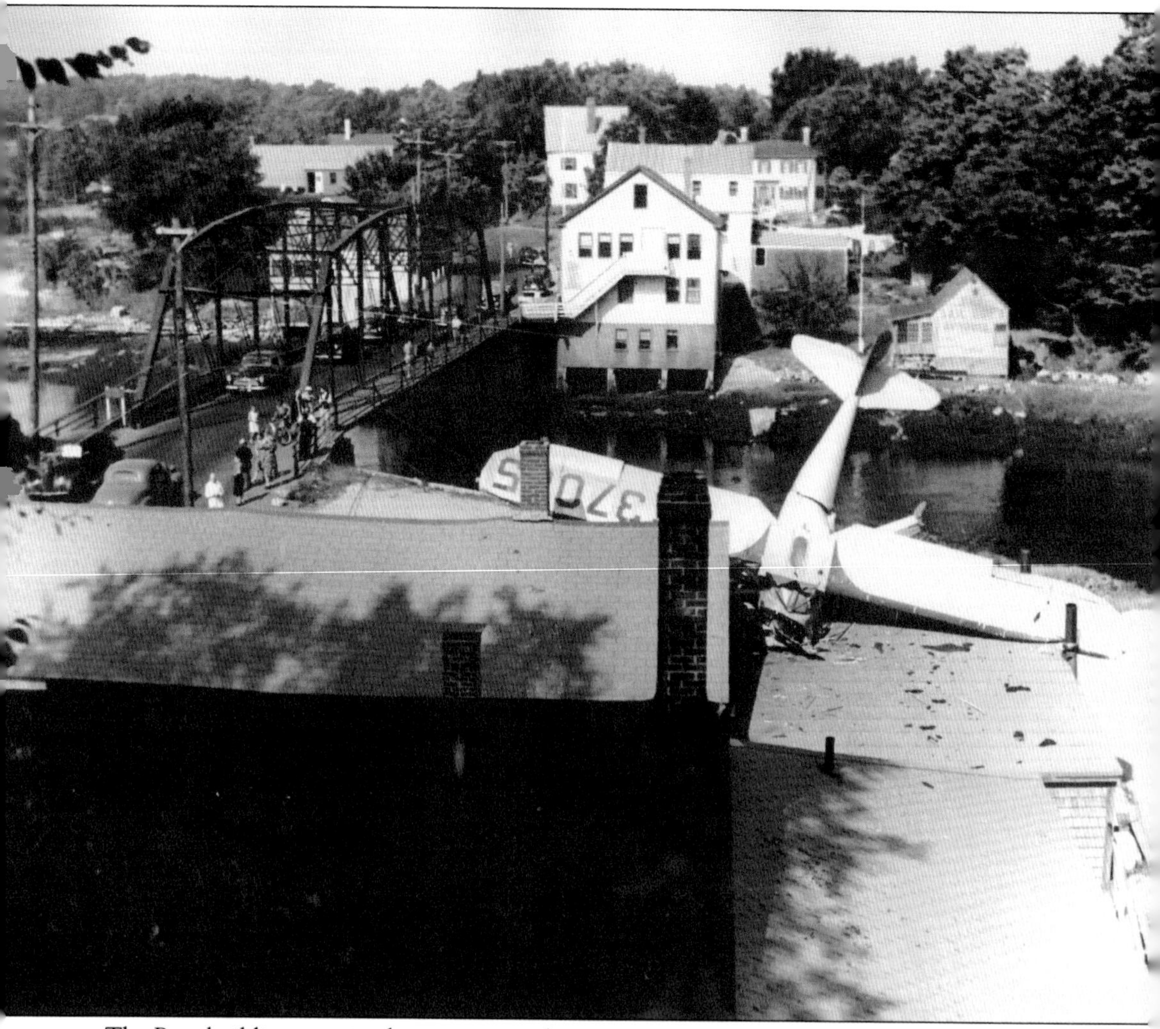

The Page buildings received an unexpected visitor on September 5, 1948, when this small plane became entangled in wires near the bridge and crashed into the roof. The floatplane was one of three carrying friends to visit Edward Freeman, owner of Round Top Farms; instead of touching down on Pemaquid Lake as originally planned, the three planes were attempting a river landing. The New York City pilot, who was able to crawl out of the aircraft, was hospitalized with facial lacerations and a broken nose. The other two planes landed safely. The next day state police ordered the plane dismantled and removed from the premises because sightseers were blocking the flow of traffic at the Damariscotta end of the bridge. (David Page)

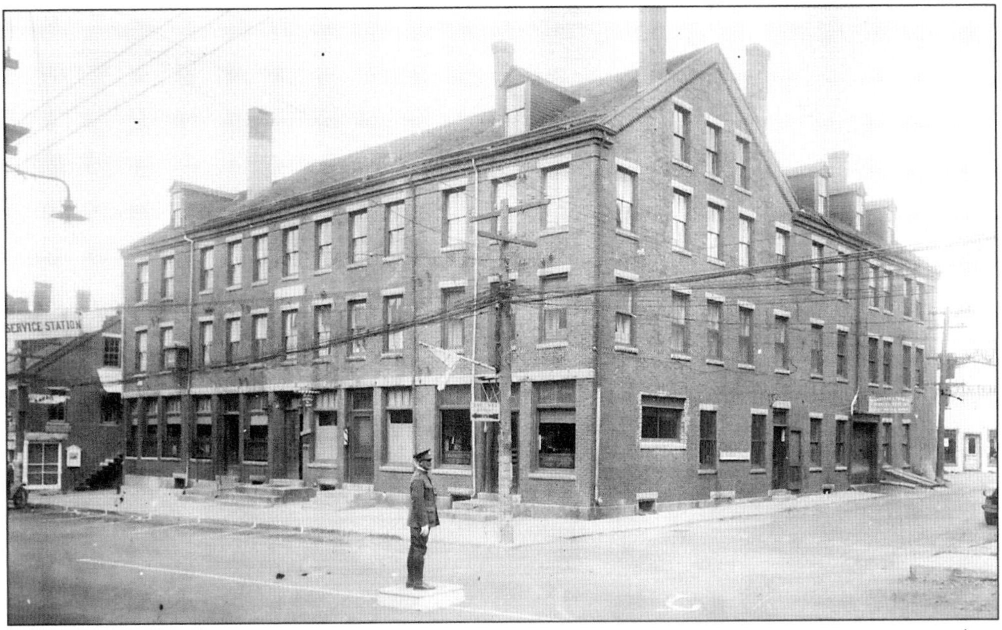

The mid-Maine coast appears to have been "undiscovered" in 1925 as Damariscotta Police Officer Joseph Lewis waits patiently for some traffic to direct. Behind him is the Day Block, built in 1850 by shipbuilder Joseph Day, just a few years after a disastrous fire leveled Main Street's wooden buildings. On the first floor of the building on the left were the offices of the First National Bank; in the center was a barbershop; and on the right was the Damariscotta Post Office. The large doorway in the center led, originally, to the second- and third-floor rooms of the Maine Hotel, but by 1925 those floors housed offices and apartments. (Nobleboro Historical Society, Ivan Flye Collection)

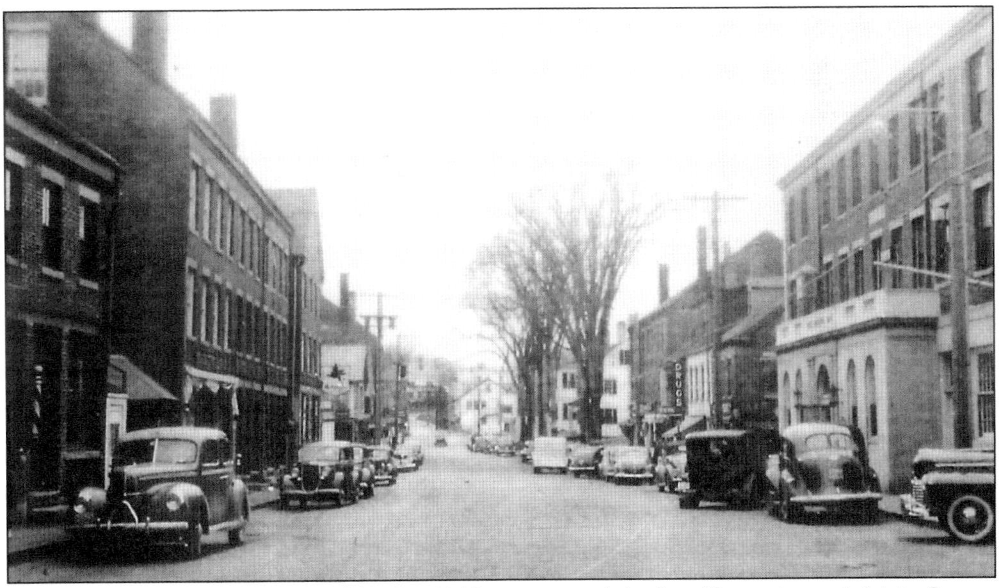

Traffic appears to have increased by the 1940s as automobiles line Damariscotta's Main Street. Note the changes in the façade of the Day Block, right, made by the First National Bank as it expanded to occupy most of the first floor. (Norman Kelsey)

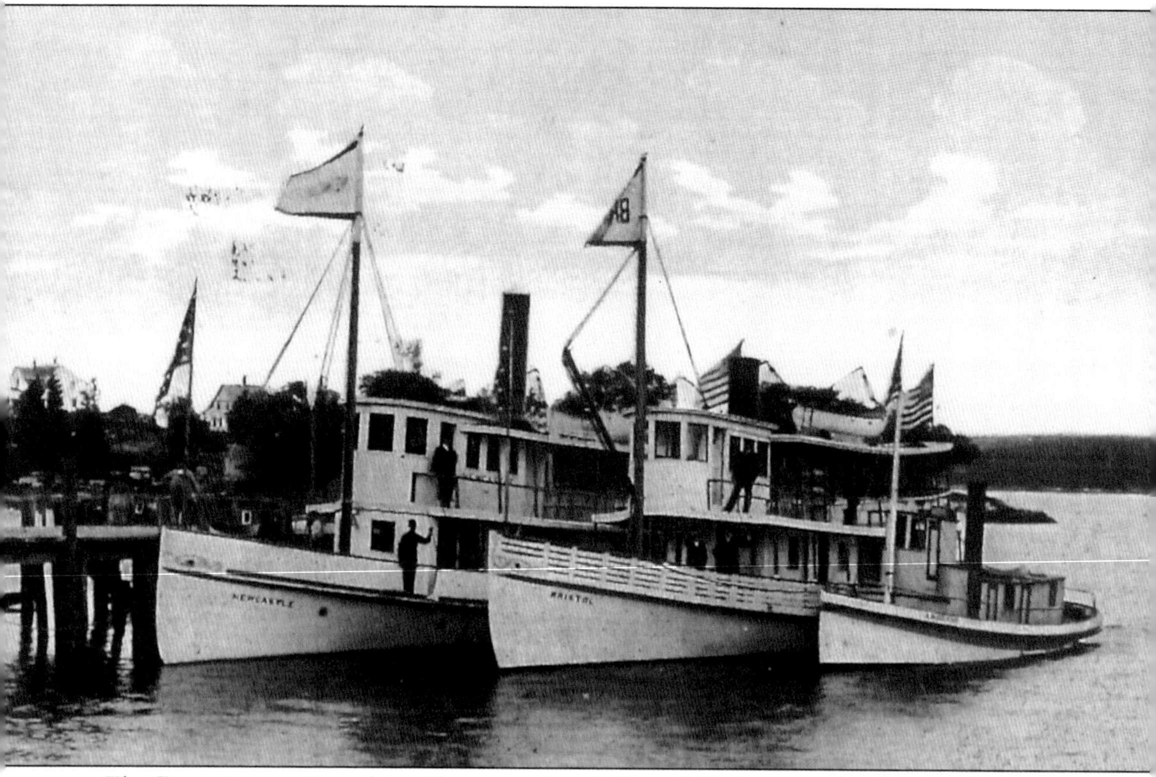

The Damariscotta Steamboat Company, founded in 1900, lines up the fleet, including from left to right: the 80-foot *Newcastle*, the "Queen of the Fleet," which operated on the river from 1902 to 1928; the slightly smaller *Bristol*, built in 1901 and in operation until 1909; and the first and smallest of the fleet, the 36-foot *Anodyne*, which was in service from 1895 to 1922. All of the steamers were built at the A. & M. Gamage shipyard in South Bristol. This photograph was actually taken in South Bristol, but all of these vessels made trips on the river with scheduled stops at East Boothbay, Poole's Landing, Clark's Cove, and Damariscotta, as well as at South Bristol. (William Kelsey)

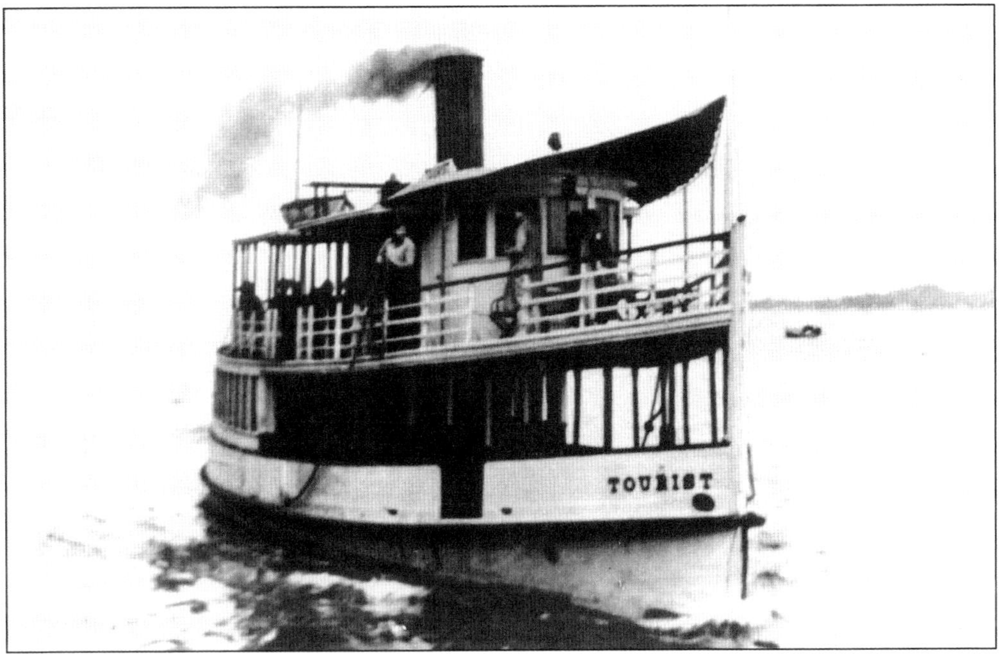

The *Tourist* also carried passengers on the river in the early years of this century. The steamer, which listed its home port as Damariscotta, was built in East Boothbay at the W.I. Adams & Son shipyard in 1908. (Boothbay Region Historical Society)

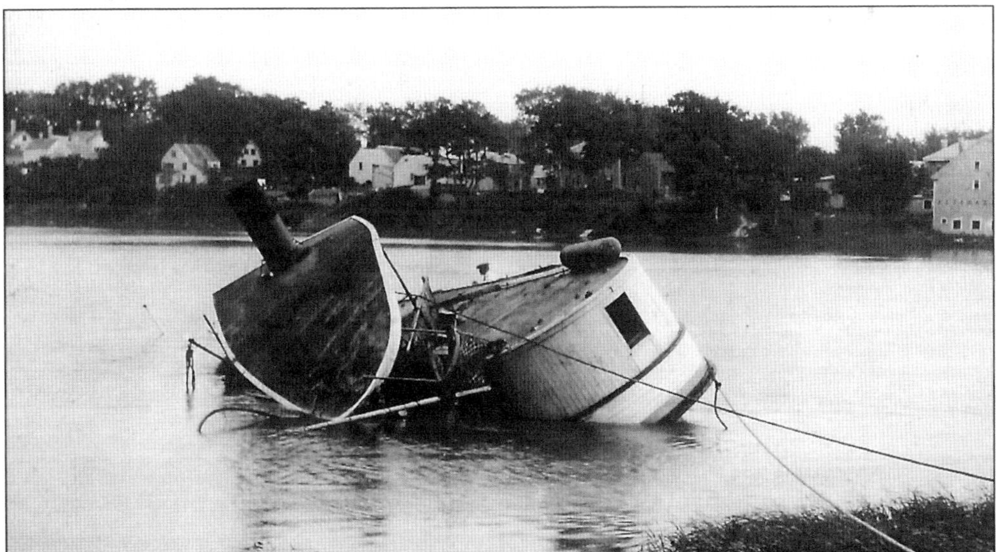

On August 26, 1918, the engineer of the *Tourist*, because of an injury to his arm, failed to reverse the engines as the steamer was landing at the dock in Damariscotta. The vessel (with nineteen passengers aboard) surged ahead and struck the bridge, tearing off the hurricane deck. The engineer drowned in the mishap. The steamer drifted upriver and is shown tied to the Newcastle shore above the bridge waiting for a salvage crew. The *Tourist* was bought and taken to Boothbay where she was refitted and renamed *Sabino*. Eventually she was sold and used to haul freight out of Portland for a few years before being taken to Connecticut where she still runs excursions at Mystic Seaport. (William Kelsey)

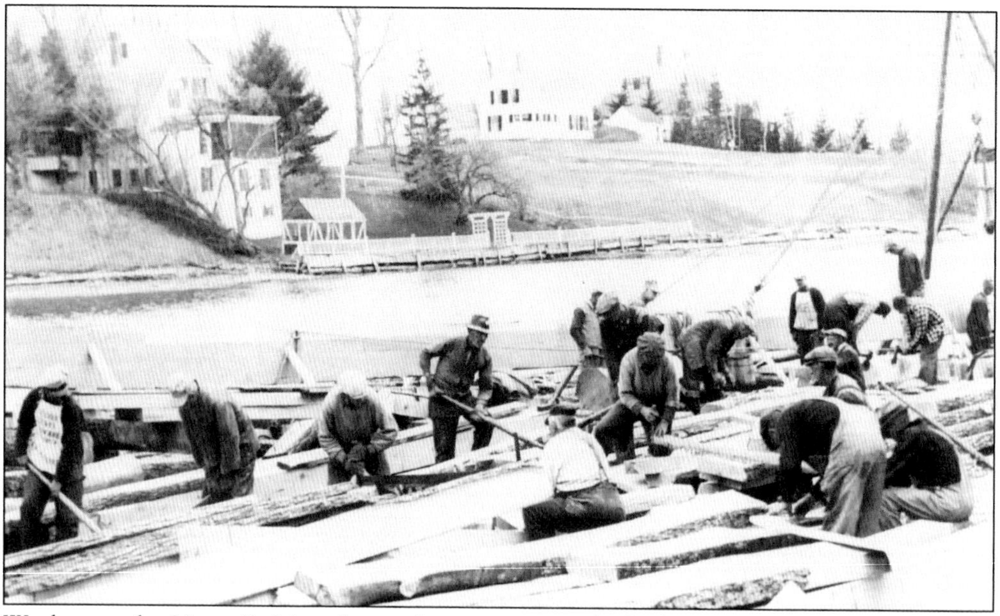

Workers at the Harry O. Marr shipyard are preparing planks for the construction of a vessel, probably a minesweeper or transport for the U.S. government, as this photograph was taken during World War II. Maine shipyards were busy during the early 1940s when they were called upon to produce several different types of vessels for the war effort. The Marr shipyard was located where the municipal parking lot is today and was the last shipyard to operate in Damariscotta. (Nobleboro Historical Society, Ivan Flye Collection)

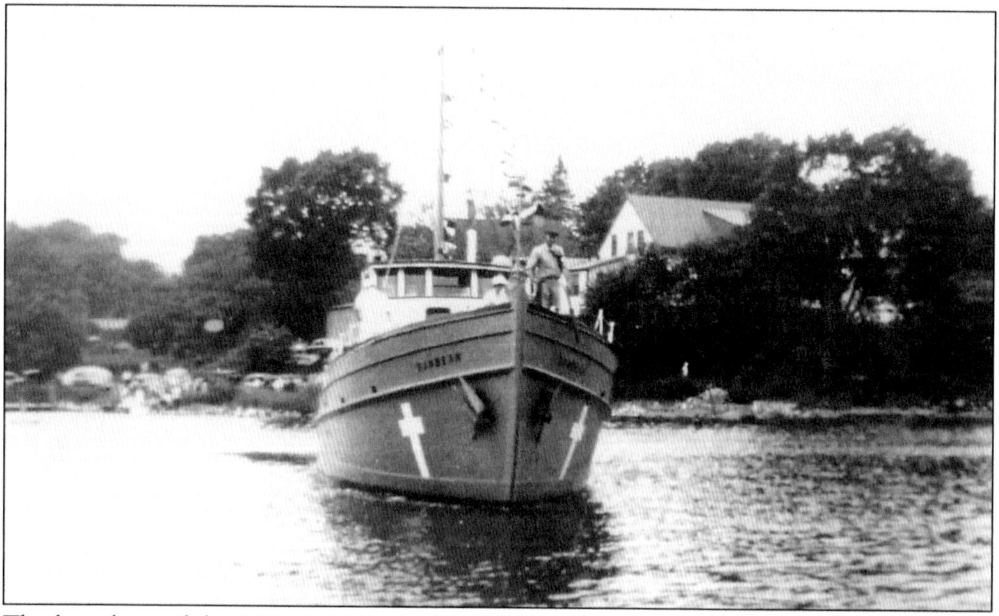

The launching of the 66-foot *Sunbeam III* in 1939 at the Marr shipyard was the second such vessel commissioned by the Maine Seacoast Missionary Society to be built in Damariscotta. Nicknamed "God's Tugboat," the *Sunbeam* carried its ministry to isolated communities and islands off the Maine coast. In 1926 the 37-ton *Sunbeam II* slid down the ways at the Jonah P. Morse yard, the Marr shipyard's predecessor. (David Belknap)

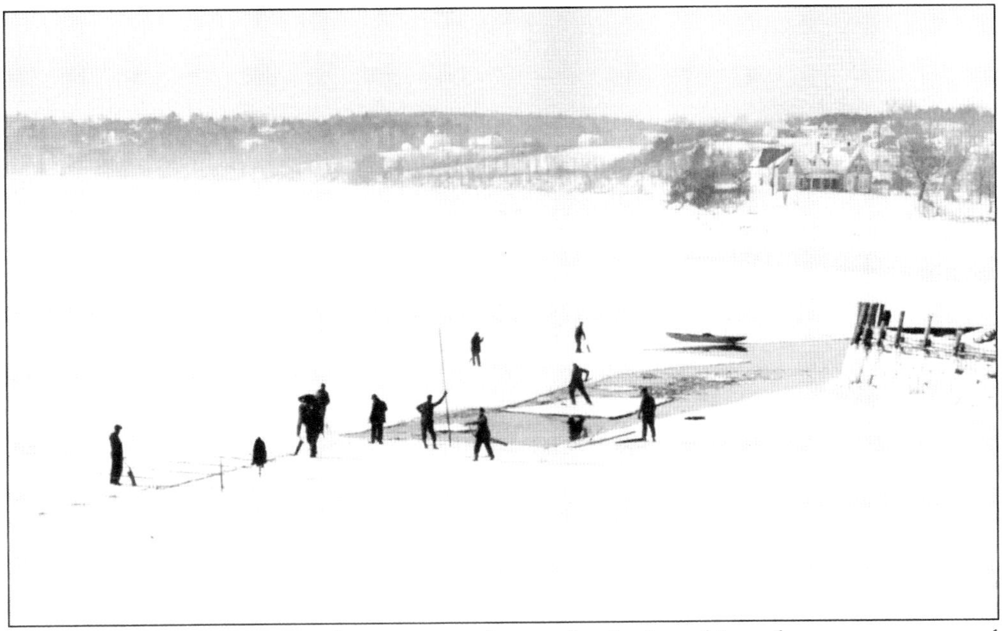

These men are cutting ice on the river to make way for the launching of a government vessel from the Marr shipyard in January of 1942. Later the *Sunbeam III*, acting as an icebreaker, cut a channel so the A.P.C. could safely reach the open ocean. Harry O. Marr took over the Morse yard in 1939 and operated it until it closed permanently in 1947. (Nobleboro Historical Society, Ivan Flye Collection)

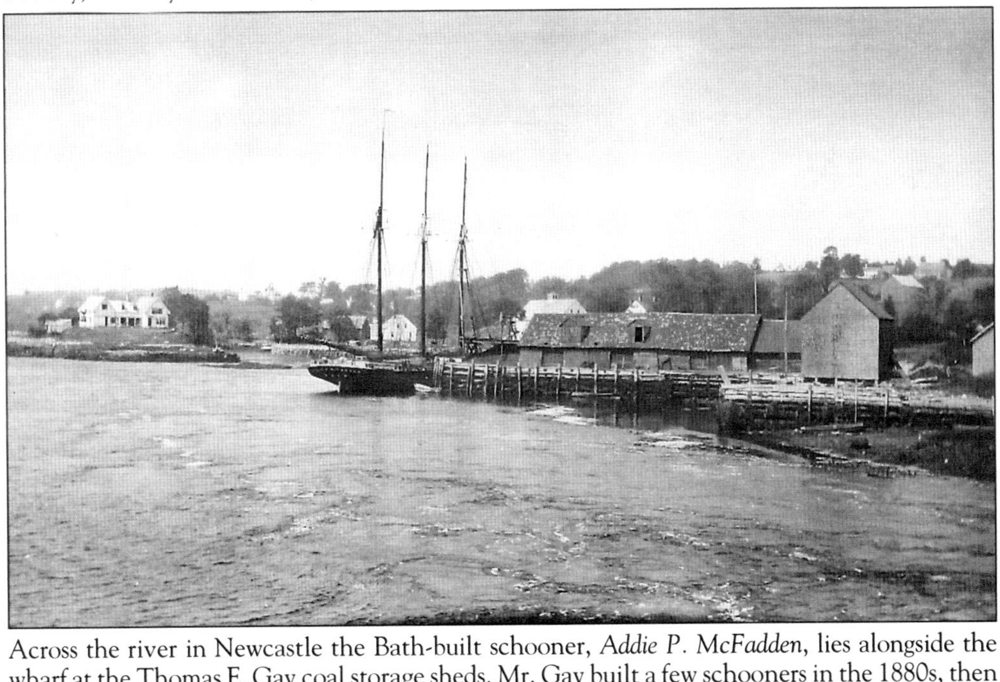

Across the river in Newcastle the Bath-built schooner, *Addie P. McFadden*, lies alongside the wharf at the Thomas E. Gay coal storage sheds. Mr. Gay built a few schooners in the 1880s, then turned his talents toward managing his grocery store and coal business. Five generations of the Gay family owned the store on Main Street at the west end of the bridge. (Marjorie Dodge)

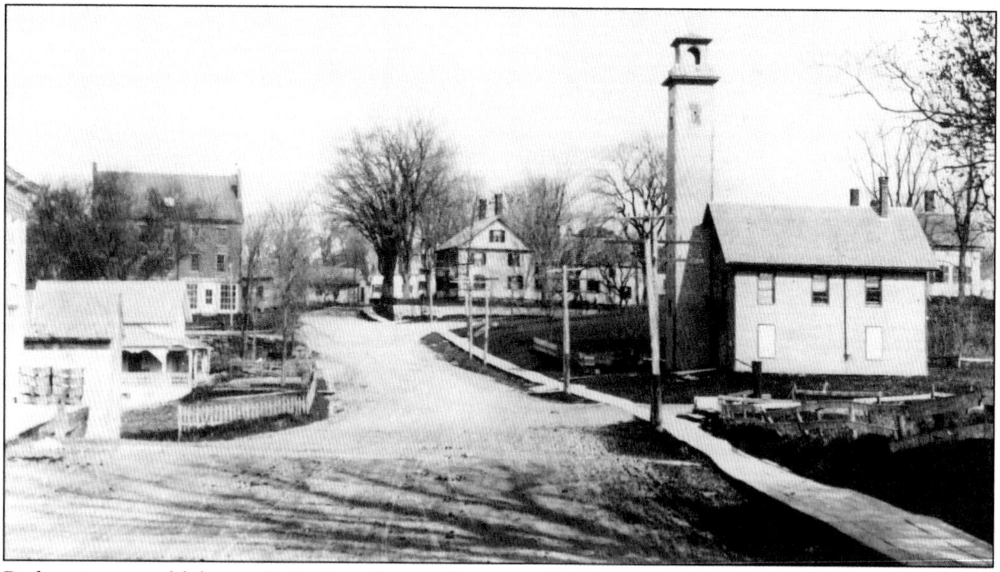

Pedestrians could keep their feet dry walking on Newcastle's wooden sidewalks soon after the turn of the century. The Main Street buildings are, counterclockwise from the right: the Taniscot Engine House with its high tower for drying hose; the Genthner house on the corner of the Mills Road (whose iron fence is now in front of Skidompha Library); and the Austin Block (now Newcastle Square), which originally housed the Newcastle National Bank before it moved to the Glidden Block just west of the bridge. (Nobleboro Historical Society, Ivan Flye Collection)

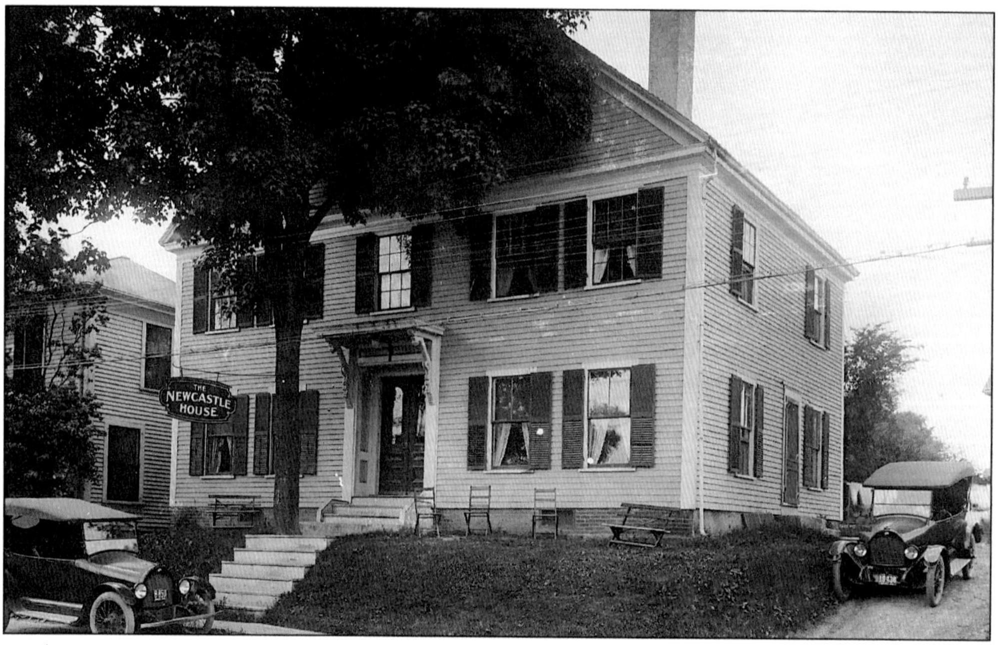

In the 1920s accommodations in town could be found at the Newcastle House, also located on Main Street (currently site of the Maritime Farms convenience store). Earlier, in 1908, this house and the one next door, the St. Andrews Parish House, became the temporary quarters for the Newcastle National Bank after the Glidden Block burned. (Arthur Jones)

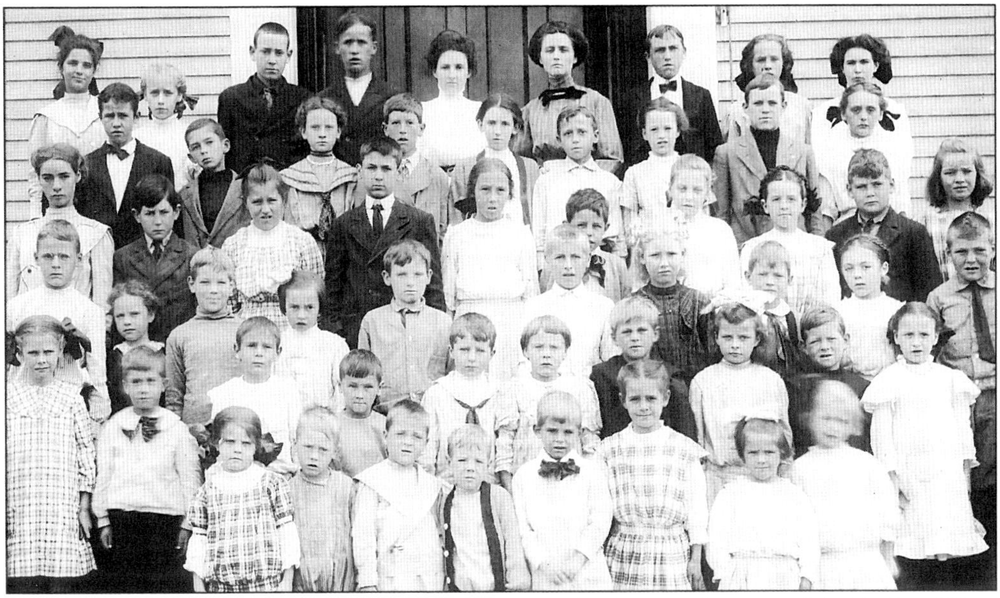

In the fall of 1910 these children had a group photograph taken on the steps of the Bridge Village School on Mills Road. This building had been built in 1901, and thirty years later was renamed Franklin Grammar School by the student body. After a 1950 addition was made to consolidate Newcastle's remaining rural schools, Franklin served as the town's elementary school until 1980 when Great Salt Bay Community School officially opened. The only person identified in the photograph is Walter Rand (second row from the back, second left). (Arthur Jones)

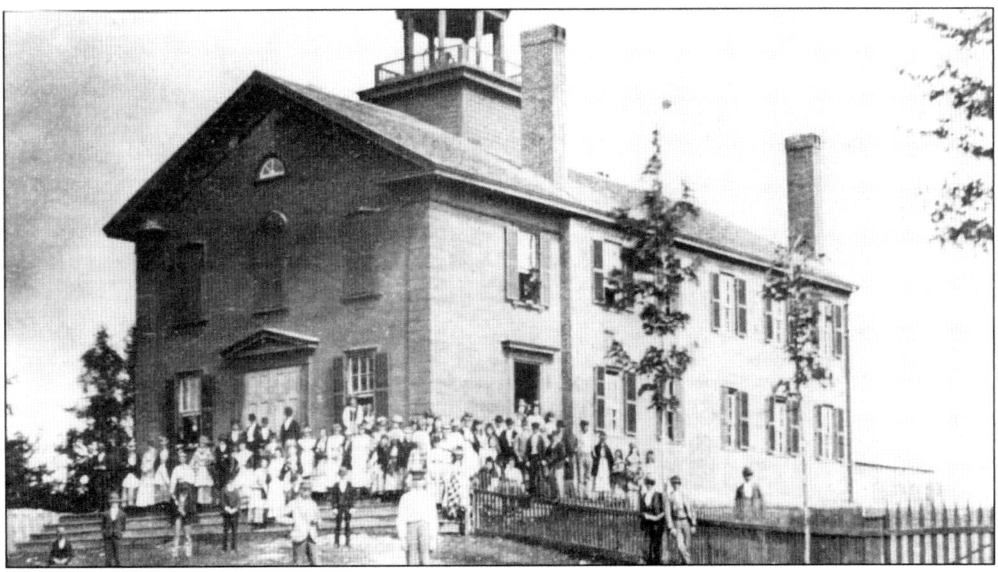

Students at Lincoln Academy line up for a group picture in 1890. The front portion of this building was built in 1829 after the original building on the River Road burned. Around the turn of the century Lincoln Academy attracted more students from towns along the river because of the reliable transportation offered by the steamers. During the winter when the steamboats were not running many of those students boarded with residents of Newcastle and Damariscotta. (Nobleboro Historical Society, Ivan Flye Collection)

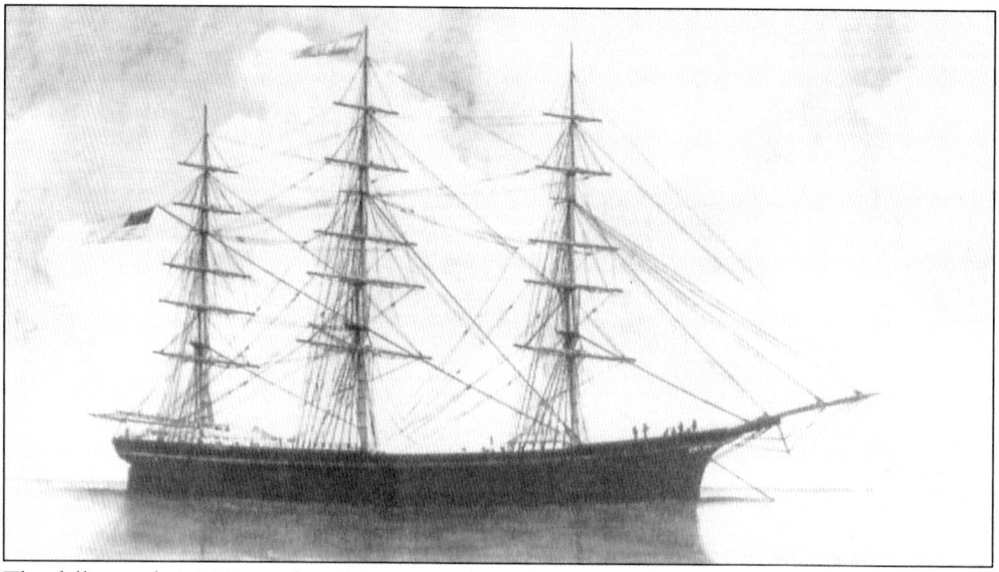

The full-rigged, 1,155-ton ship, *Norris*, was built by Elbridge Norris in 1874, and was one of seven vessels launched that year at "The Bridge." Norris built several large sailing vessels during Newcastle and Damariscotta's boom years, many of them with Benjamin Metcalf. Later, on his own, he built at least one Down Easter, a full-rigged ship, not quite as sleek and fast as a clipper, but sturdier and with a greater carrying capacity. These vessels transported grain, lumber, and guano from Pacific Coast ports, and helped extend the era of large sailing vessels for a few more years. (Lillian Hale)

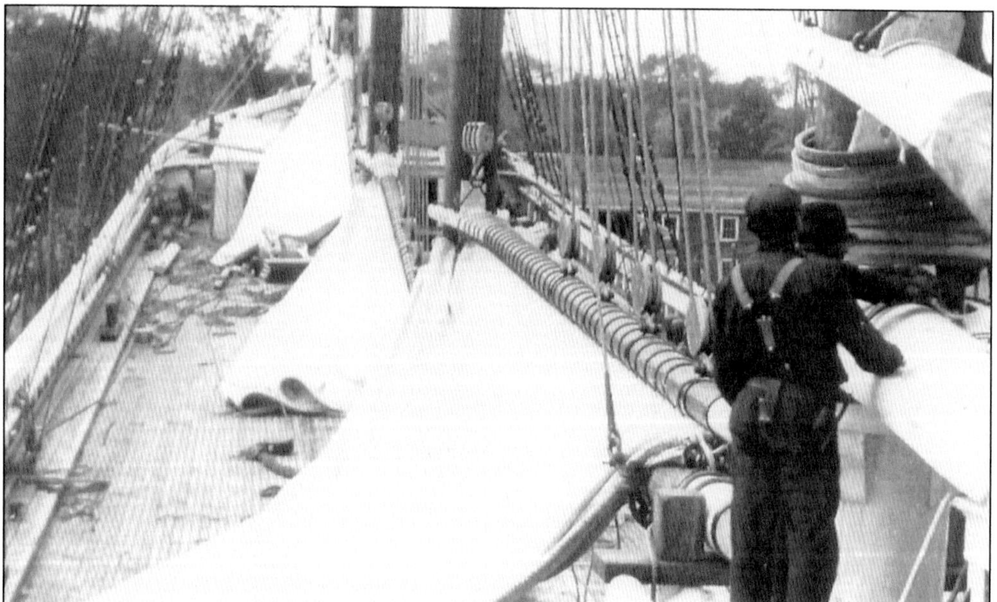

By 1885 iron and steam had made great inroads in New England shipbuilding and although Maine did not abandon the wooden vessel, her shipbuilders were forced to turn their efforts toward the more maneuverable schooners for the coastal trade. These vessels had a less complicated rigging and required fewer men to sail them. Here, workmen put the finishing touches on the *Virginia Dare*, a four-masted schooner built in Newcastle. (Lillian Hale)

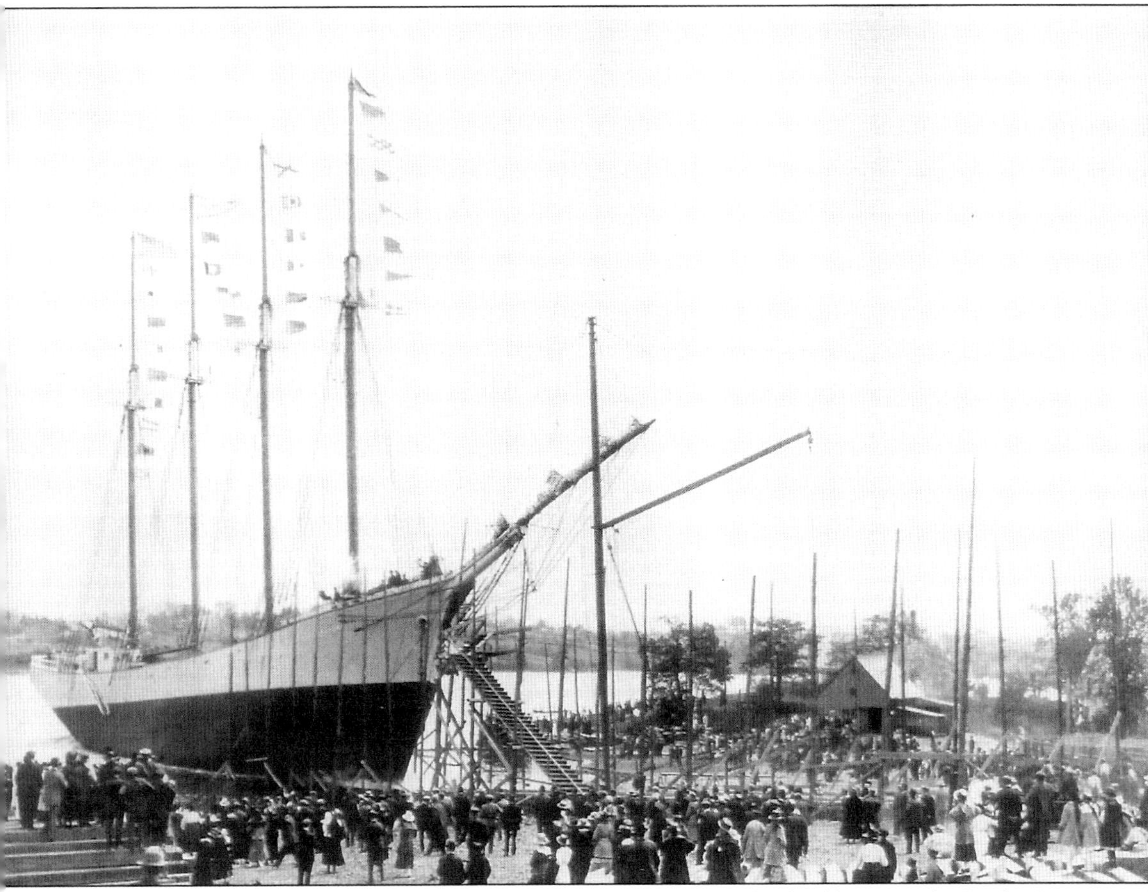

The years at the turn of the twentieth century were lean ones for shipbuilders at "The Bridge." Many Maine yards benefitted from the World War I building boom, but not so Damariscotta and Newcastle. Just after the war, however, Richard Diebold took over the old Haggett yard (in the cove by the Lincoln Home) and began to build, hoping to revive a sagging industry. On June 5, 1919, hundreds of people attended the launching of his first vessel, the *Virginia Dare*, a 1,525-ton four-masted schooner which was sold to a New York man and chartered to haul coal to Europe. The vessel was christened by Inez Colcord (of the Searsport seafaring Colcords) while Lowell Sidelinger and his fife and drum corps played "Yankee Doodle." (Lillian Hale)

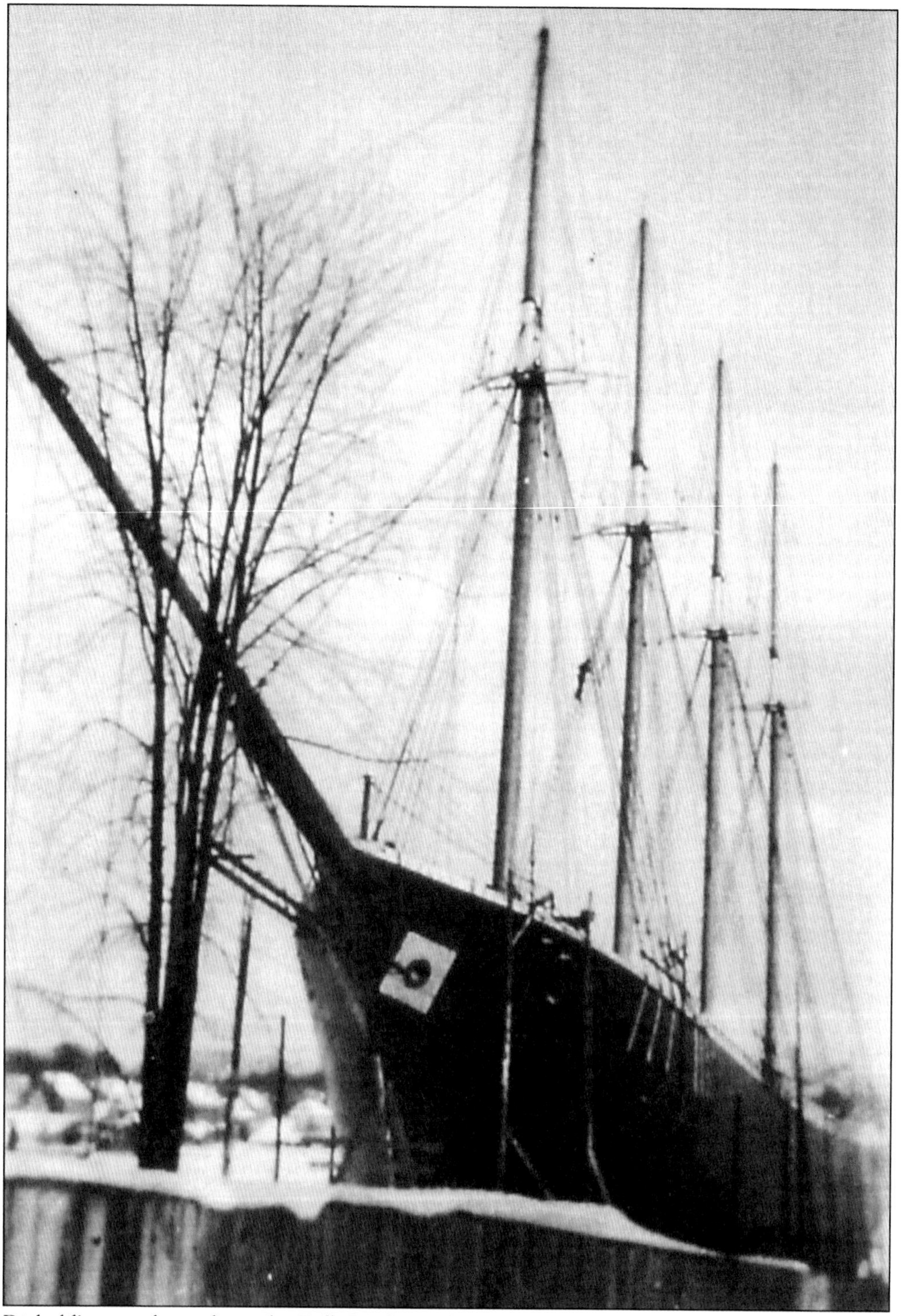

Diebold's second vessel was the *Dolly Madison*, also a four-masted schooner. At a total length of 224 feet, the *Madison*, with its bowsprit, extended over the sidewalk on the River Road. Lillian Hale remembers walking under it on her way to school at Lincoln Academy. (Lillian Hale)

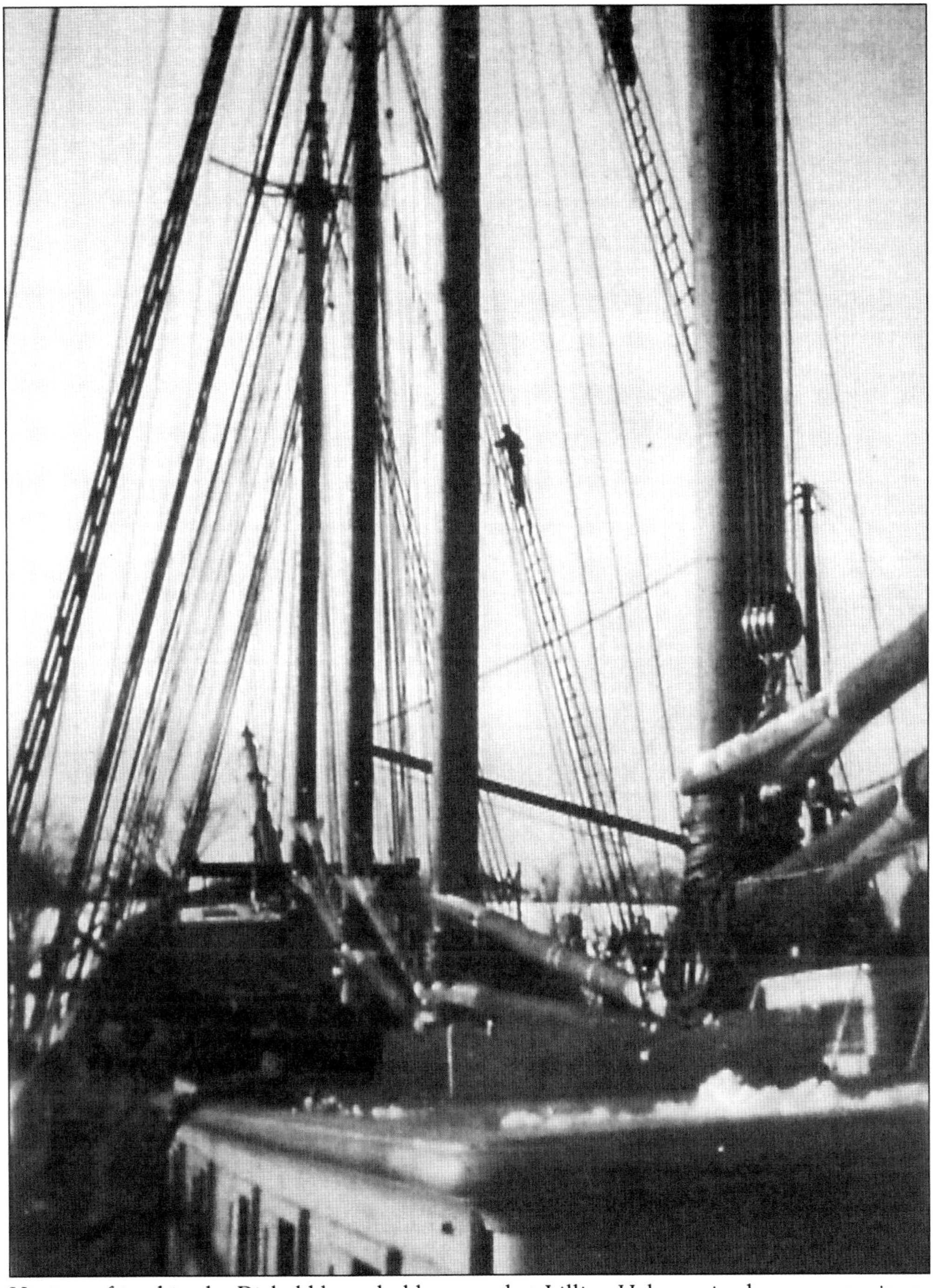

Having a friend in the Diebold household meant that Lillian Hale received an opportunity to go aboard the *Dolly Madison* during construction. She took along her camera and snapped the pictures on these two pages. Note the men working on the ratlines. This vessel was launched on April 5, 1920, after 9 feet of ice had been removed from the stern. The *Dolly Madison* was towed down the river the next day, bound for Norfolk where she would carry coal to San Juan, Puerto Rico. (Lillian Hale)

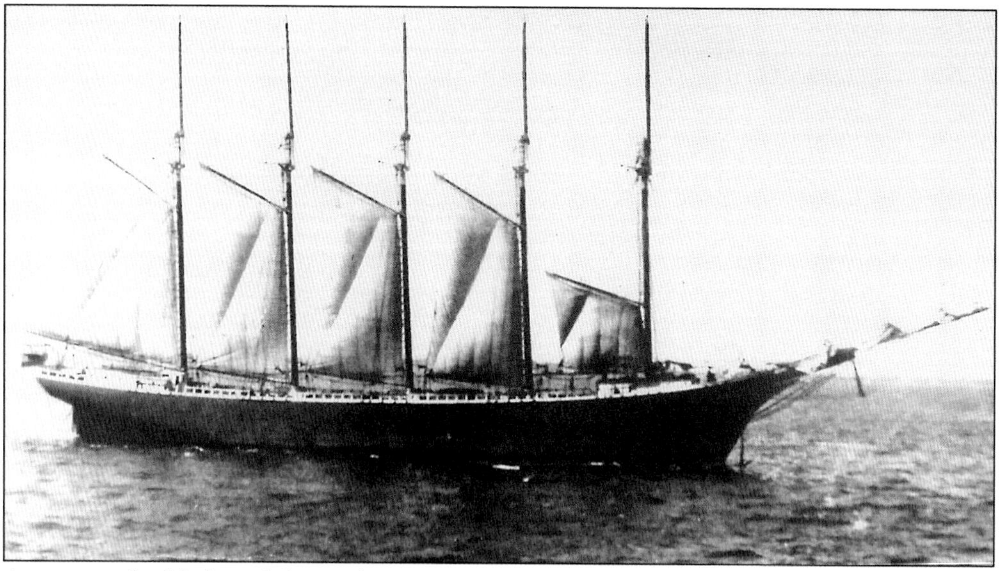

As soon as the *Madison* slid into the river, construction began on the Newcastle Shipbuilding Company's third large schooner, the *Mary H. Diebold*. The crew worked steadily through the summer and fall without time off so the vessel could be launched before the river froze. She was a five-masted schooner, 1,425 tons in weight, and the last large vessel built at the Diebold shipyard. (Lillian Hale)

C&T

The Boston Maritime Corporation

invites you to attend the launching

of the

Schooner "Mary H. Diebold"

on Saturday, November 27, 1920

at 11.30 o'clock, A. M.

from the Shipyard of Richard Diebold

Newcastle, Maine

Crowell & Thurlow
Agents

An invitation to the launching of the *Mary H. Diebold*. Mr. Diebold built one more vessel, the 127-foot fishing schooner *Lark*, but escalating materials and labor costs prevented him from continuing the business that had for three years brought employment to the community. The closing of the Diebold shipyard marked the end of 150 years of the construction of wooden sailing vessels in Damariscotta and Newcastle. (Lillian Hale)

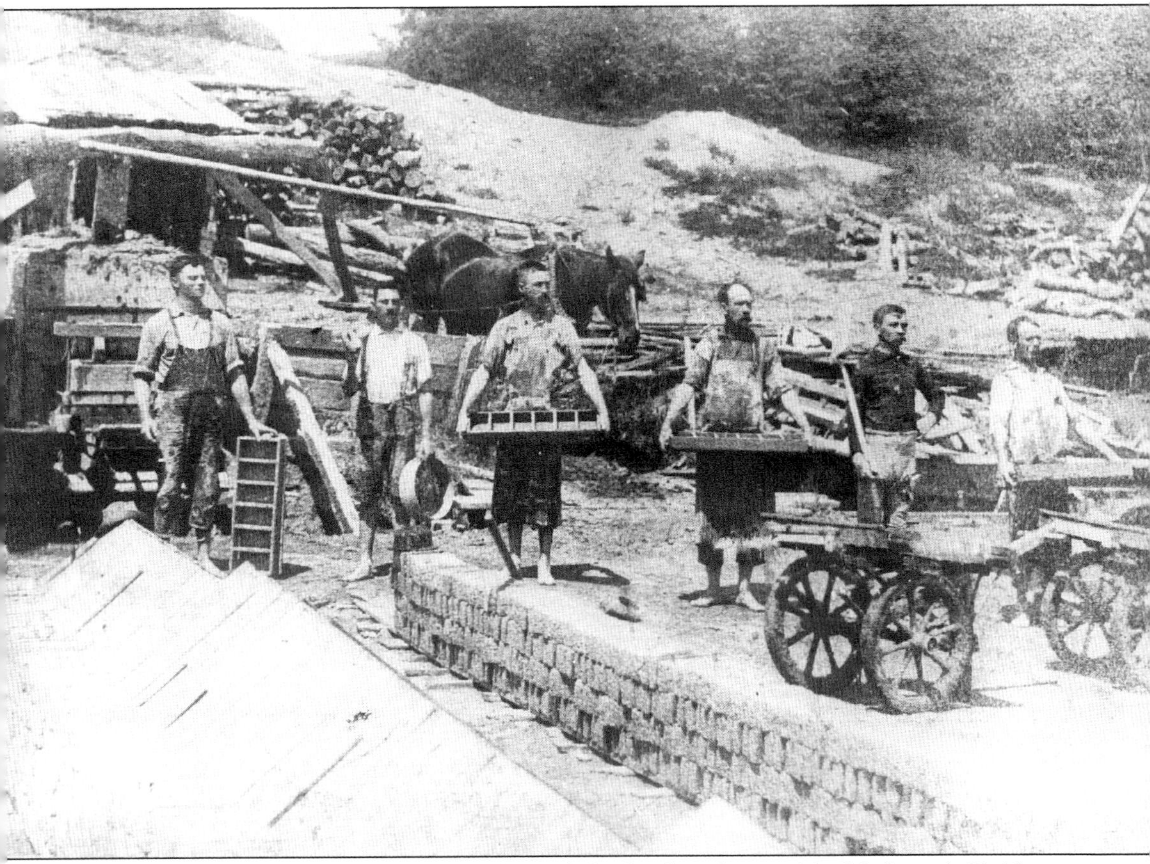

Just downriver from the Diebold shipyard stood the brickyard owned by Nathaniel Glidden Bryant. This yard, still making bricks c. 1900, was one of the last to continue operating after financial problems closed the larger brickyards in the late 1870s. The mid-nineteenth century saw the industry flourish, however, as workmen took advantage of the large deposits of marine clay along the riverbanks. It was backbreaking work and the men labored, barefoot, in the mud throughout their twelve-hour workday. The season began in the spring as soon as the clay could be dug and continued until fall; in the winter men cut wood and stacked it next to the kilns, where 150–200 cords were needed to fire the newly-made product. All of the bricks used in Newcastle and Damariscotta's Main Street buildings were of local manufacture, and hundreds of thousands were shipped on coastal schooners to Boston, Halifax, and other eastern seaboard ports. (Nobleboro Historical Society, Ivan Flye Collection)

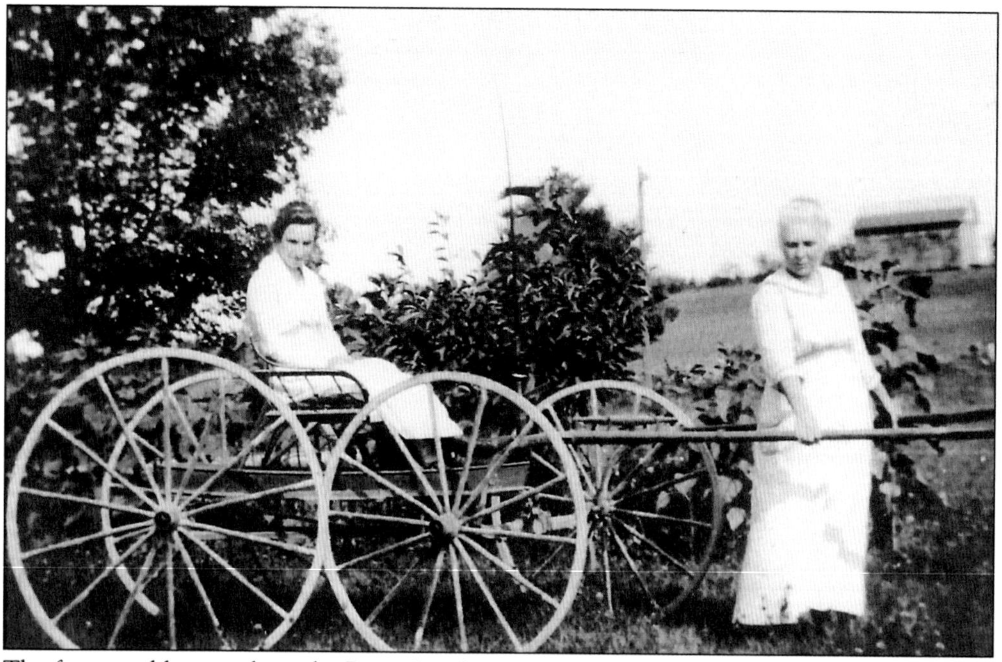

The farms and homes along the River Road are some of the prettiest in the area as they take advantage of the natural beauty of a saltwater shoreline. Alice Boynton and her mother, Mabel, pose for sister Lillian's camera at their home just outside the village. (Lillian Hale)

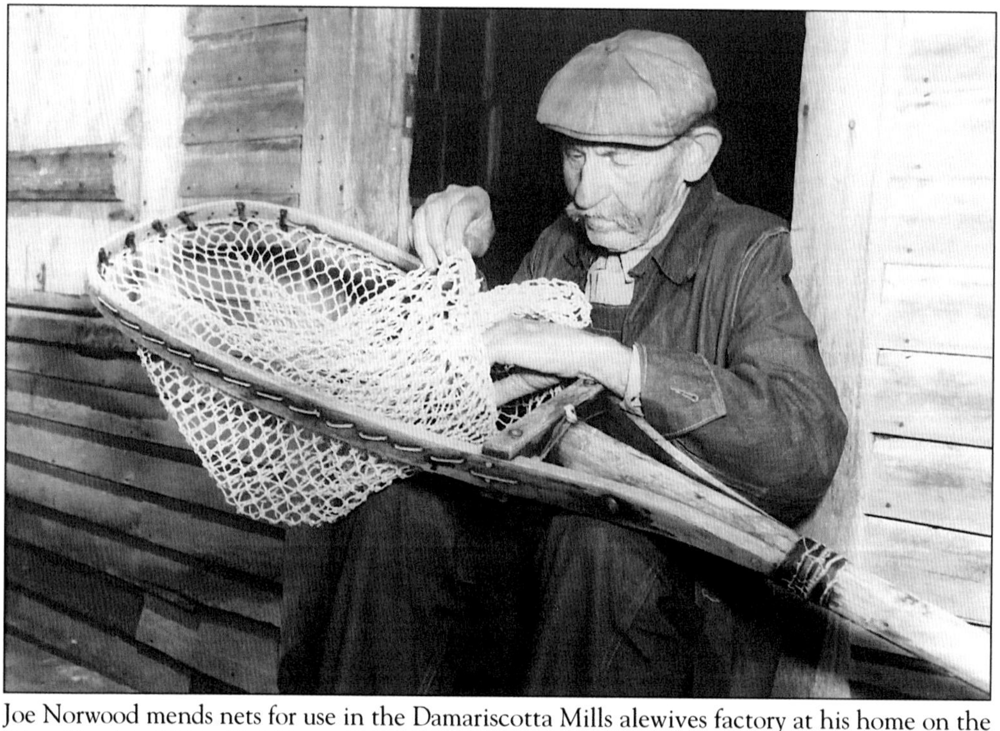

Joe Norwood mends nets for use in the Damariscotta Mills alewives factory at his home on the River Road in 1949. (Nobleboro Historical Society, Ivan Flye Collection)

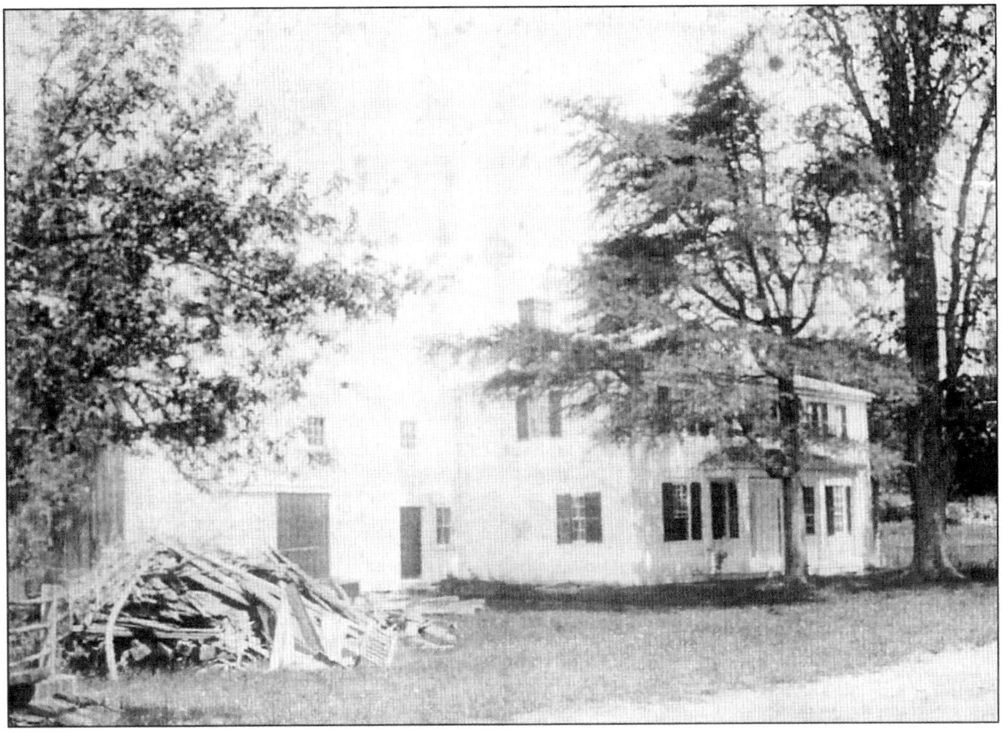

The Merry house on the River Road in Edgecomb, shown here in the late nineteenth century, was home to several distinguished members of that family. Among them were Charles Glidden Merry, who built twelve vessels in Damariscotta from 1868 to 1877, and his son John Fairfield Merry, who volunteered his service to the Union fleet at the beginning of the Civil War and retired many years later a Rear Admiral in the U.S. Navy. (Howie Davison)

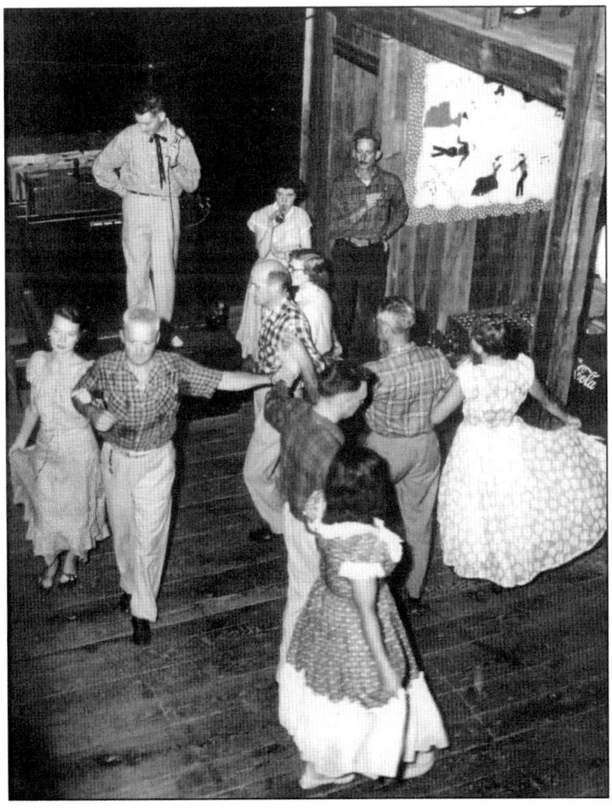

Howie Davison bought the Merry property in 1951, and the following year began to hold square dances in the barn across the road. Always popular, dances at the Merry Barn drew large crowds and were enjoyed by young and old alike. Mr. Davison is shown calling this dance during the Merry Barn's first season. (Howie Davison)

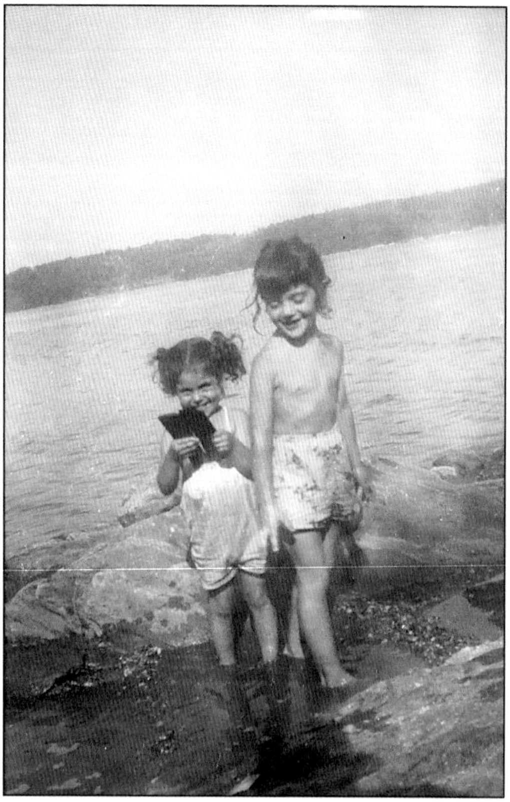

The Damariscotta River has always been a place for recreation to those who live and vacation along its shores. Paula Barletta and her younger sister, both of Boston, were summer visitors at the Albert and Flora Tonry cottage on the Merry Island Road, and are shown here playing in the water on a hot summer day in 1949. (Phyllis Tonry)

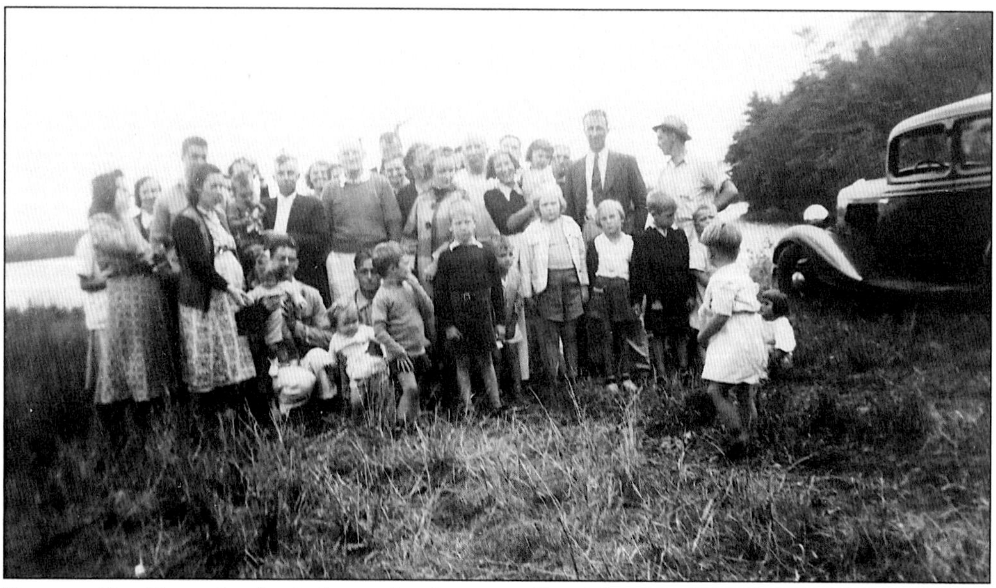

Dermont Reed hosted a clambake on the shore near Page's brickyard for the Reed family reunion in September 1939. This was an annual tradition in the 1930s and an affordable one, as several family members participated in digging the clams on the nearby flats. (Dot Hathorne)

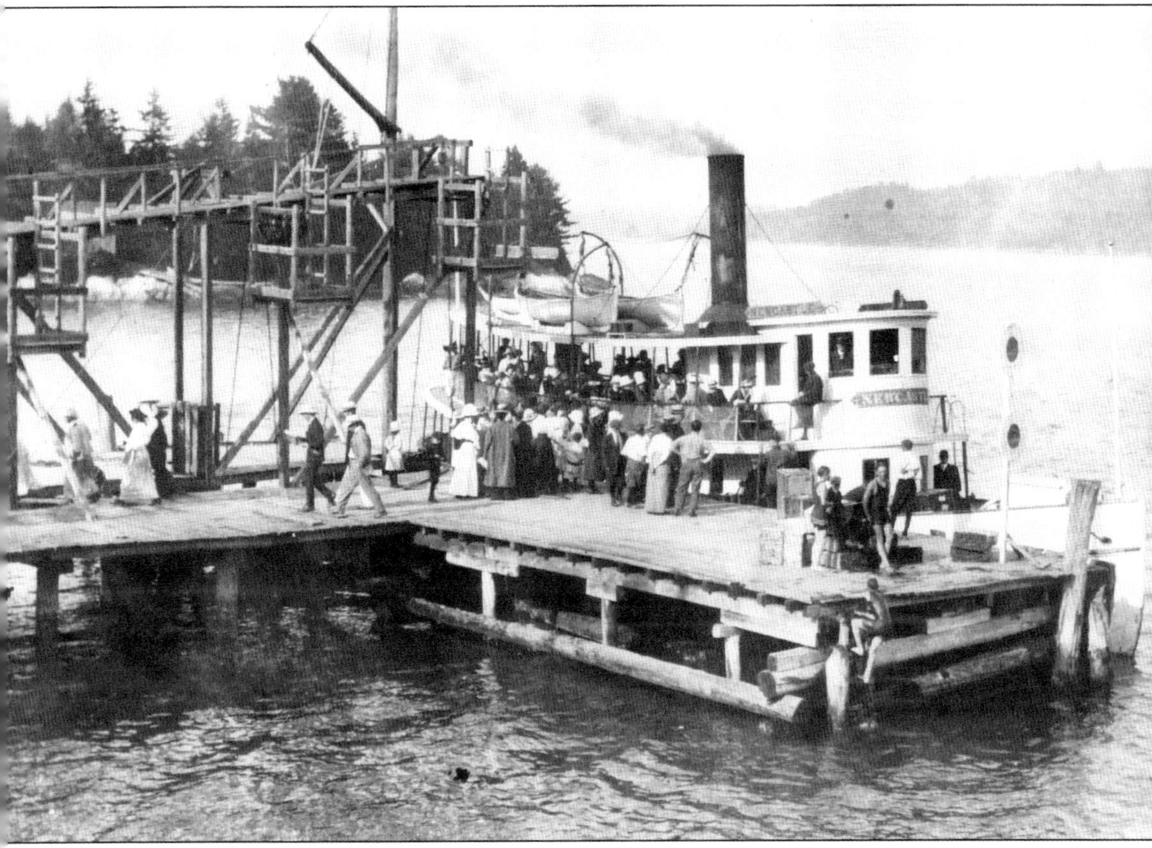

The steamer *Newcastle* stops for passengers at Poole's Landing in East Edgecomb. This was one of the regular stops on the schedule as the steamer made its way along the river. Part of the Damariscotta River Steamboat Company's fleet, the *Newcastle* began operating in the spring, making two round trips daily until late fall. She carried passengers, freight, and mail, and also made stops at Heron Island, Christmas Cove, South Bristol, East Boothbay, and Clark's Cove. Note the ice lift, the wooden apparatus which carried blocks of ice from the storage sheds to waiting vessels. The ice was cut from the pond at the head of Salt Marsh Cove, and sent by means of a long ramp to the ice house at the shore in an operation similar to those at other locations along the river. (Nobleboro Historical Society, Ivan Flye Collection)

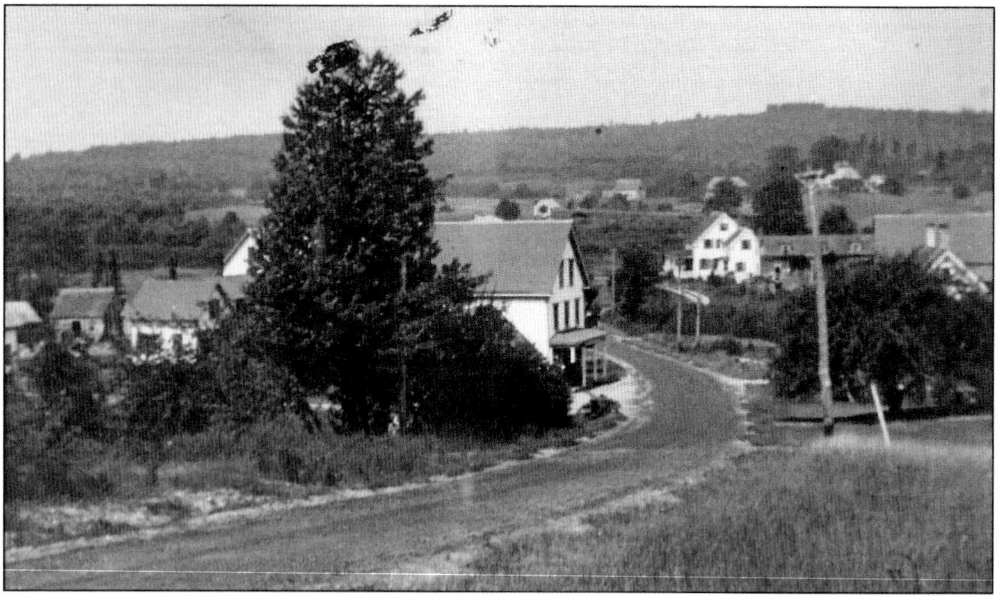

John Burnham's store and the Dodge farm are the most prominent buildings looking north through the village at East Edgecomb. The obvious clump of trees on Mt. Hunger (background) was known as the Square Pines, an uncut area of old-growth pine which could be seen for miles and was a landmark for mariners. (Boothbay Region Historical Society)

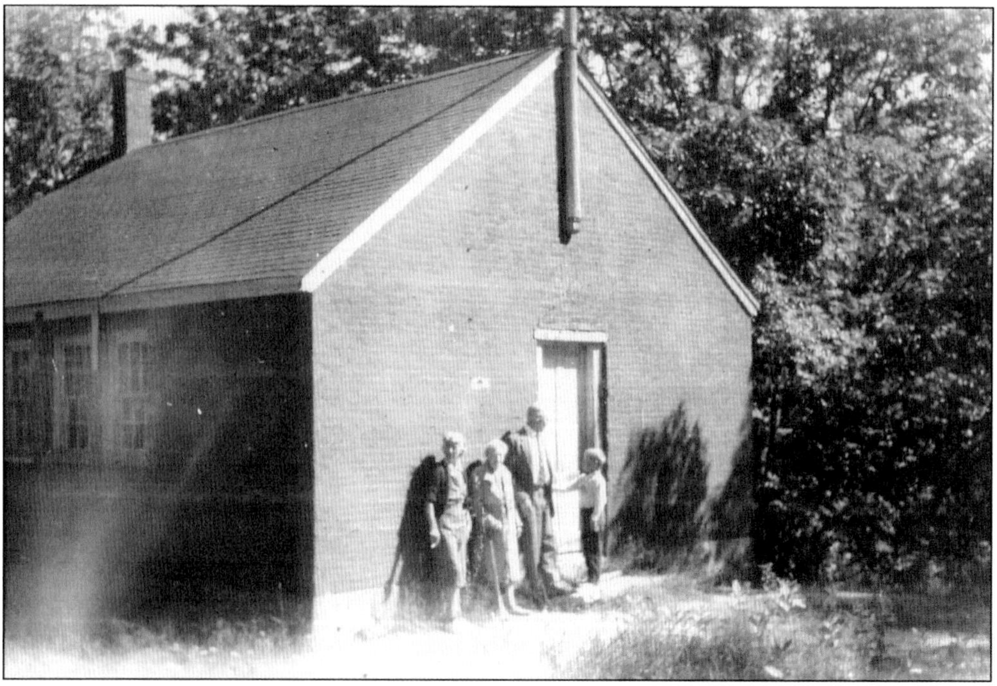

The Salt Marsh School served students in East Edgcomb and was one of several district schools in the town of Edgecomb at the turn of the century. Student population steadily declined after 1900 forcing several of the buildings to close. Residents Abbie Dodge (second from the left) and Robert Brown (the boy on the right) were photographed at the Salt Marsh School soon after it closed in the mid-1940s. The brick building is now a private residence. (Robert Brown)

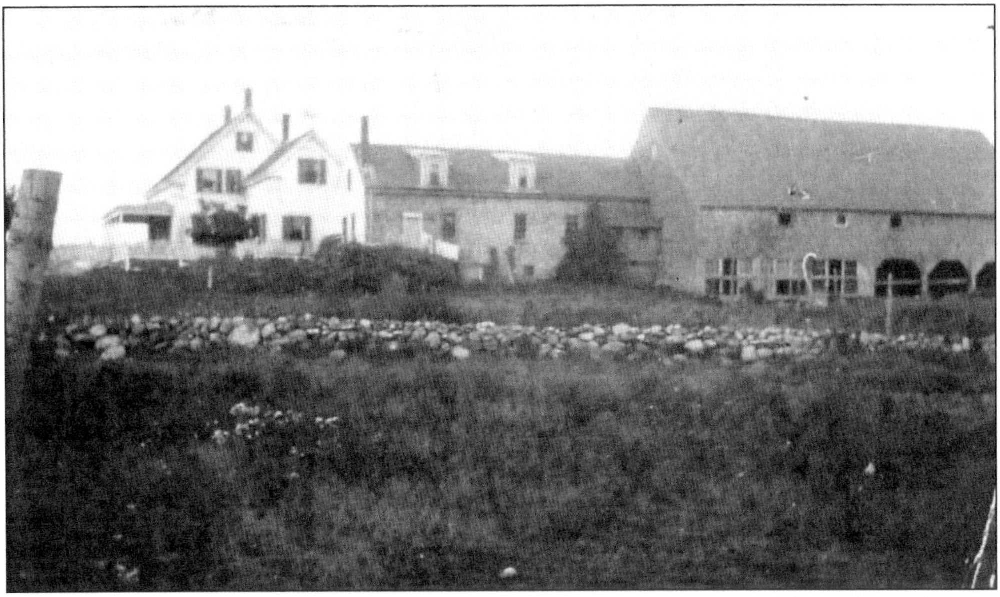

This classic set of connected farm buildings in East Edgecomb was owned by Abbie and Rosie Dodge, long-time residents of the community. To supplement their income the ladies opened the house to guests: in the winter they housed men who were employed cutting ice, and in the summer they catered to tourists. Miss Abbie Dodge was also postmaster in East Edgecomb for a number of years. (Robert Brown)

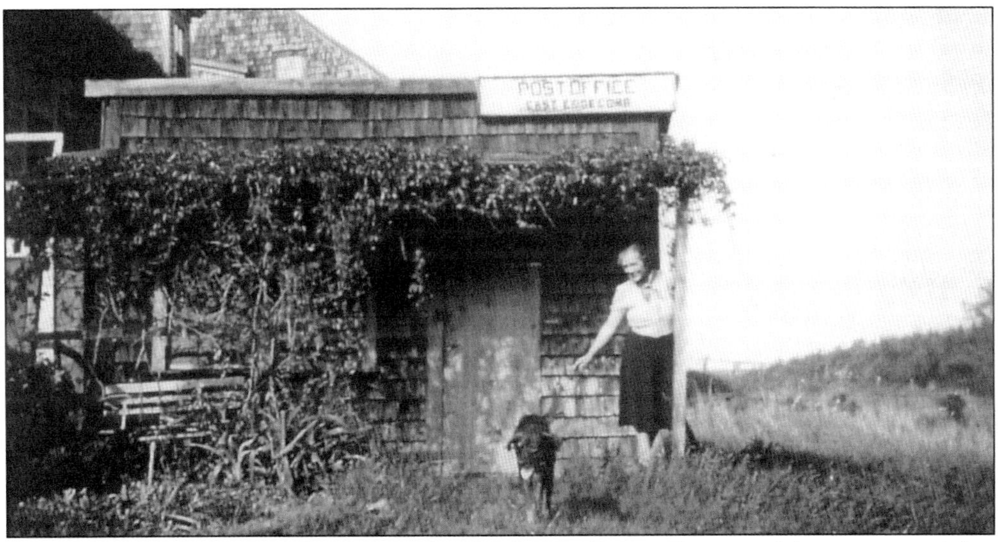

The East Edgecomb Post Office was said to be the smallest in the state. Measuring just 6 feet by 12 feet, it was also said to do the least amount of year-round business! A newspaper article written in the 1930s noted that the post office was active only in the summer; in winter business was "practically nil." Finally, in 1940, when this picture was taken, it closed permanently. Abbie Dodge is shown at the building where she worked for so many years. (Robert Brown)

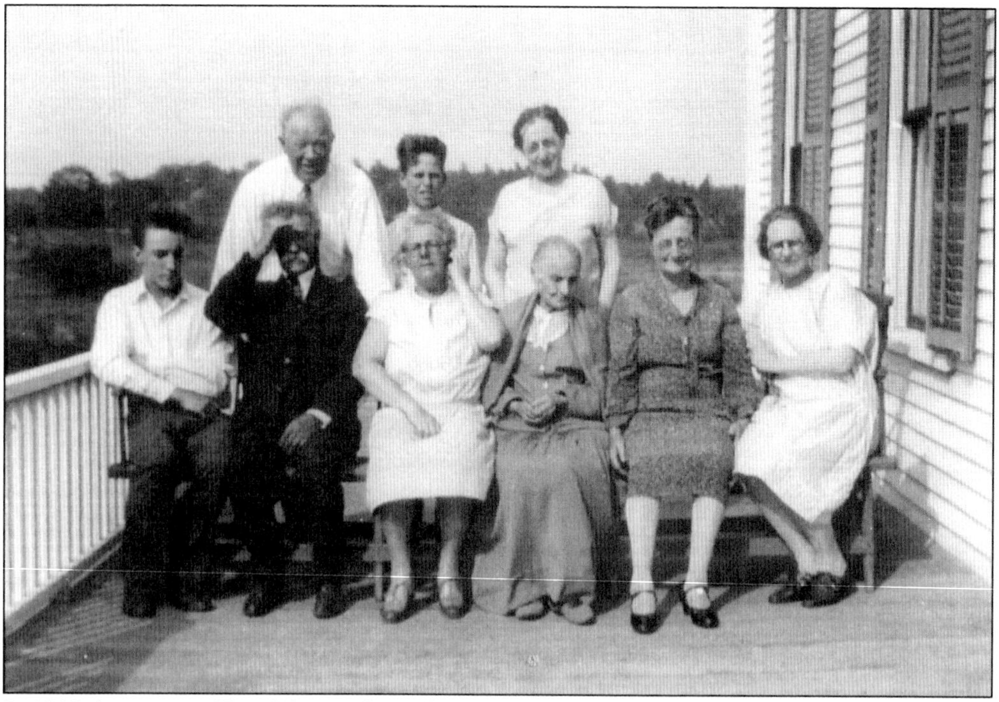

In 1928 this group of East Edgecomb residents gathered on the porch of the Dodge house during a Fourth of July celebration. From left to right are: (standing) Frank Eddy, Robert Poole, and Abbie Dodge; (seated) Allen Brown, James R. Brown, Martha Eddy, Fannie Dodge, Rosie Dodge, and Arzetta Poole. (Robert Brown)

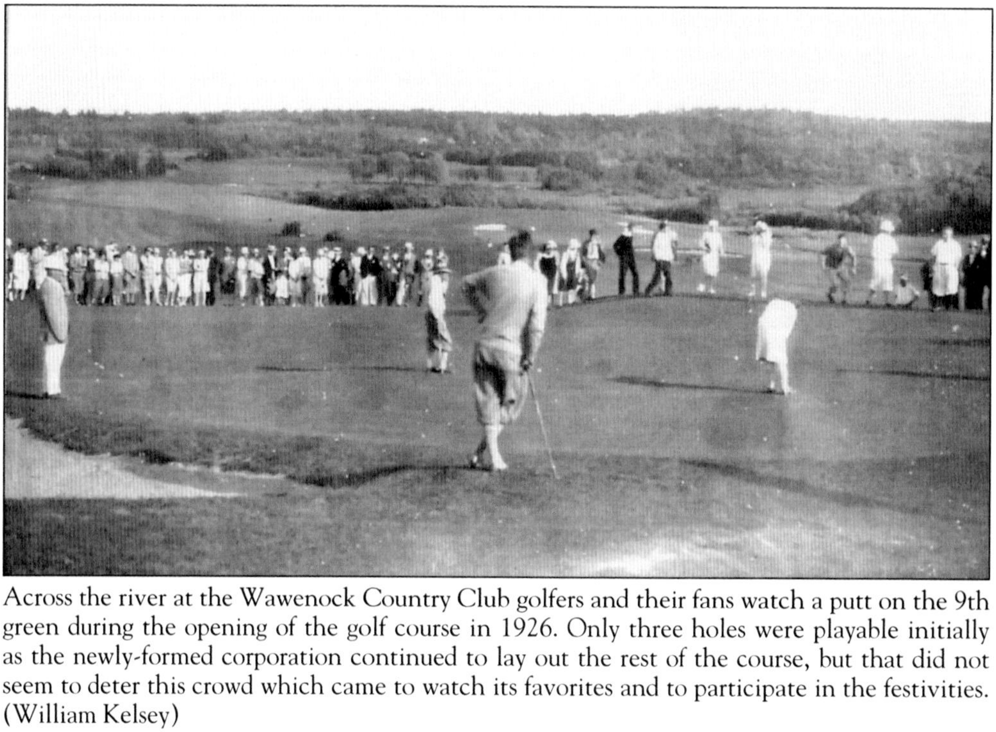

Across the river at the Wawenock Country Club golfers and their fans watch a putt on the 9th green during the opening of the golf course in 1926. Only three holes were playable initially as the newly-formed corporation continued to lay out the rest of the course, but that did not seem to deter this crowd which came to watch its favorites and to participate in the festivities. (William Kelsey)

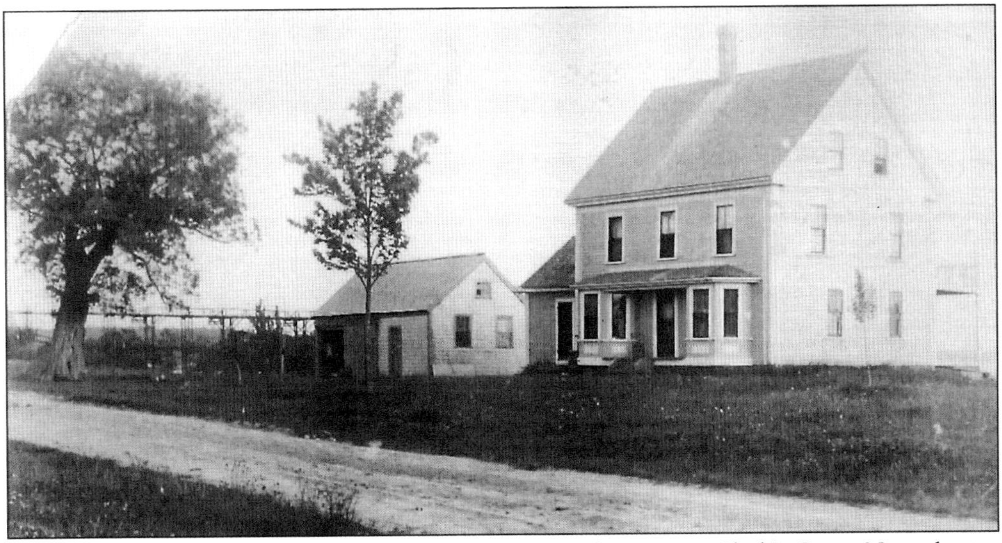

The Kelsey (now Myers) house in Walpole overlooks the river at Clark's Cove. Note the ice slide at the left. Ice harvesting had become a major industry in Maine during the waning years of the nineteenth century with ninety vessels loaded at various ice works along the Damariscotta in 1889, according to a Damariscotta newspaper. But by 1900 New York and Boston merchants who held a monopoly on the business transferred all operations to the Hudson River, almost entirely eliminating Maine producers. Ice cut after the turn of the century was generally sold locally. The last year of the operation at Clark's Cove was 1916. (Norman Kelsey)

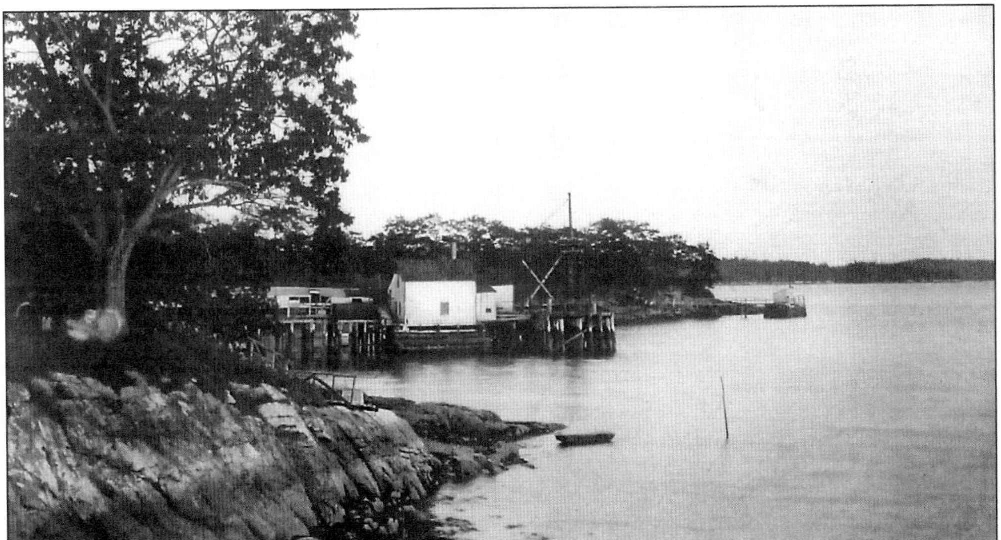

Storage buildings in Clark's Cove housed ice until it was ready to be shipped. After the ice business declined, Everett Kelsey moved one of the white buildings across the river on a scow to Pleasant Cove where it was used as an artist's studio. The steamer landing juts into the river beyond the freight wharf. (Norman Kelsey)

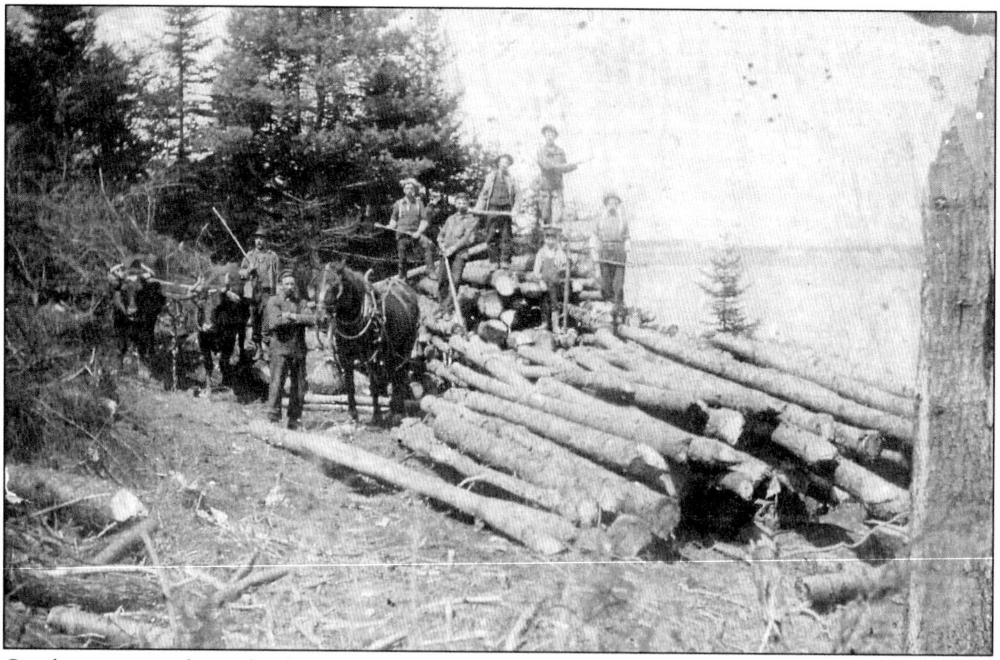

On the opposite shore this logging crew was cutting timber along Pleasant Cove in 1911 for the DuPont Powder Company. The only man identified is Charles Campbell, standing to the left on the pile of logs, wearing a slouch hat and holding an axe. Barely visible in the background are the houses across the river in Clark's Cove. (George Campbell)

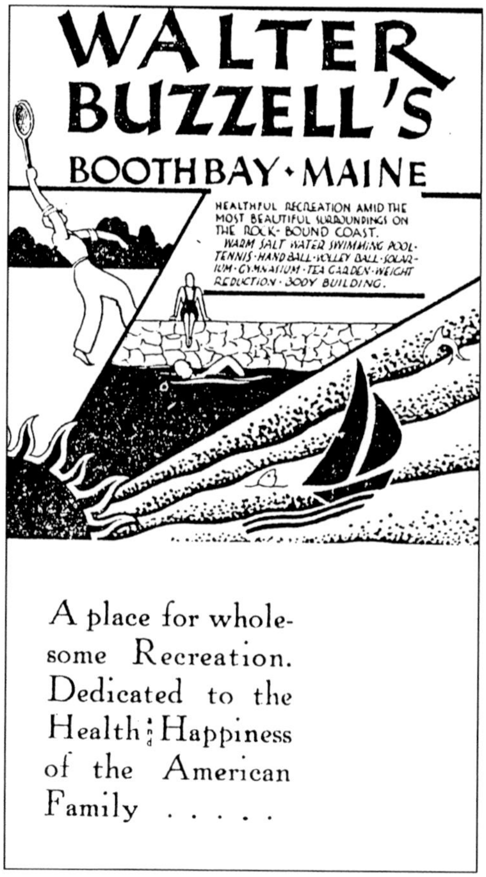

A brochure for Walter Buzzell's Health Resort at Back Narrows proclaims health-building activities for all ages on its spacious grounds beside the Damariscotta. Operating during the 1930s and '40s, it offered daily, weekly, and seasonal memberships, and promoted fitness through recreation. The idea was to "provide a beautiful, wholesome environment where people of all ages could be encouraged and instructed in improvement of their well-being." (Boothbay Region Historical Society)

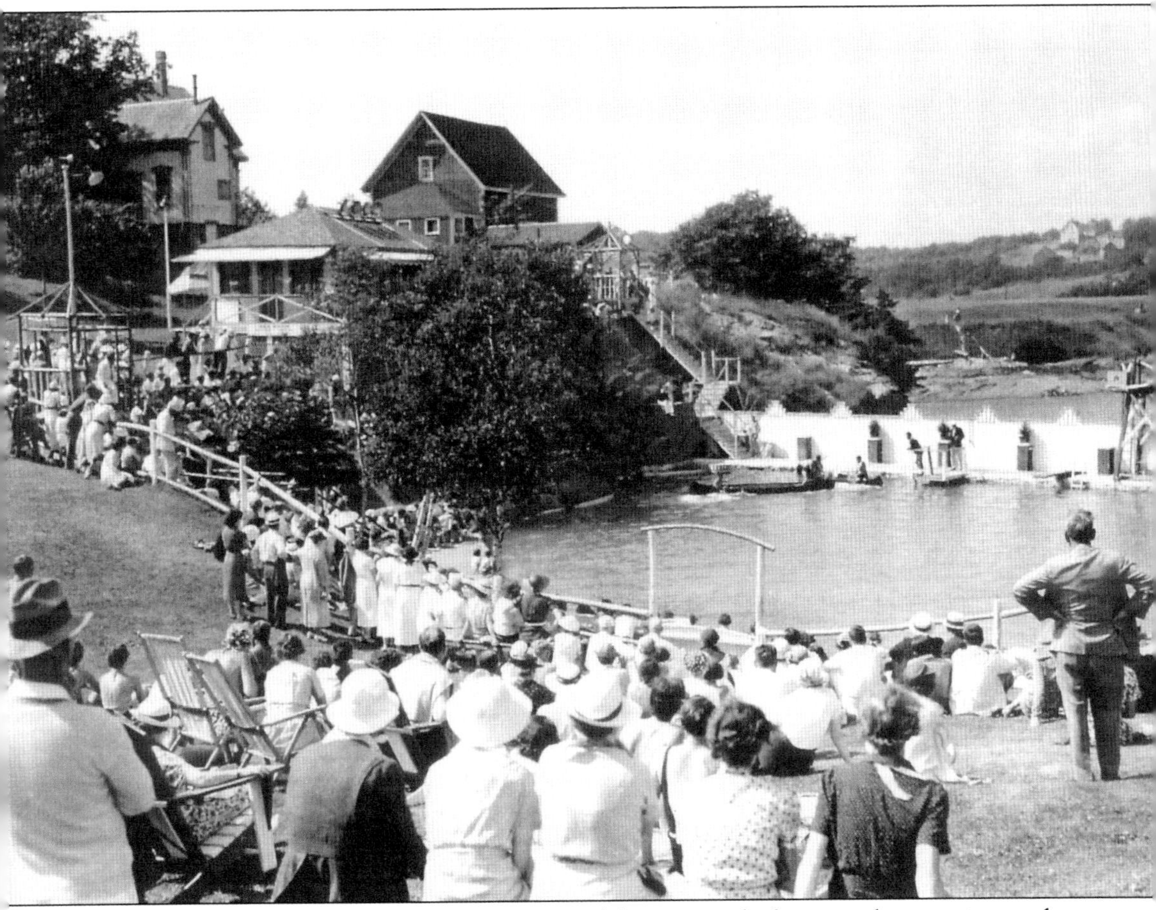

The salt water pool at Walter Buzzell's attracted large crowds for special swimming and diving events. Note the high diving tower at the right. Local organizations often held field days and promoted competitions at this well-maintained facility which offered swimming, tennis, volleyball, handball, a gymnasium, a solarium, and a tea garden. In 1944 the resort was authorized by Governor Sewall and the Executive Council to become the site of a rehabilitiation experiment for World War II veterans. Much publicity surrounded the facility as Walter Buzzell and his staff sought to restore the health and spirit of combat-weary veterans through exercise and fitness. In the mid-1950s the entire complex was purchased and presented to the newly-organized YMCA and was used for a number of years for the youth and family activities of that organization. (Boothbay Region Historical Society)

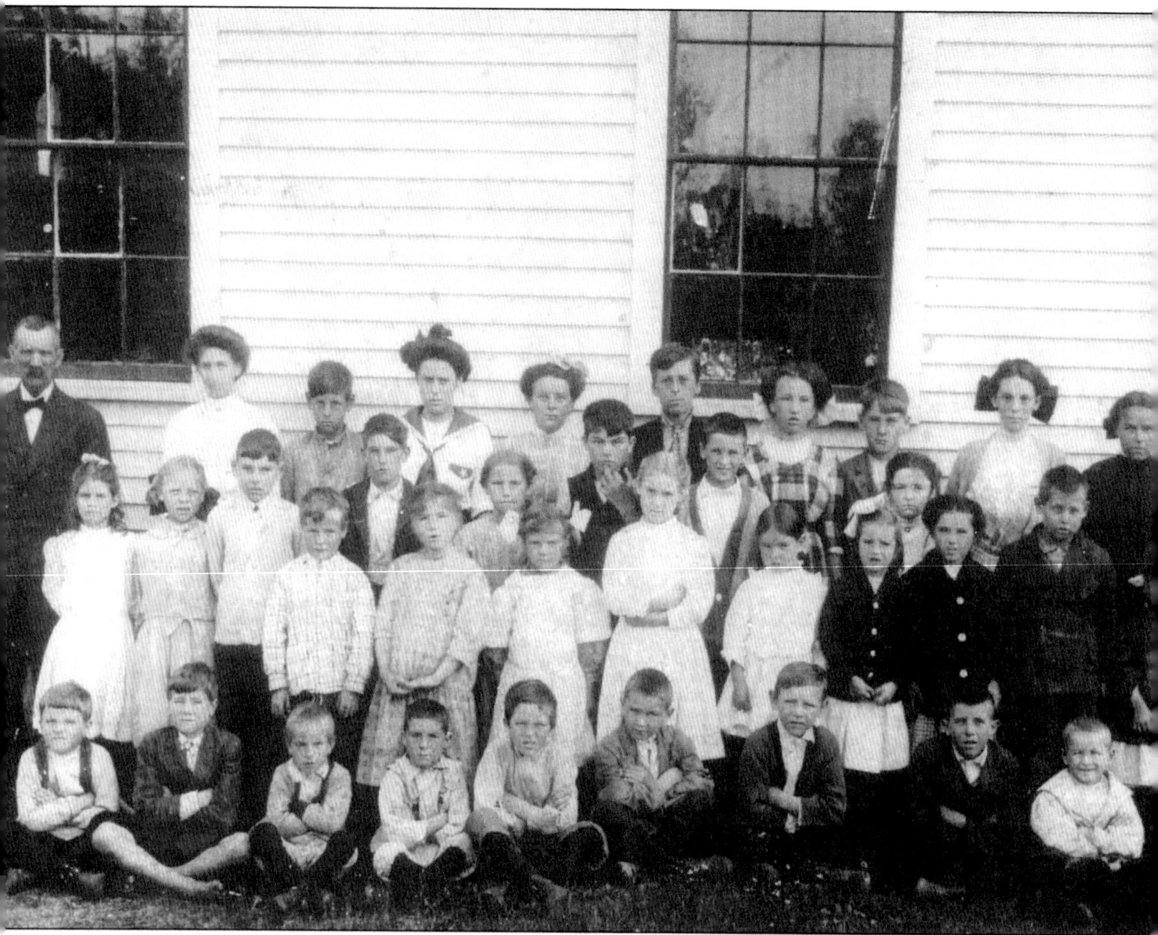

Students at the Back Narrows School, *c.* 1920, pause for a group photograph with their teacher, Benjamin Giles. From left to right are: (front row) Burton Hutchins, Lawrence Blake, Donald Blake, Kenneth Gray, Elmer Bryer, Leander Murphy, Lester Dickinson, Lewis Gray, and Samuel Murphy; (second row) Charles Bryer, Doris Doughty, Hazel Lord, Barbara Lord, Beryl Bryer, Mildred Blake, Jessie Joyce, Merrill Burnham, Mildred Joyce; (third row) Pearl Nason, Amy Dickinson, Russell Lane, Roland Nason, Beatrice Bryer, Ralph Doughty, Edward Murphy, and Celia Boyd; (back row) Mr. Giles, Evelyn Nason, Henry Dickinson, Beulah Burnham, Annie Burnham, Arnold Dodge, Marion Doughty, Roscoe Bryer, Dora Blake, and Elsie Cunningham. (Boothbay Region Historical Society)

Four

The Sea

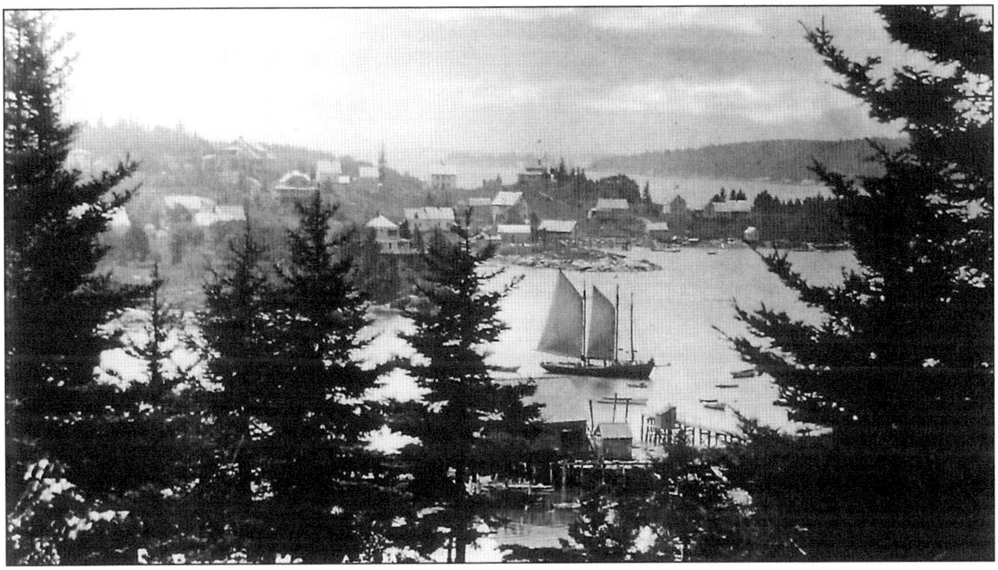

The villages of East Boothbay and South Bristol are oriented toward the sea where traditional fishing and shipbuilding industries have coexisted with summer cottage communities since the late nineteenth century. There were Europeans at the mouth of the Damariscotta in the 1600s, but not until well into the next century did they experience the security necessary to create permanent settlements. Fishing, farming, and the occasional sawmill characterized the early days of settlement until the shipbuilding boom of the nineteenth century created the industry which is still carried on today. Pinkies and power boats, sloops and steamers, minesweepers and replicas of famous sailing vessels have all found a place in the history of East Boothbay and South Bristol, and at the end of the nineteenth century an influx of summer visitors began which was to have an even greater impact on the communities of the lower Damariscotta. (William Kelsey)

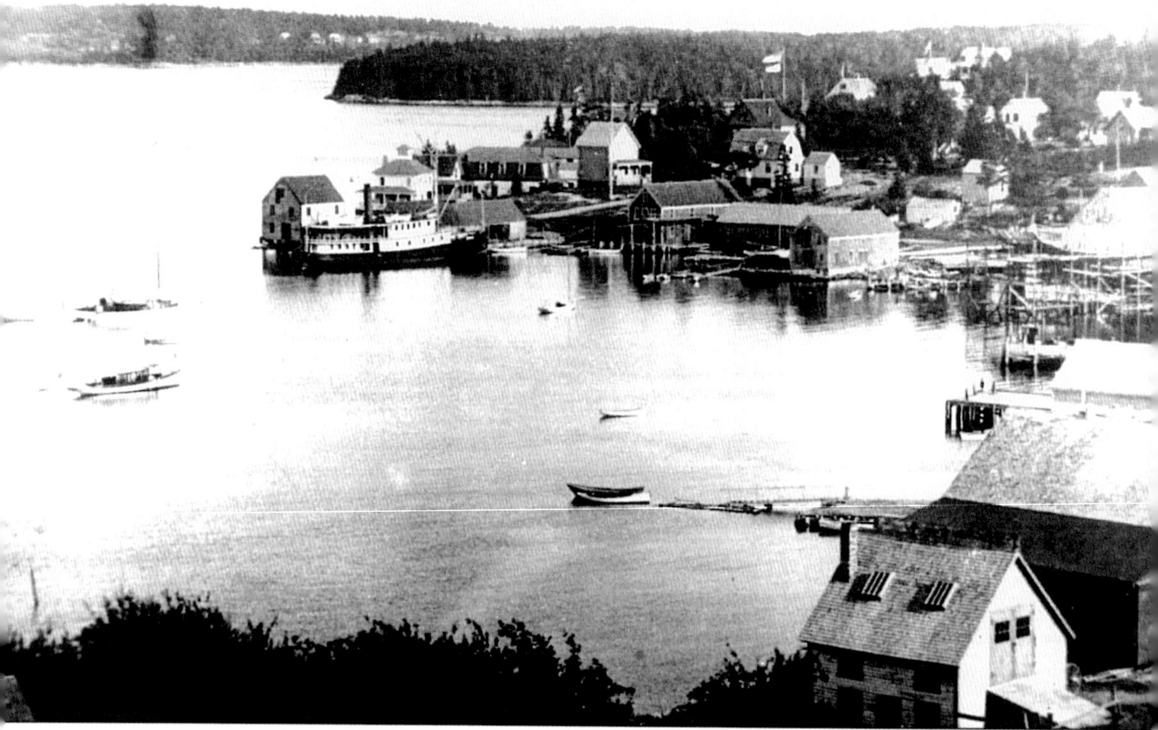

East Boothbay in 1903 had an active waterfront. On the south side of the harbor at the steamer landing is the black-hulled *Enterprise* which operated between the Boothbay region and Portland carrying both passengers and freight; the buildings in the center housed a sail loft and spar shop with the Vannah & Jones coal shed located between them; and the vessel under construction on the right is the four-masted schooner, *Eleanor F. Bartram*, at 1,000 tons the largest vessel ever built by the W.I. Adams & Son shipyard. (Boothbay Region Historical Society)

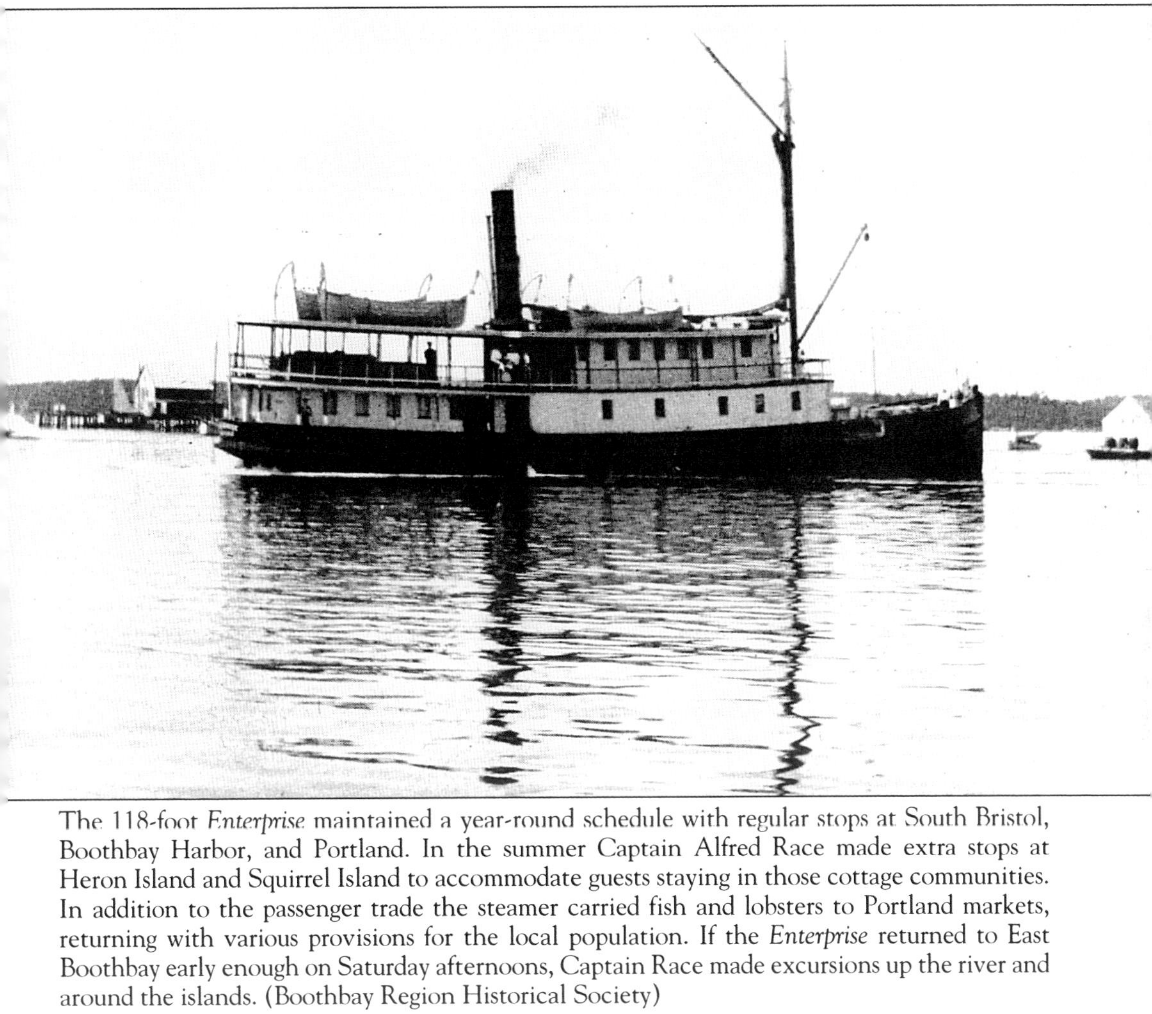

The 118-foot *Enterprise* maintained a year-round schedule with regular stops at South Bristol, Boothbay Harbor, and Portland. In the summer Captain Alfred Race made extra stops at Heron Island and Squirrel Island to accommodate guests staying in those cottage communities. In addition to the passenger trade the steamer carried fish and lobsters to Portland markets, returning with various provisions for the local population. If the *Enterprise* returned to East Boothbay early enough on Saturday afternoons, Captain Race made excursions up the river and around the islands. (Boothbay Region Historical Society)

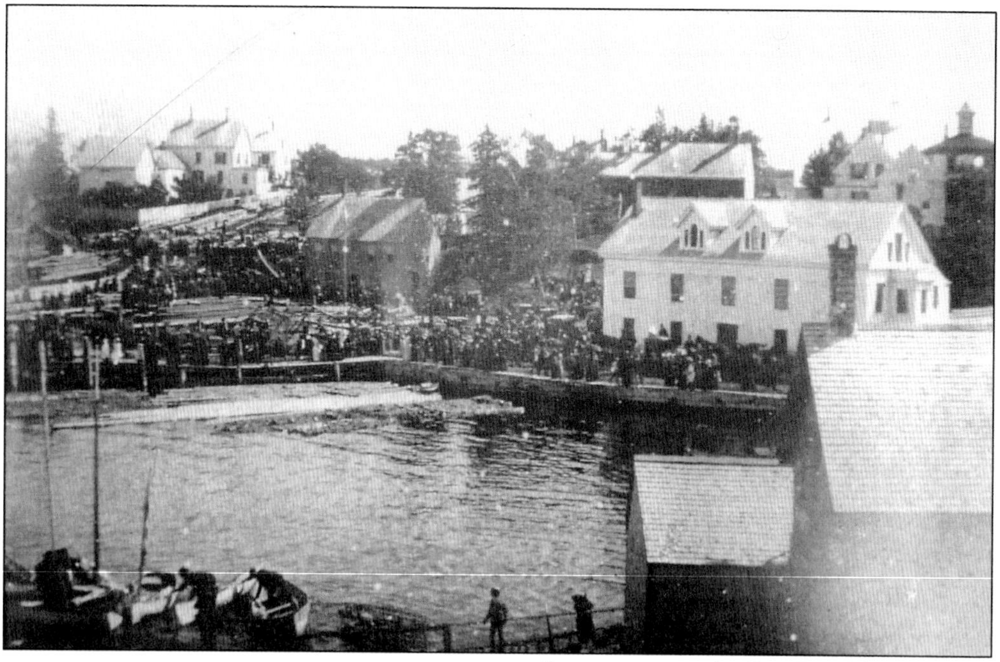

For many years the East Boothbay waterfront was dominated by the Benjamin Reed house. Squire Reed, as he was called, was a merchant, shipbuilder, and owner of a great deal of real estate. He managed his yard and vessels from the store which was in the basement of the house. (Boothbay Region Historical Society)

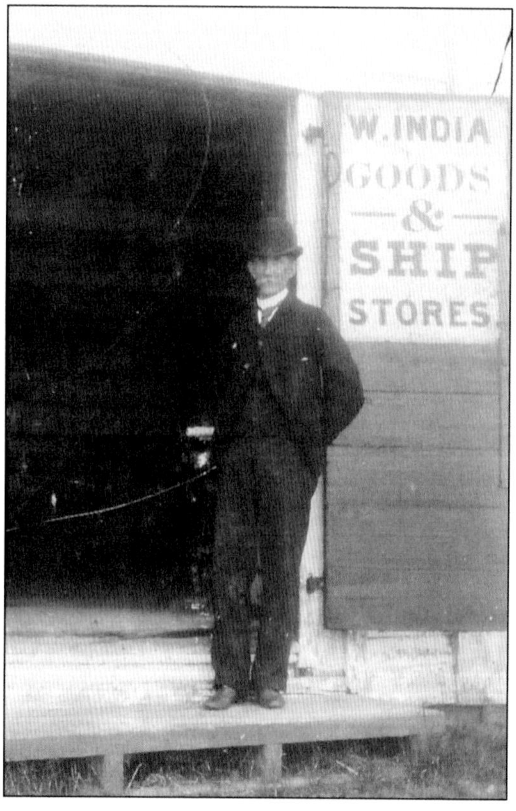

William Reed, son of Benjamin Reed, assumed ownership of his father's businesses and continued to run the store, which advertised West India Goods and molasses. Inside the building sat a barrel of rum and a tin dipper which might have increased the popularity of the business, and perhaps even contributed to the high praise given William Reed on his death, for it was said that he was a man "who held the esteem and confidence of those who knew him." (Boothbay Region Historical Society)

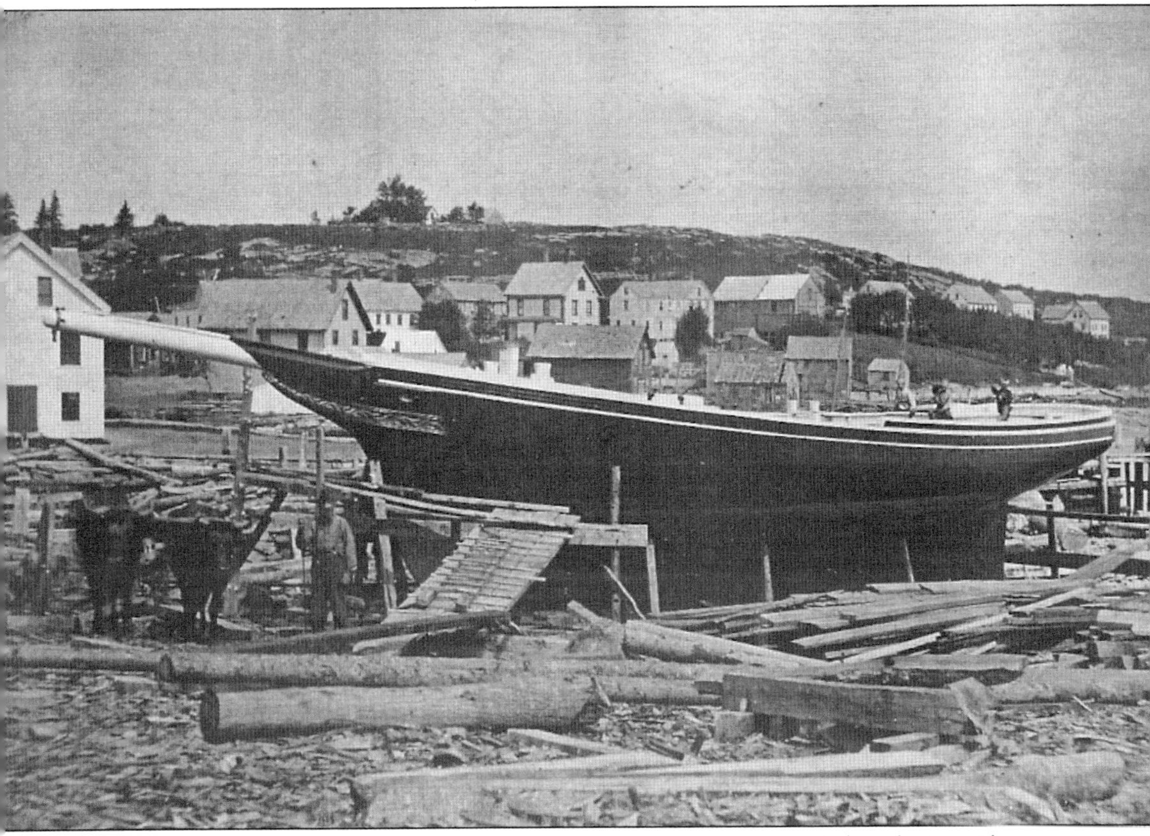

The construction of a vessel at the W.I. Adams shipyard c. 1885 is helped along by Mr. Chase, who lived on nearby School Street and often worked around the waterfront with his oxen. The view is looking north toward Barlow's Hill with the Benjamin Reed house on the left. East Boothbay, like most other Maine shipbuilding communities, built large sailing vessels before the Civil War, but by the 1880s the yards were generally filling orders for schooners and fishing craft. East Boothbay yards were noted for quality work and most of them were active in the declining years of the nineteenth century, principally because they adapted well to changes in the industry. (Boothbay Region Historical Society)

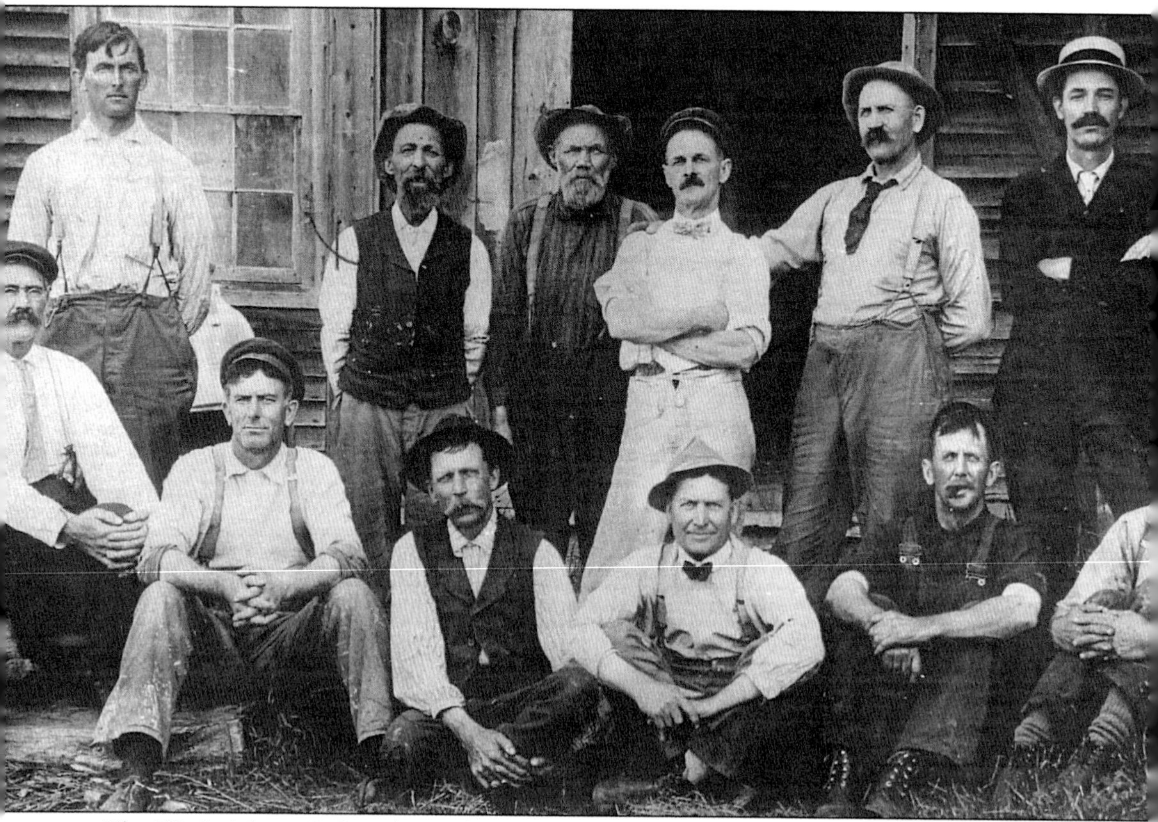

The W. I. Adams & Son shipyard c. 1905 had recently launched its one hundredth vessel. The yard, operated by the Adams family since the middle of the nineteenth century, employed this crew in the early 1900s: (front row) Philip Seavey, Bert Odlum, unknown, James Hunter, George Martin, and John Hodgdon; (back row) Frank Adams, Irving Adams, Jim Fishburn, Len Webster, James Dodge, and James Bishop. (Boothbay Region Historical Society)

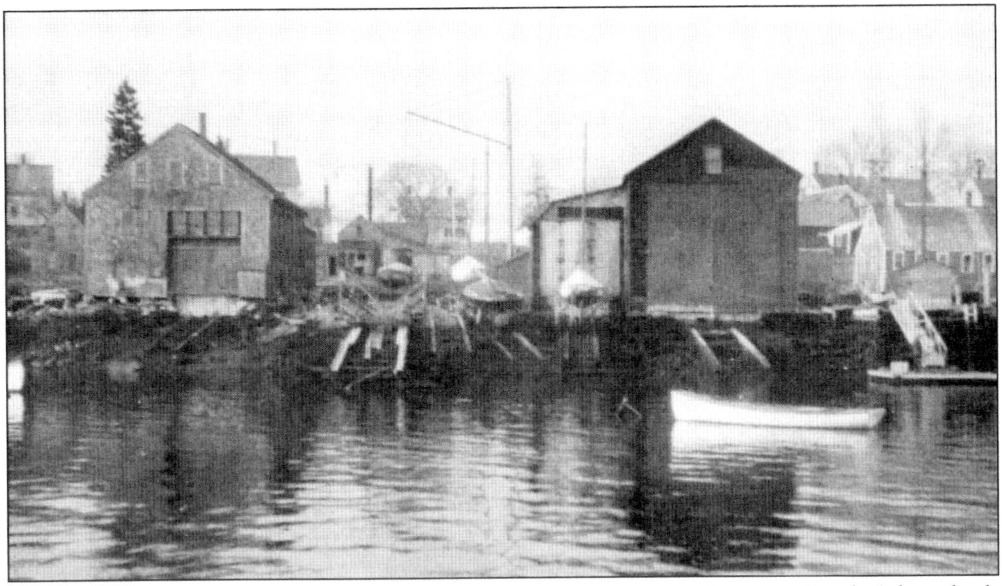

In 1912 W. Irving Adams died and his son, Frank, took over the business. Frank Adams built a few yachts, a tugboat, and several fishing schooners before selling out to Goudy & Stevens in 1924. This photograph was taken soon after the new owners began operating. The building on the left is the old Presbyterian Church, which was moved by ox team from Boothbay Center in the nineteenth century and which served as a shop at both the Adams and Goudy & Stevens shipyards until 1942. (Boothbay Region Historical Society)

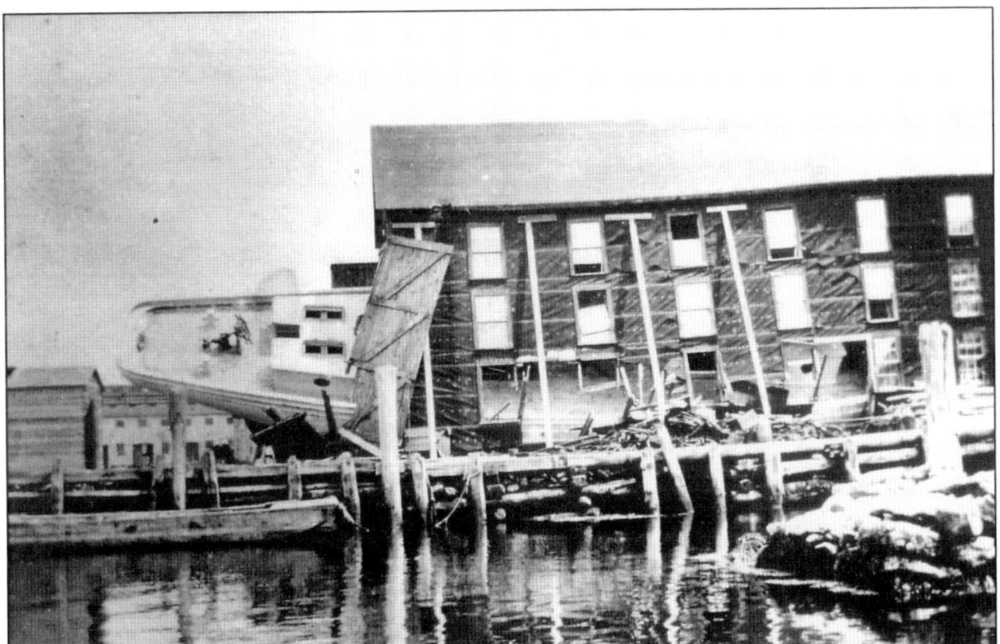

An accident at the Adams shipyard occurred in 1920 when the *Seaward* fell off its double cradle and smashed through this building as it was about to be launched. Rather than right the yacht, shipyard workers built a third cradle and launched the *Seaward* sideways. (Boothbay Region Historical Society)

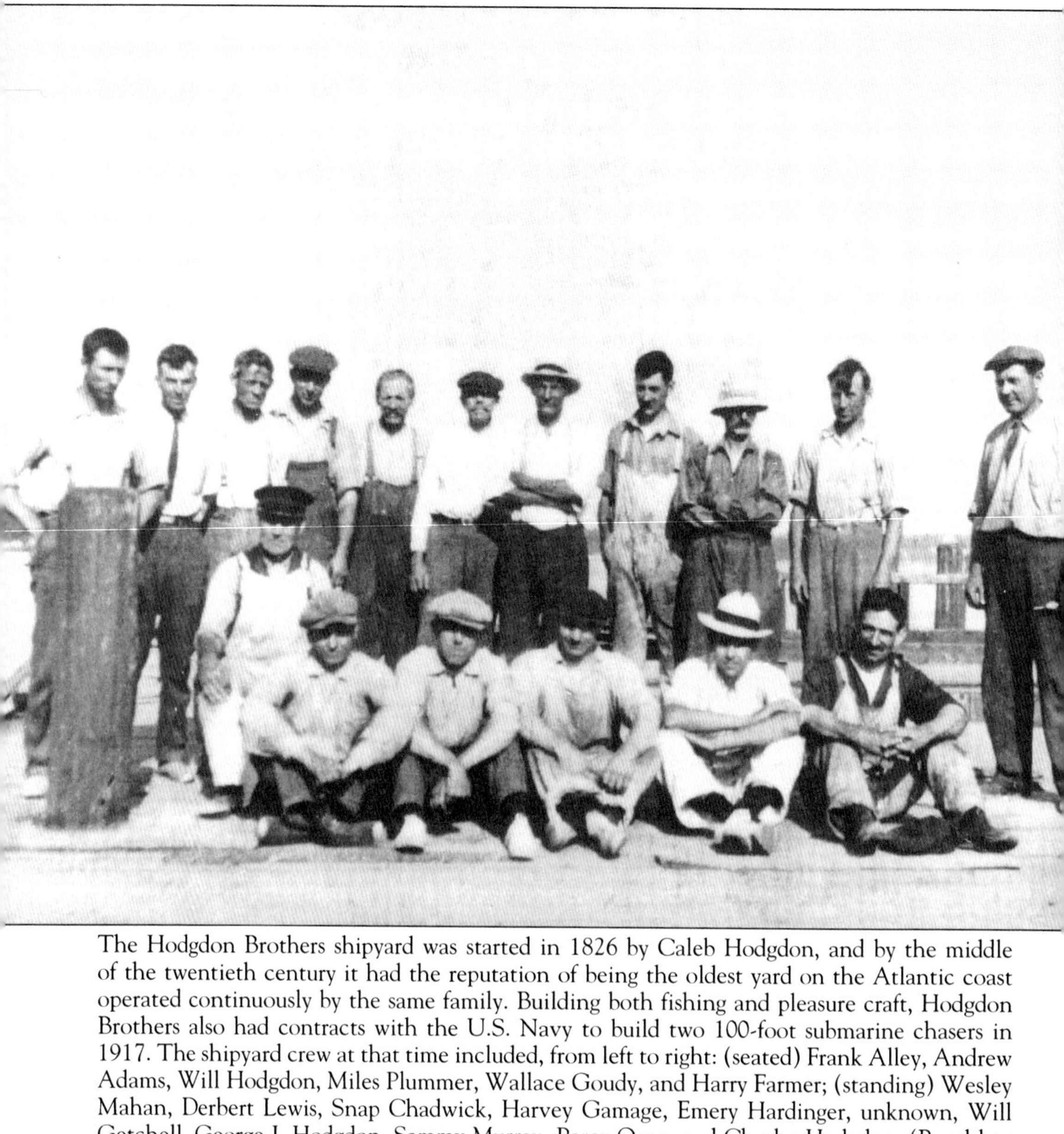

The Hodgdon Brothers shipyard was started in 1826 by Caleb Hodgdon, and by the middle of the twentieth century it had the reputation of being the oldest yard on the Atlantic coast operated continuously by the same family. Building both fishing and pleasure craft, Hodgdon Brothers also had contracts with the U.S. Navy to build two 100-foot submarine chasers in 1917. The shipyard crew at that time included, from left to right: (seated) Frank Alley, Andrew Adams, Will Hodgdon, Miles Plummer, Wallace Goudy, and Harry Farmer; (standing) Wesley Mahan, Derbert Lewis, Snap Chadwick, Harvey Gamage, Emery Hardinger, unknown, Will Getchell, George I. Hodgdon, Sammy Murray, Percy Orne, and Charles Hodgdon. (Boothbay Region Historical Society)

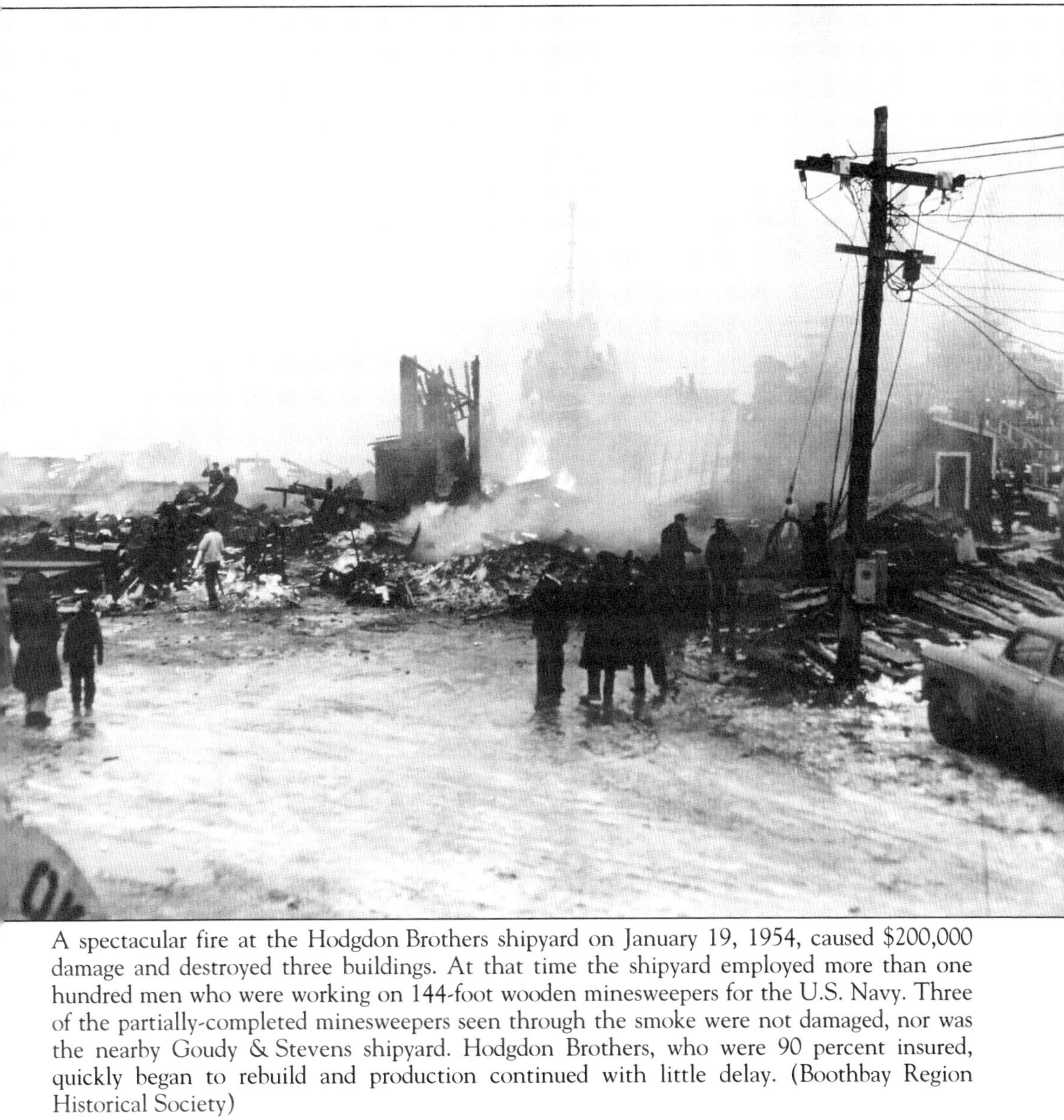

A spectacular fire at the Hodgdon Brothers shipyard on January 19, 1954, caused $200,000 damage and destroyed three buildings. At that time the shipyard employed more than one hundred men who were working on 144-foot wooden minesweepers for the U.S. Navy. Three of the partially-completed minesweepers seen through the smoke were not damaged, nor was the nearby Goudy & Stevens shipyard. Hodgdon Brothers, who were 90 percent insured, quickly began to rebuild and production continued with little delay. (Boothbay Region Historical Society)

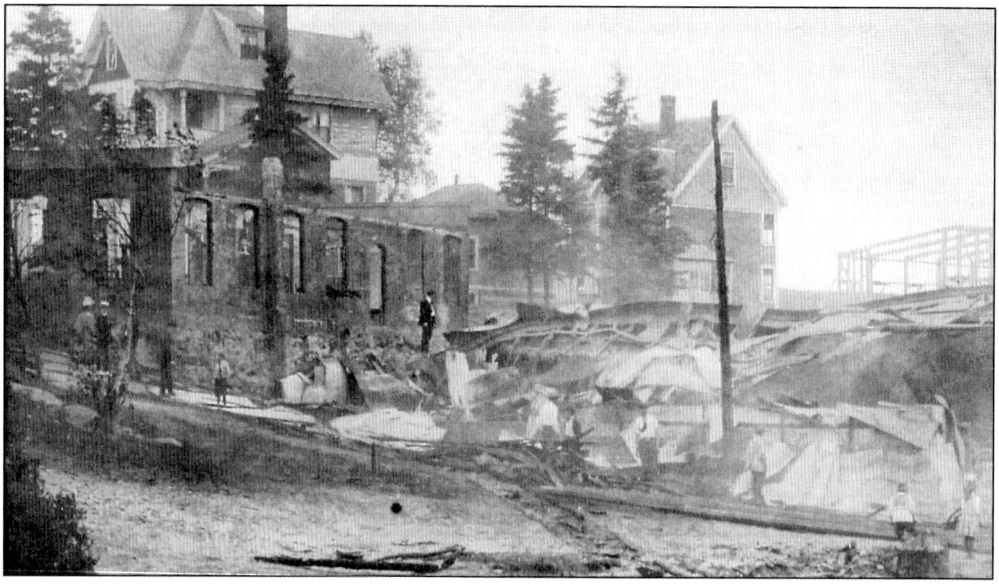

Fires have taken a toll on East Boothbay shipyards over the years. This one at the Rice Brothers shipyard in July of 1917 destroyed fifty stock pleasure boats that were finished and ready for shipment. A partially completed lightship under contract for the U.S. Government was also destroyed. The twisted wreckage of the lightship is visible in the ruins. The loss, estimated at $130,000, was partially covered by insurance, and Rice Brothers rebuilt. (Boothbay Region Historical Society)

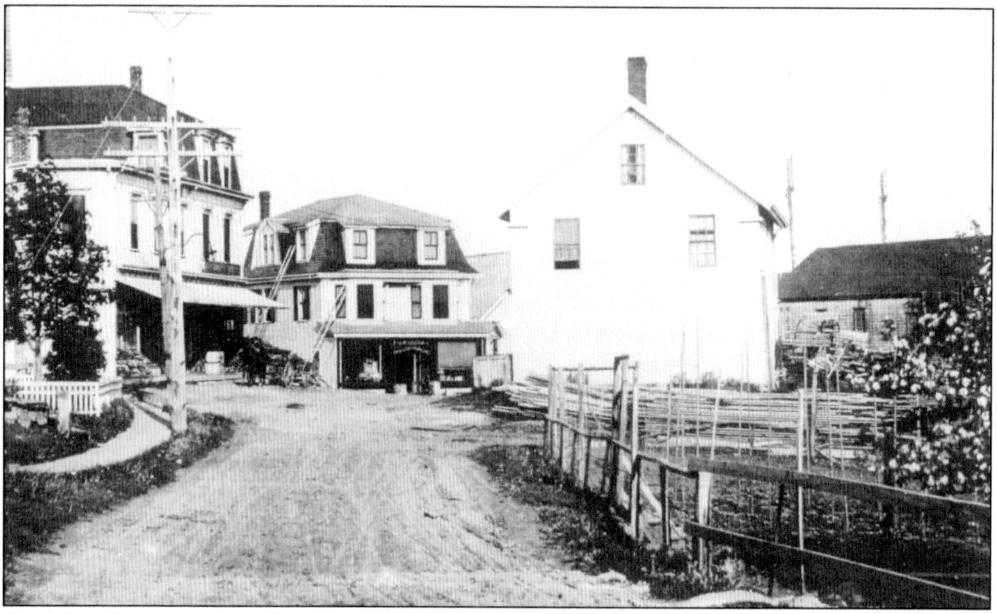

On Main Street in East Boothbay the two grocery stores of J.R. McDougall (left) and A.O. McDougall (center) stand ready for business, *c.* 1906. In the 1920s half of the building on the left served as the post office run by Everett Vannah. Mrs. Barlow had a millinery shop in the white building in the center, which later housed Len Webster's barbershop. Two masts of a vessel under construction at the Adams shipyard tower over the old tide mill on the right. (Boothbay Region Historical Society)

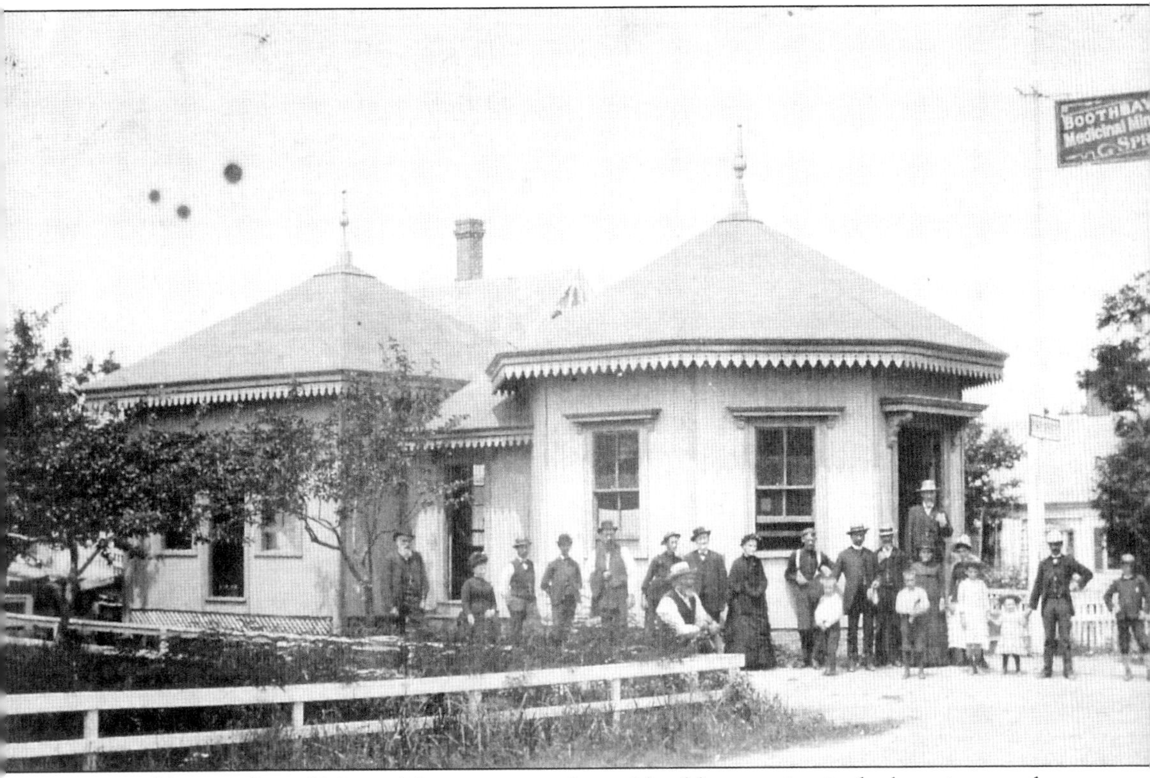

The Boothbay Medicinal Mineral Spring attracted considerable attention in the late nineteenth century. The spring, which was on land owned by E.E. Race, had been known locally for many years, but in the 1880s Mr. Race decided to advertise its curative properties. In true entrepreneurial spirit he bottled the water, sold it at the spring house, peddled it around the area in a wagon pulled by his two coal-black horses, and according to a newspaper article had plans to build a hotel. The spring drew hundreds of health seekers who proclaimed "strikingly wonderful" cures for every ailment, known or imagined. The venture was short-lived, however, and by the early 1900s the building had become a drugstore, with a soda fountain and ice cream parlor. (Boothbay Region Historical Society)

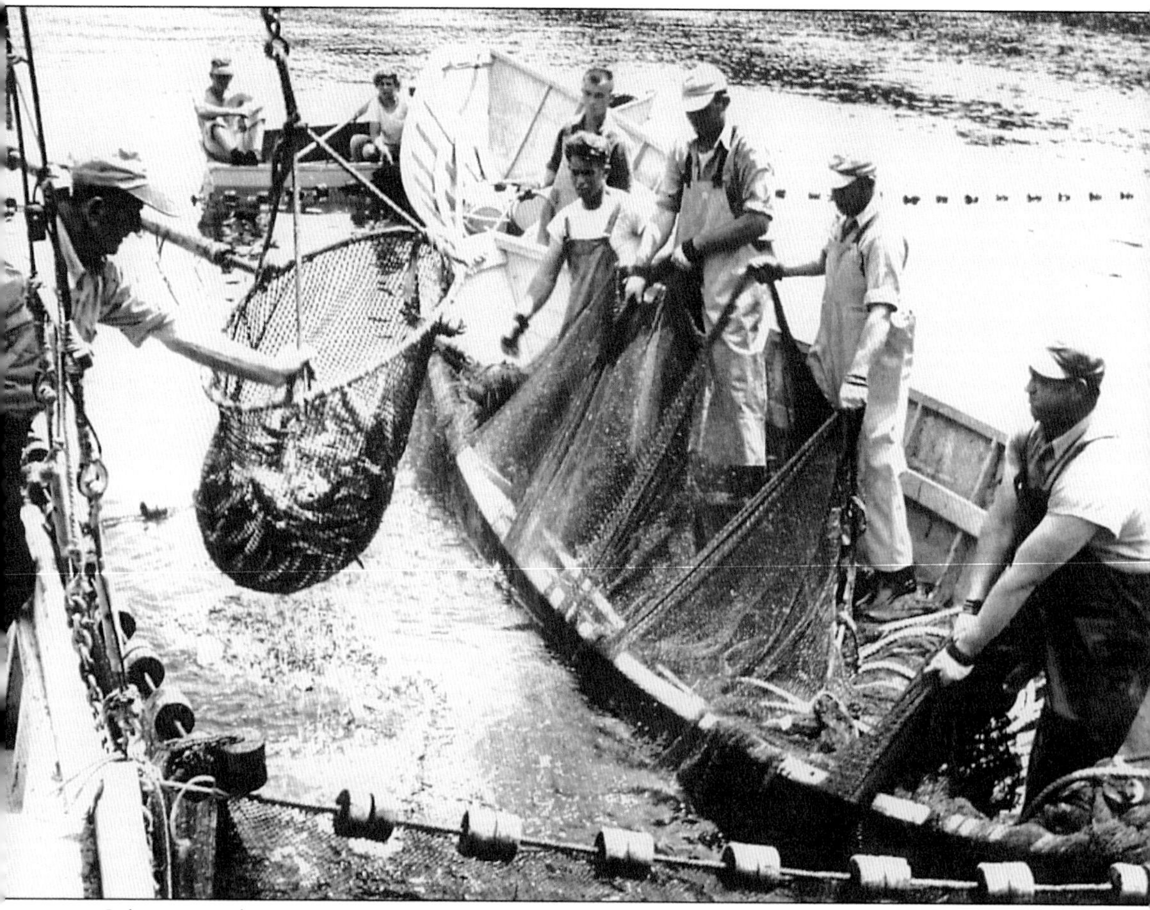

Like most other Maine coastal communities, East Boothbay sends its families to sea for their livelihood. Dick Tibbetts, left, and his crew from Linekin Neck are shown "drying up" mackerel so the fish can be scooped up and loaded aboard the carrier (left). Stop-seining requires the men to row out quietly into a cove at night, startle the fish by striking the bottom of the boat, and then watch for the fish to "fire up" (make a phosphorescence on the water) so they will know where to set the stop-seine. When the tide ebbs, the net is gathered in, the carrier comes alongside, and the fish are loaded onto the larger boat. Stop-seining occurred in several coves on the river as far north as Clark's Cove. Other members of the Tibbetts crew are, from left to right: Leon Tibbetts, Max Tibbetts, Ed Poore, unknown, and Clinton Tibbetts. (Boothbay Region Historical Society)

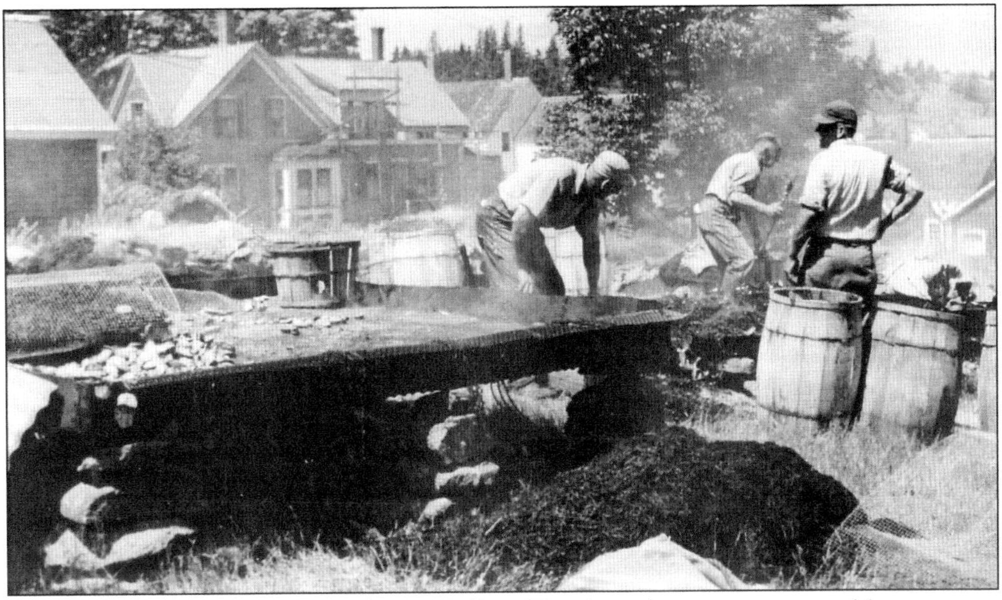

In 1947 East Boothbay held a Fishermen's Fair. The three-day event sponsored boat races, a street dance, a ball, and the crowning of Miss Downeaster. Maine's governor, Horace Hildreth, made an appearance, and what was billed as the "biggest clambake on earth" was prepared for the event. These men on the cooking crew are steaming the lobsters and clams for the large crowd that gathered on School Street. (Boothbay Region Historical Society)

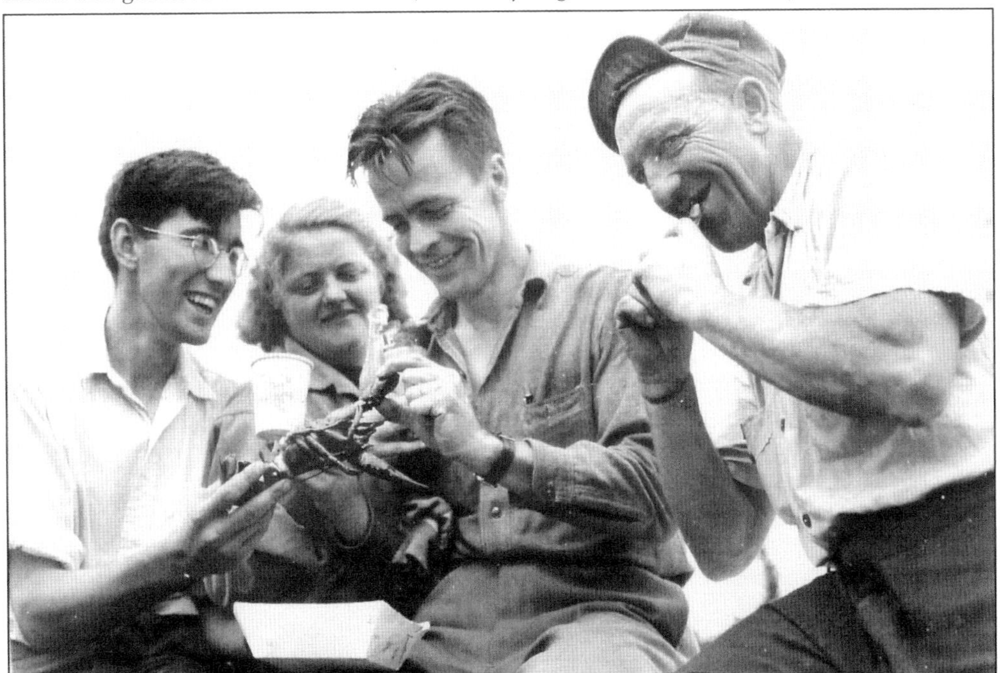

Demonstrating the finer points of lobster dissection at the Fishermen's Fair are these East Boothbay residents, from left to right: Sonny Hodgdon, Eva (Stevens) Cummings, Jiggs Jacobson, and Lester Burnham. The well-attended fair was enjoyed by residents and tourists alike, and by all accounts was a huge success. (Boothbay Region Historical Society)

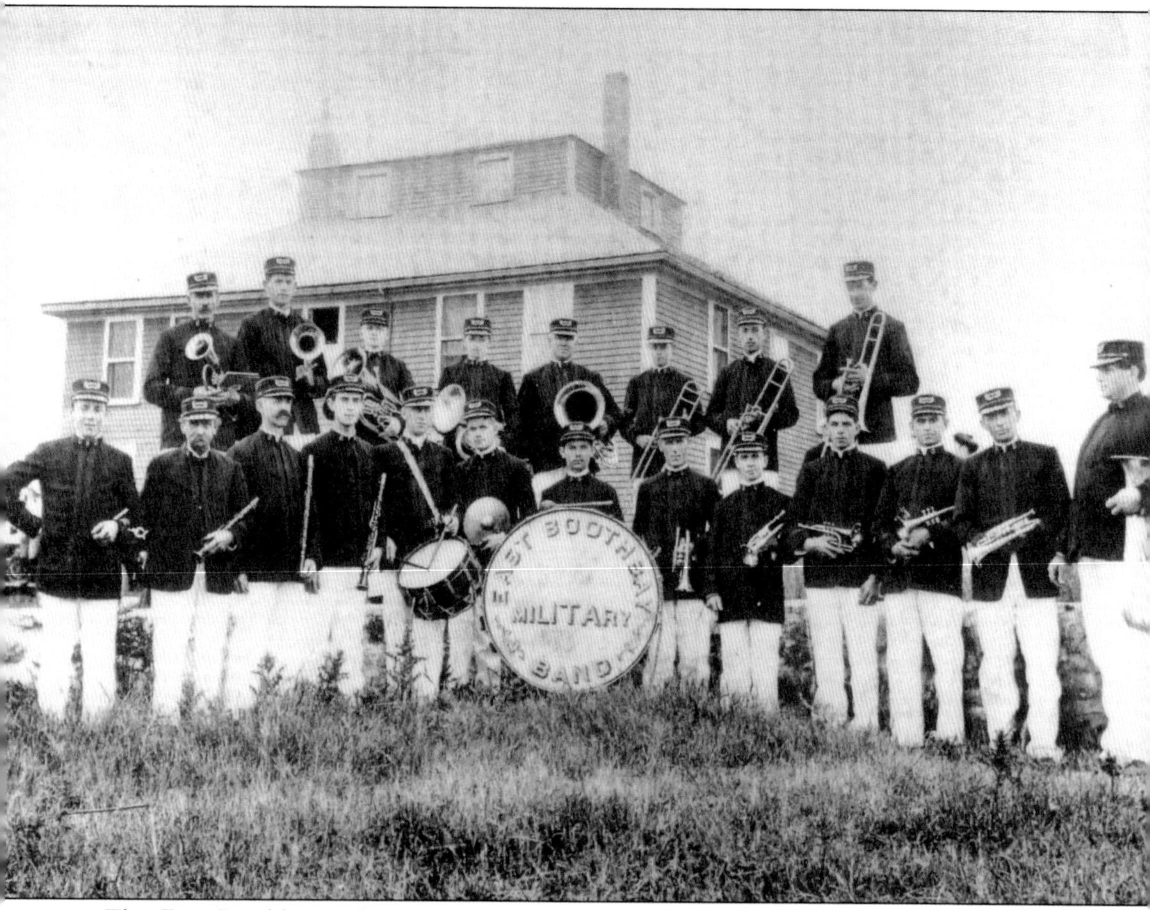

The East Boothbay Military Band performed at parades, concerts, and special functions throughout the region. This photograph taken at the Old Fort House in Pemaquid in the early 1900s suggests the band may have taken part in the dedication ceremonies for the newly completed Fort William Henry Memorial. From left to right are: (front row) Lawrence Bishop, Dan Race, Evander Gamage, Alton Lailer, Percy Orne, Charles Seavey, Edwin Gamage, Melvin Alley, Howard McDougal, Charles Hyson, C. Tyler Hodgdon, Luther Barlow, and Harold H. Selig; (back row) Lester McFarland, Everett M. Vannah, James L. Race, Clifford Murray, Merrill Blake, Rendall Damren, William Durfee, and George I. Hodgdon. (Boothbay Region Historical Society)

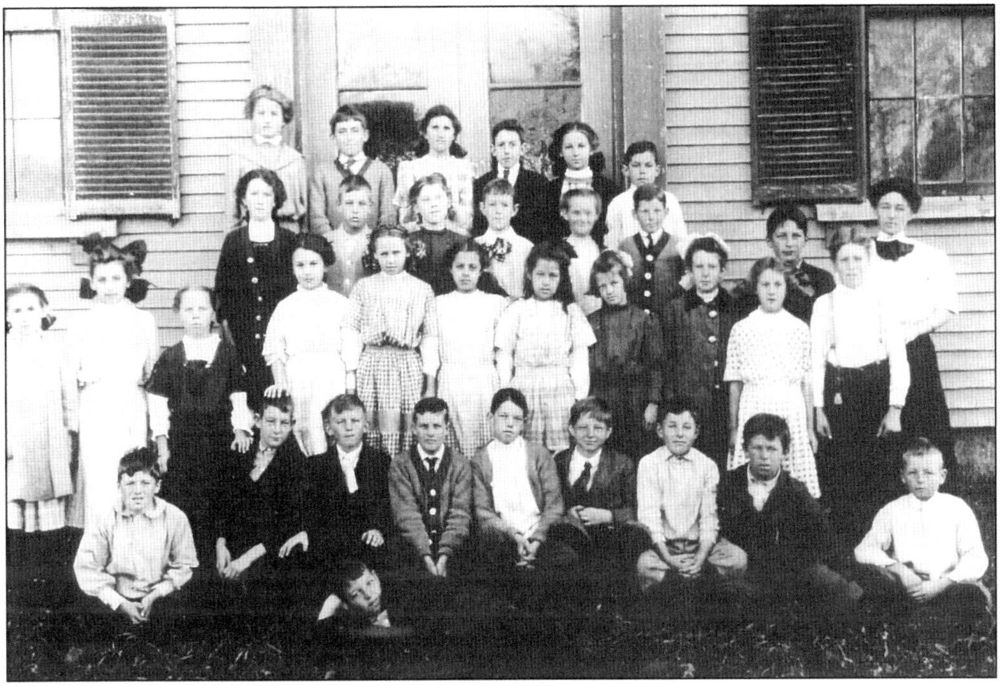

Miss Jennie Hagan stands with her students at the East Boothbay School *c.* 1914. The original building was doubled after this photograph was taken, and by the early 1920s the school housed nearly one hundred students from first grade to the second year of high school. Other schools in the area were at Linekin and Back Narrows. (Boothbay Region Historical Society)

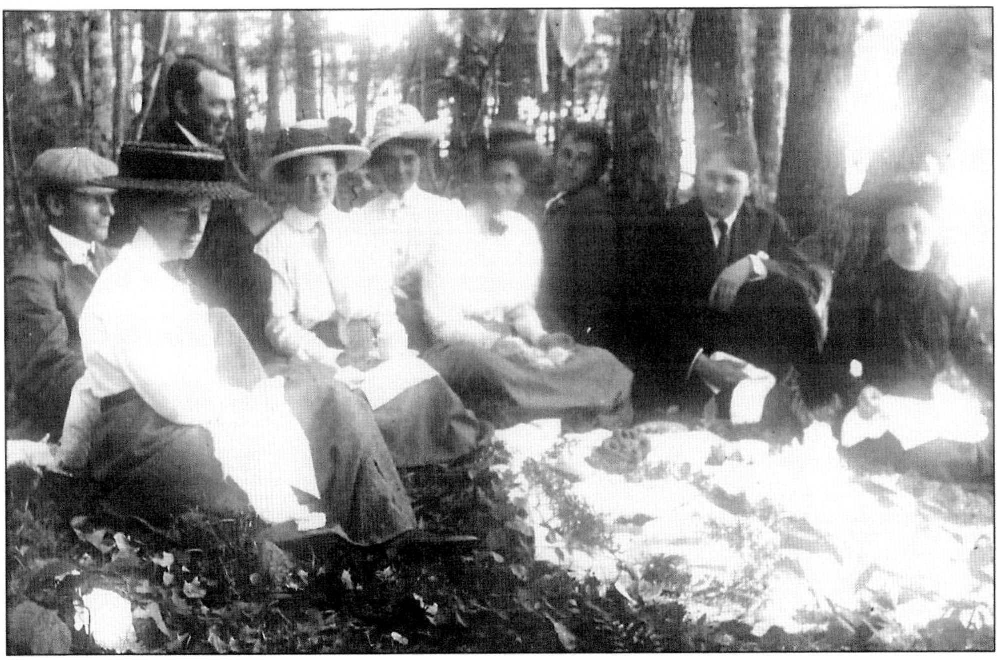

Picnics at the shore have always been popular for Lincoln County residents who lived inland. The open ocean was a pleasant day trip down the river even in 1915, as this group of young people from Damariscotta Mills suggests. (Bryant photograph, courtesy Arthur Jones)

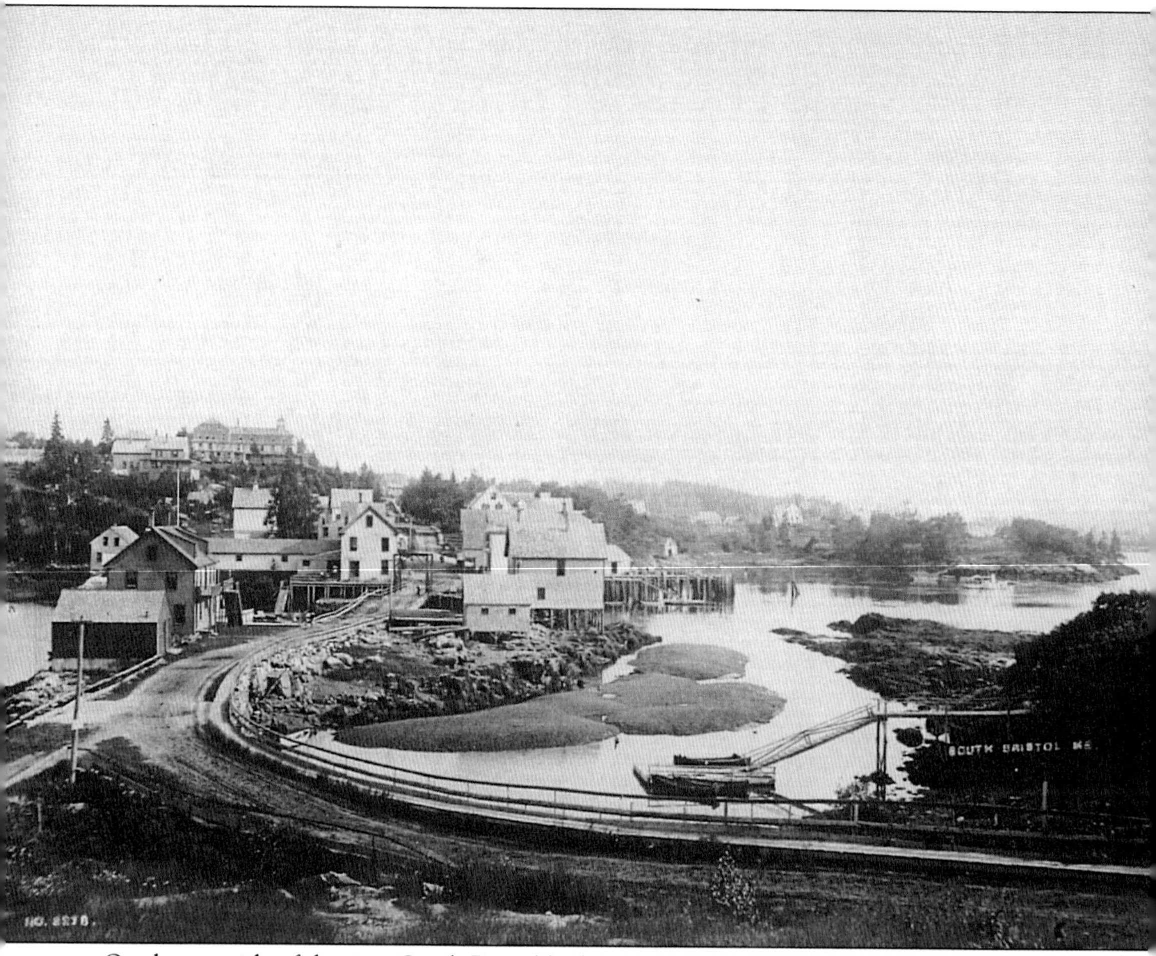

On the east side of the river South Bristol looks peaceful c. 1912. The village was still a part of Bristol at this time, but citizens, including some of the more prominent summer people, soon started a movement to create a separate community. This effort became a reality on July 2, 1915, when South Bristol was incorporated as Maine's 482nd town. The view is looking south toward Rutherford Island with the Summit House clearly visible on the hill overlooking the water. The pilings in the center of the picture are part of the steamer landing, an important structure considering that most of the town's goods came in by boat. (Margaret House)

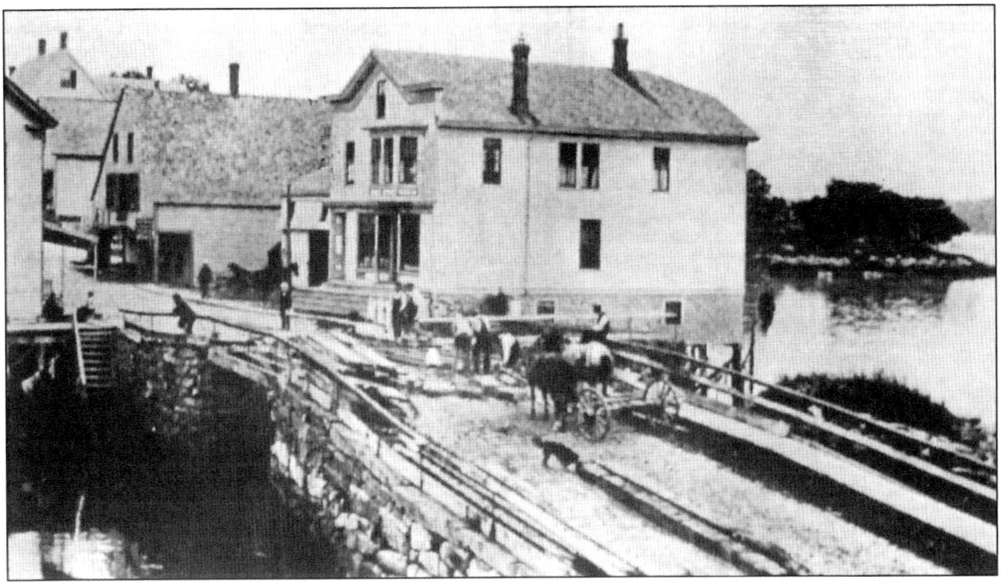

In this early photograph work is progressing on the plank bridge at the Gut. Prior to its construction only a footbridge linked Rutherford Island to the mainland. The bridge in the photograph had developed a reputation over the years and was known as the "notorious dangerous bridge." According to local historians problems over repairing the bridge were among the reasons South Bristol separated from Bristol. (William Kelsey)

They are building a bridge at South Bristol
From the Island down to the mainland.
They've put in everything they could think of
From rockweed down to the beach sand.

They've covered the pastures all over
And taken down all the stone walls.
They wouldn't hire men from South Bristol
But brought them from Pemaquid Falls.....

The first two stanzas of a poem written by Flora (French) McFarland capture some of the strong feelings and rivalry that existed between South Bristol and the other sections of Bristol at the time the bridge was built. The poem goes on to describe how the Pemaquid workmen had to be hauled out of the water after falling in, and how the bridge was so crooked when completed "you cannot get across it at night!" (Margaret House)

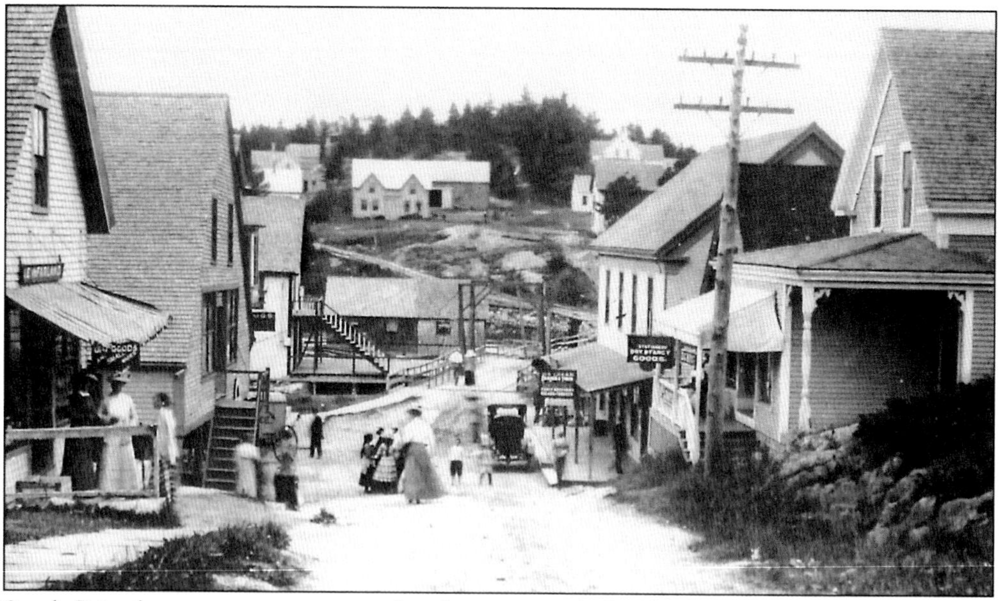

South Bristol stores are attracting a few shoppers c. 1915. Alice Pierce owned the dry goods shop on the right, while Everett Gamage sold ice cream, fireworks, and other items in the two-story building beyond. On the left side of the street another dry goods store competed with Mrs. Pierce; Merritt Thompson's grocery store can be seen next. This building later became a boat shop run by Horace Kelsey and William Alley. Beyond it is Edward Gamage's drugstore. (William Kelsey)

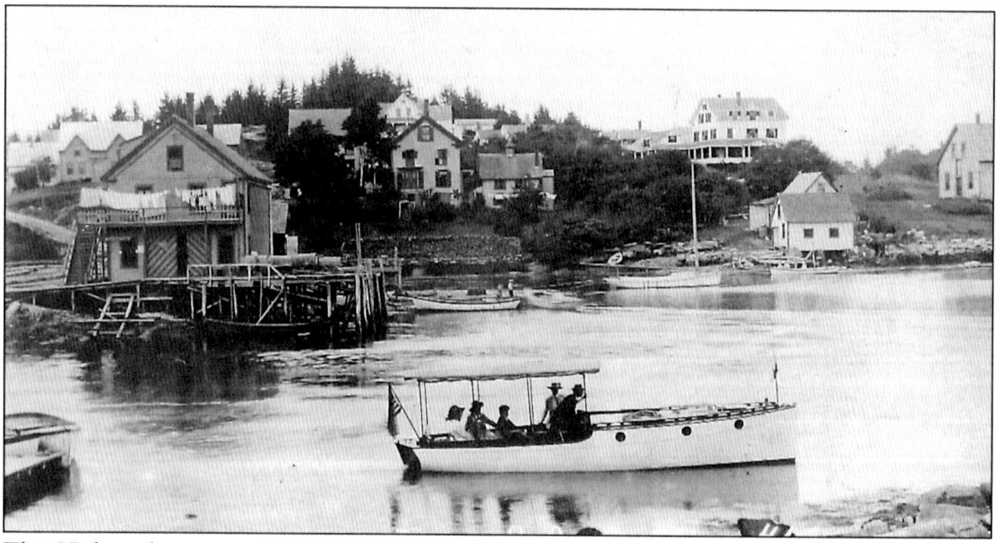

This 27-foot pleasure cruiser gliding through the Gut was built at Rice Brothers in East Boothbay in 1910, and remained on the west side of the river for a number of years before being bought c. 1930 by Harold Mott-Smith, a summer resident of South Bristol. The first thing Dr. Mott-Smith (a professor of physics and a member of the Atomic Energy Commission) did to his boat was to remove the canopy because he felt it looked undignified. The boat (minus the canopy) is still used on the river by its present owner, Bruce Farrin. The large white house on the hill (at right center) is the Thompson Inn "a comfortable and refined home for about thirty-five quiet people," according to an early brochure. (William Kelsey)

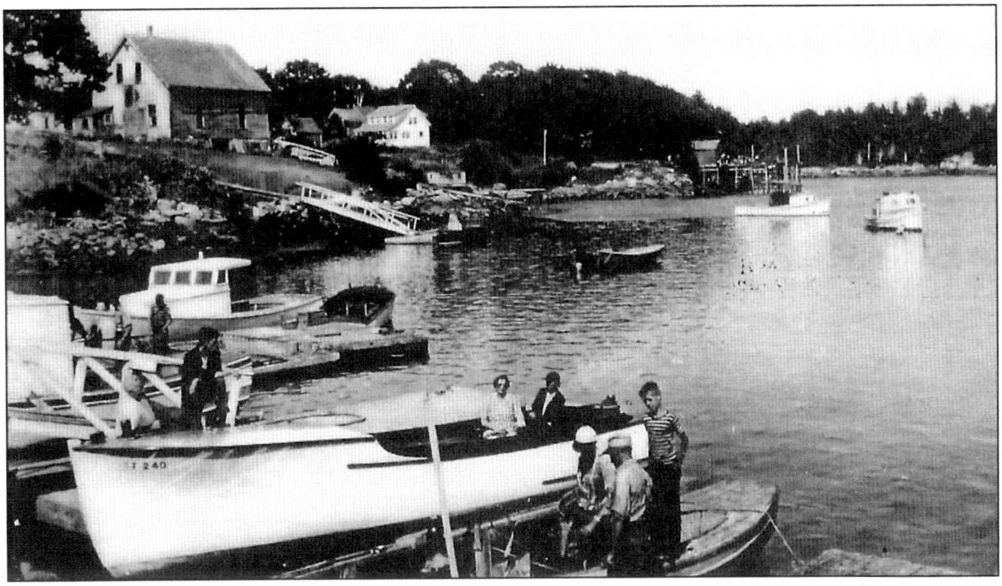

Activity on the waterfront east of the Gut indicates both fishing and pleasure boats were at home in South Bristol. Richard Swain, left, and Fred Hinck, III (with his foot on the deck of the white boat), along with Luise Hinck and Frances Swain in the *Luise II*, observe Richard Thorpe and his son, Albert, discussing important maritime matters with a local fisherman. (William Kelsey)

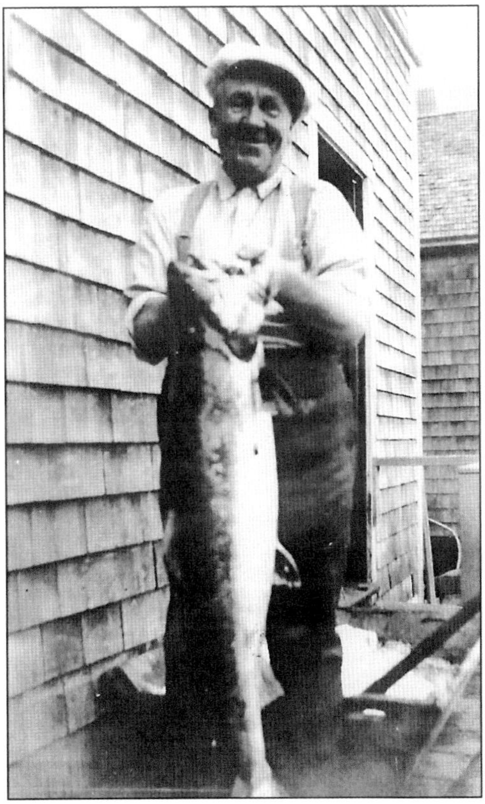

Irving Clifford's business at the north end of the bridge was his pride and joy. He ran a successful fish market with a clientele of both residents and summer people who came in as much to see the proprietor as to buy his fish. A good-natured fellow whose antics and conversation earned him a reputation that far outlived his mortal life, Mr. Clifford is still remembered with a chuckle by those who knew and did business with him. (William Kelsey)

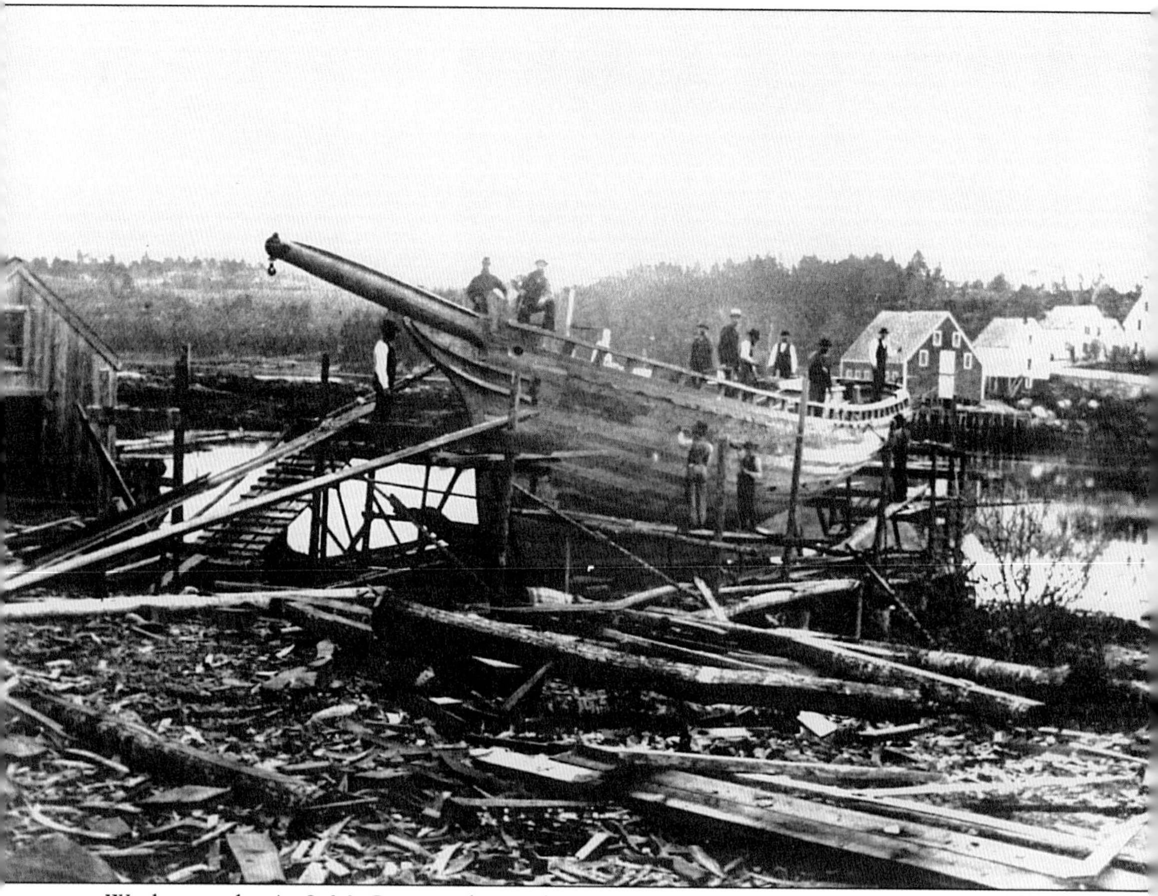

Workers at the A. & M. Gamage shipyard put the finishing touches on the schooner, *Arwilda Morse* in 1872. The Gamage brothers started building in 1854, turning out nearly one hundred vessels during their fifty years of operation. The company also built several steamboats, including the *Anodyne*, launched in 1895. This little steamer was originally built to advertise and sell Johnson's Anodyne Liniment up and down the Maine coast, but in addition to his regular run Captain Elliott Gamage occasionally found time to take a few passengers on excursions. This part of the business was an immediate success, leading to the formation of the Damariscotta Steamboat Company which enjoyed profitable steamer excursions along the river for many years. (Margaret House)

Opposite, bottom: Fowler, Foote & Company's Menhaden Oil Works conducted business at their factory on the waterfront. "Pogy factories," as they were known locally, were common along the coast: South Bristol alone had four. The fish were taken in large quantities and processed for the oil which was used for the same purpose as linseed oil, while the scraps were used for fertilizer. Local residents preserved their wood-frame houses with the oil. (William Kelsey)

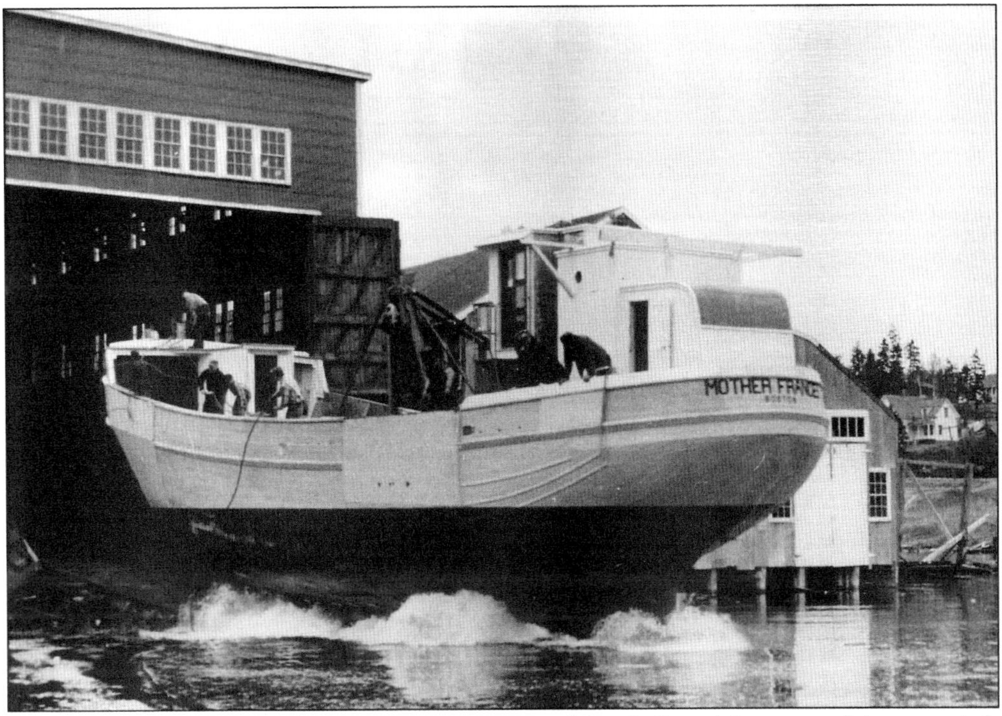

The Gamage shipyard has been an important part of South Bristol for most of the twentieth century. It was started by Harvey Gamage in the 1920s on the site of the A. & M. Gamage shipyard which at that time had been closed for about twenty years. Mr. Gamage, who worked at Hodgdon Brothers at East Boothbay early in his career, built many vessels in his South Bristol yard, about half of them fishing craft such as the 85-foot dragger, *Mother Frances*, shown here being launched on April 19, 1954. (Gamage shipyard)

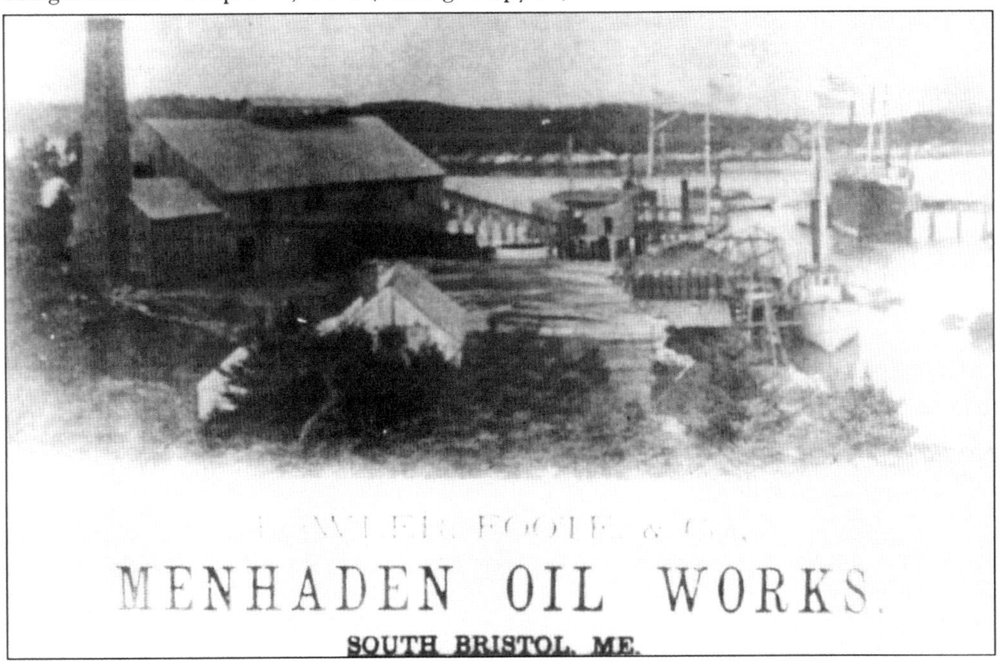

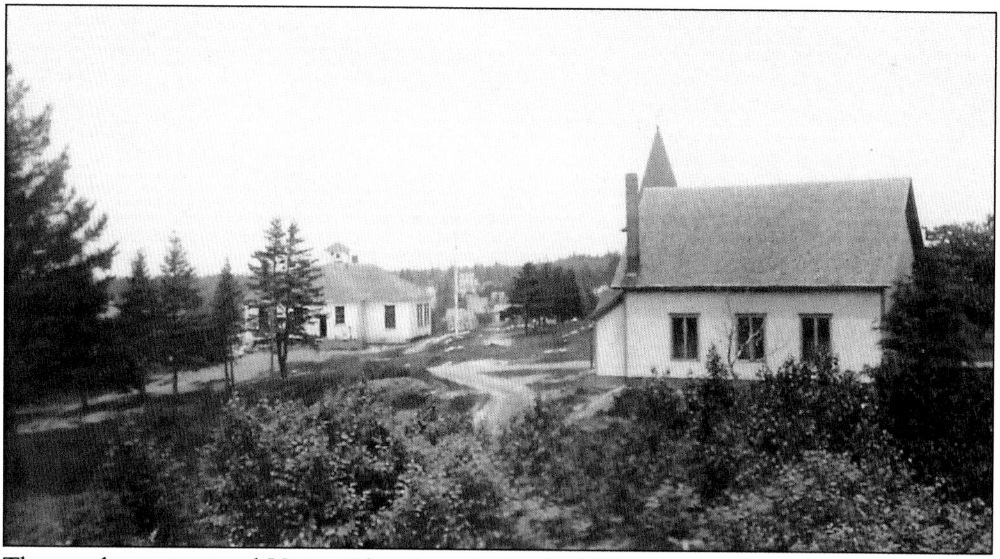

The nondenominational Union Church on Rutherford Island was dedicated August 6, 1898, with Reverend W. Henry McBride of Bristol Mills serving the new congregation until its first minister, Reverend C.W. Rogers, could assume his duties. The Lincoln Grammar School (left) was built in 1899 and, after additions, served the children of South Bristol until the present elementary school opened in January 1961. (William Kelsey)

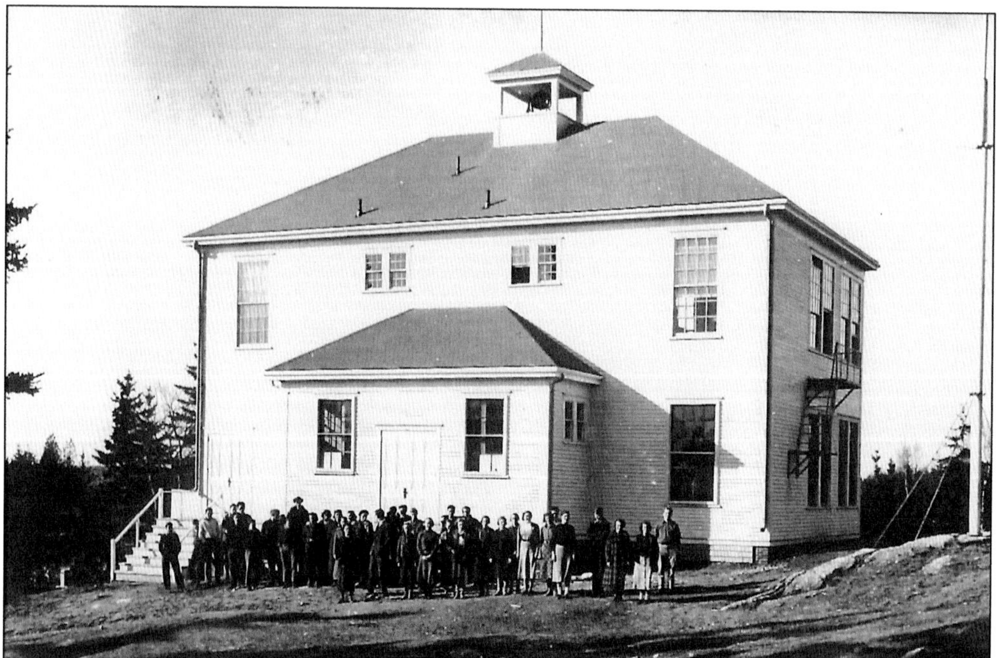

An increase in student population forced changes in the South Bristol School in the 1930s. This 1937 photograph shows the four new classrooms that were added by raising the roof to accommodate high school students. South Bristol discontinued its high school in 1962. (William Kelsey)

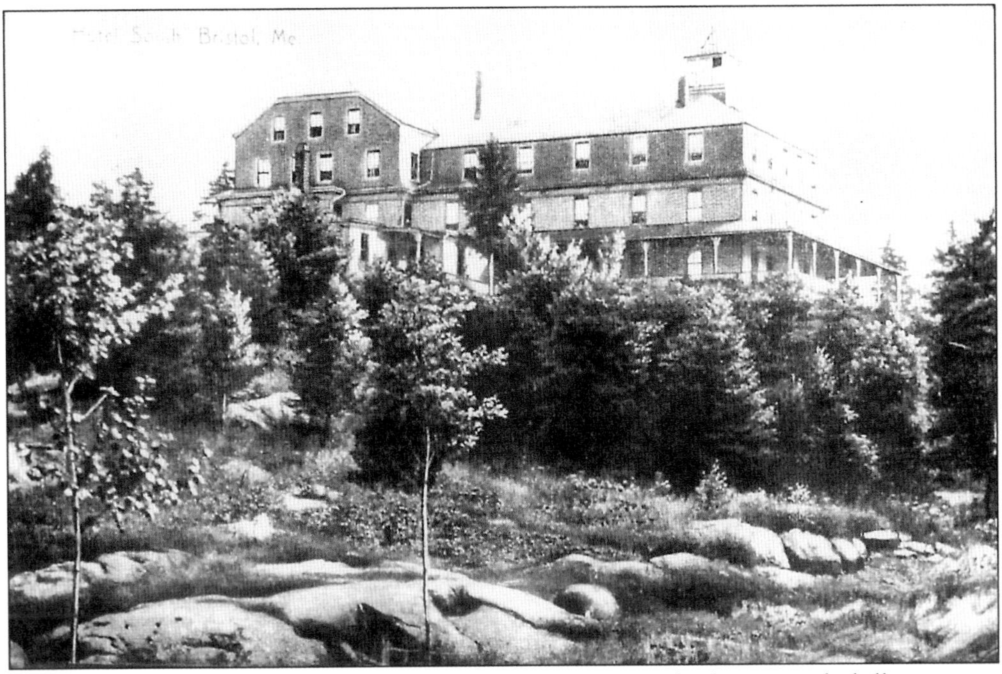

The Summit House, built by Nelson Gamage in the 1880s, took advantage of a hilltop setting on Rutherford Island to give guests beautiful panoramic views from its wide porches. Good food, indoor plumbing, and convenient railroad and steamboat connections made the hotel a popular destination at the turn of the century. The hotel burned in 1918 and was not rebuilt. (William Kelsey)

"If thou art worn and hard beset
With sorrow that thou wouldst forget.
If thou wouldst read a lesson that wouldst keep
Thy heart from fainting and thy soul from sleep,
Go to the woods and hills;— no tears
Dim the sweet look that nature wears." —Longfellow.

NATURE was in a bewitching and generous mood when she fashioned Rutherford Island, for she endowed it with wondrous charms. The grand ocean with its bold, rugged shore, on the south and east, Pemaquid Bay, and John's Bay, on the north and east. To the westward the estuary of the Damariscotta River. One hundred feet above high tide stands the Summit House. From its wide piazzas and the high land near by, there stretches forth a panorama of the mighty ocean dotted here and there with pine-topped islands, interspersed with those gray rugged rocks so peculiar to the Maine coast.

Surroundings Hard to find a spot where the air is more perfumed with the health-giving fir balsam, spruce and pine which cover a large portion of the island. These are greatly appreciated as shade and hammock trees. Nowhere are the surroundings more peaceful.

A 1913 brochure advertising the Summit House is filled with photographs, poems by Longfellow and Keats, and language designed to lure city dwellers to the healthful, peaceful environment of Rutherford Island. (Margaret House)

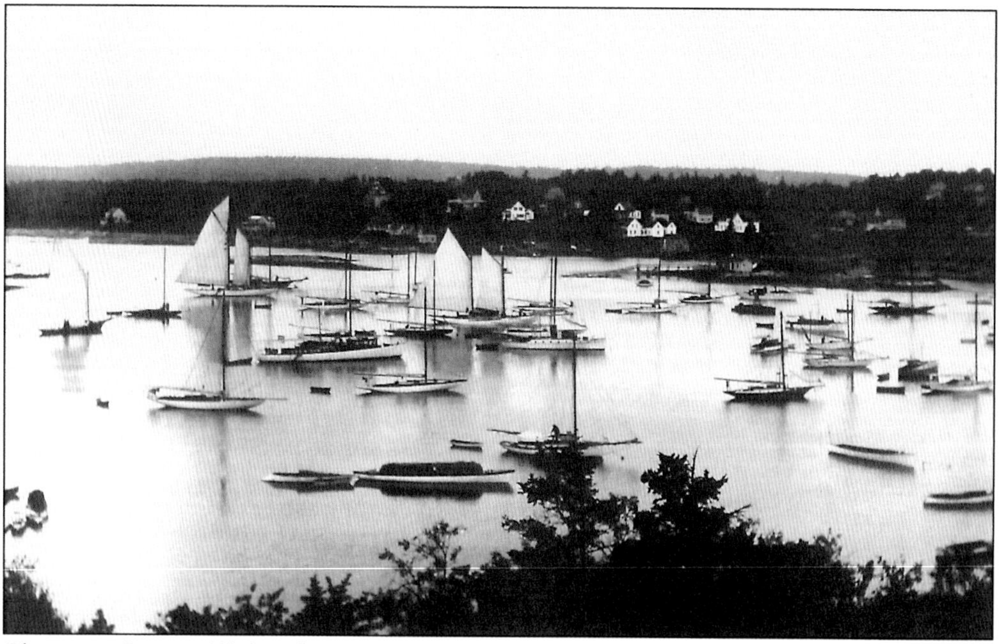

Christmas Cove is filled with an impressive array of pleasure boats c. 1920. The first summer visitors to Christmas Cove (many from the Greater Boston area) began to arrive in the mid-1880s and boarded with fishermen's families initially. In the years following they bought land and built cottages, generally arriving by steamer via Bath and Boothbay. (William Kelsey)

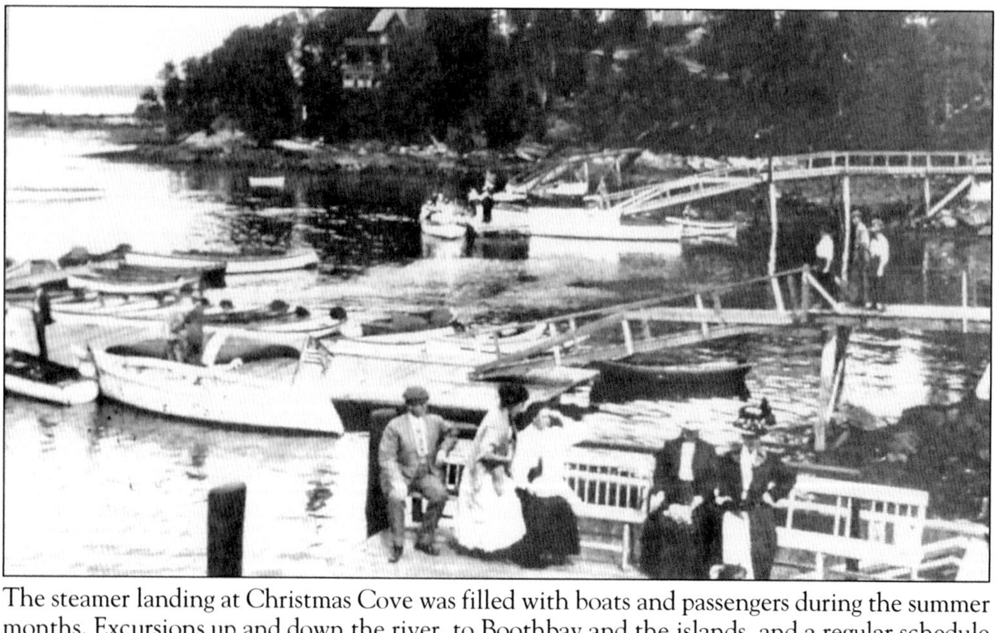

The steamer landing at Christmas Cove was filled with boats and passengers during the summer months. Excursions up and down the river, to Boothbay and the islands, and a regular schedule of steamer stops from Portland and Bath made the cove a popular place around the turn of the century. (William Kelsey)

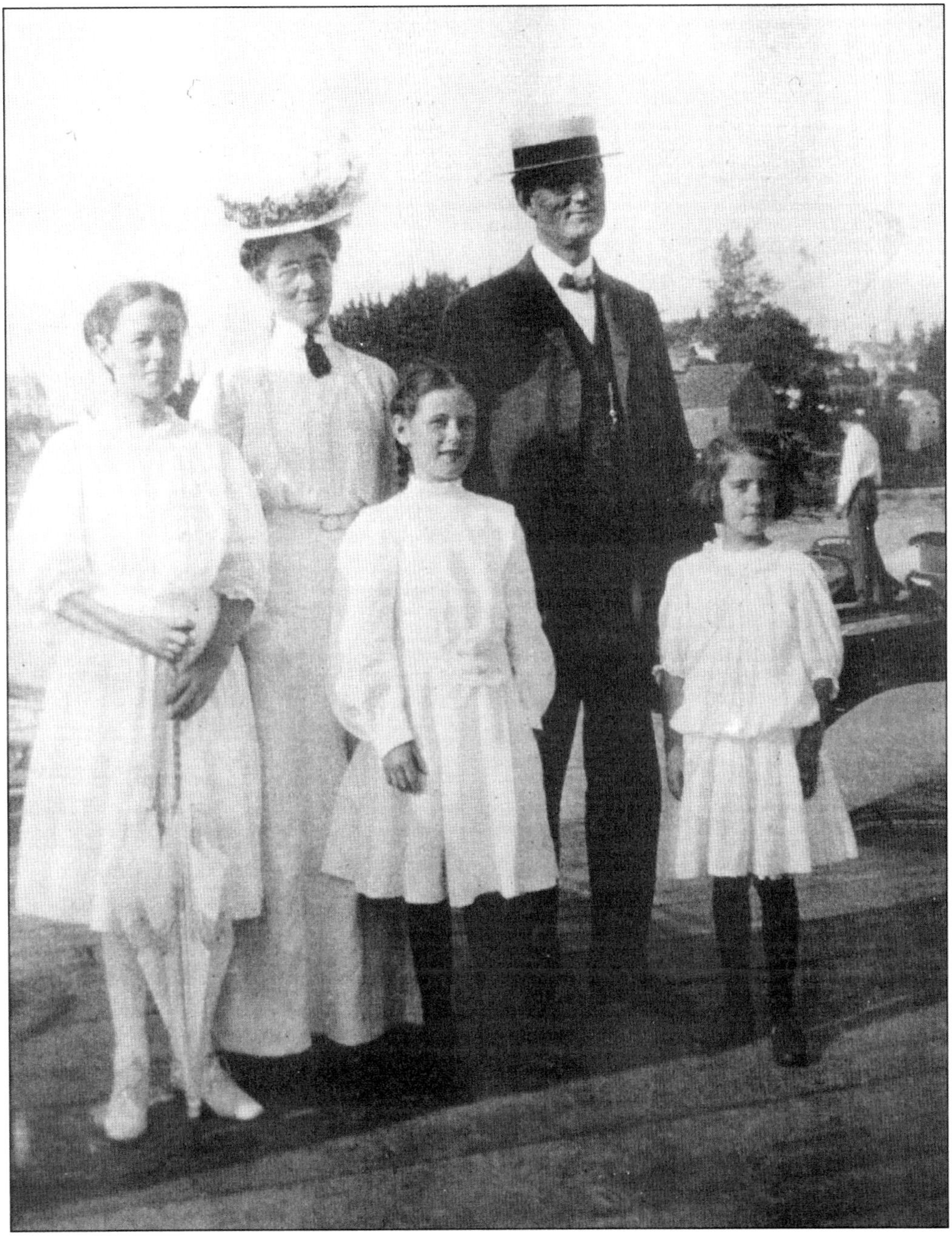

A boat trip down the Damariscotta with the prospect of spending a day at Christmas Cove was an occasion worth dressing up for in 1908. Lincoln and Josephine Chapman of Damariscotta and their daughters, Gladys, Martha, and Emily, appear to be enjoying themselves at their destination. Mr. Chapman had recently been made cashier at the Newcastle National Bank. Gladys later married Charles Brewer; Martha married Dr. Robert Belknap. (David Belknap)

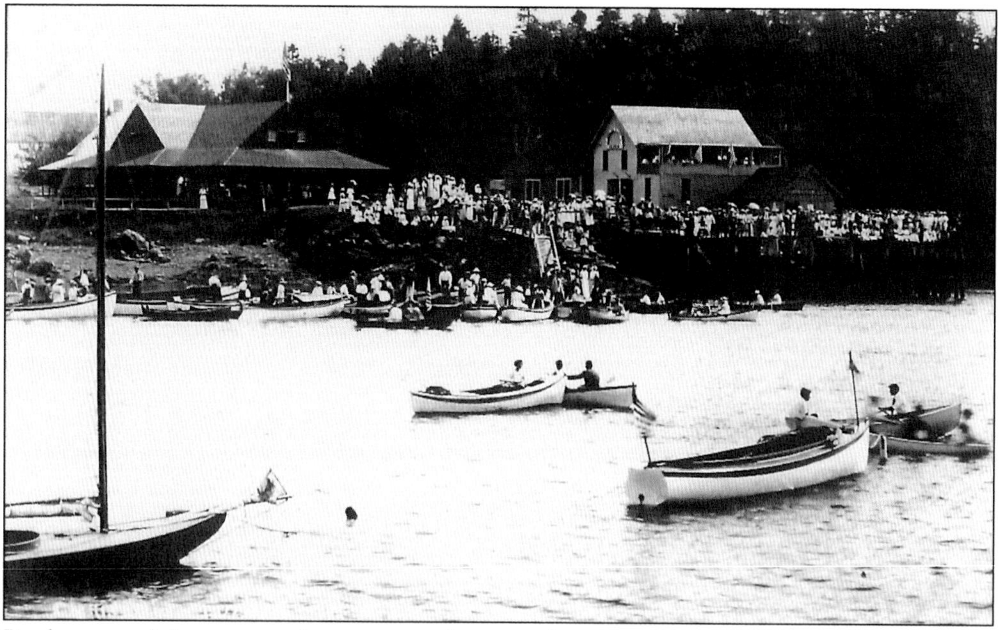

By the turn of the century the summer colony was large enough to form the Christmas Cove Improvement Association, an organization of cottage owners who originally used a converted fishhouse for recreation and religious services. In 1902 the association built the Casino, above, which served as a multipurpose building for all its activities. Boat races drew a large crowd c. 1920. (William Kelsey)

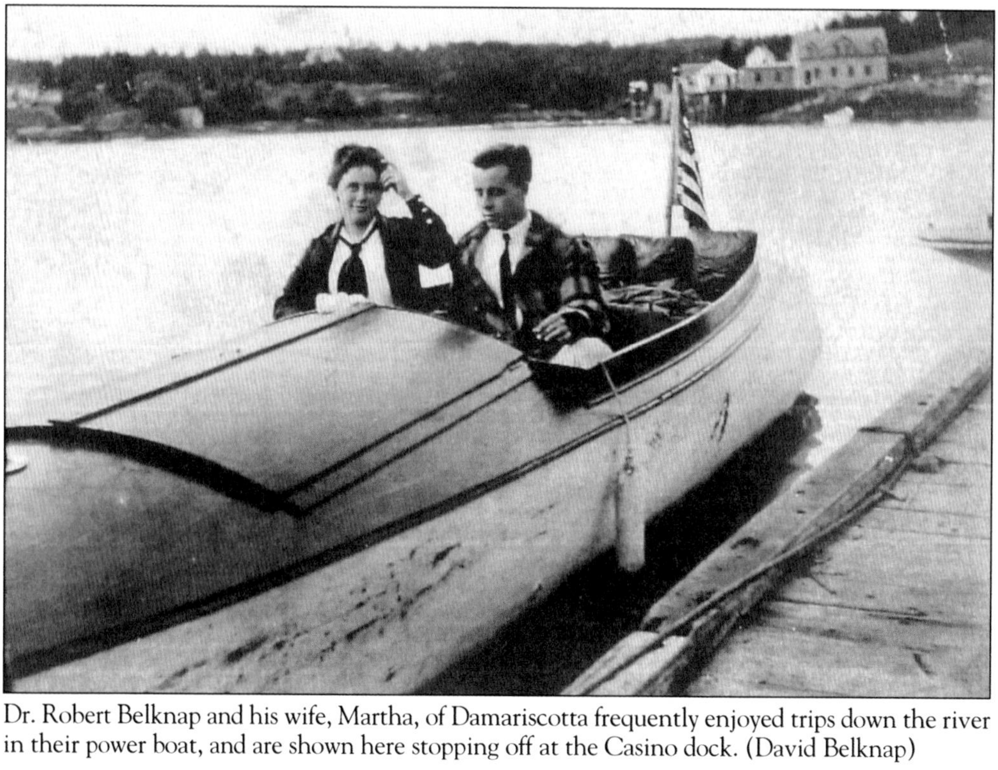

Dr. Robert Belknap and his wife, Martha, of Damariscotta frequently enjoyed trips down the river in their power boat, and are shown here stopping off at the Casino dock. (David Belknap)

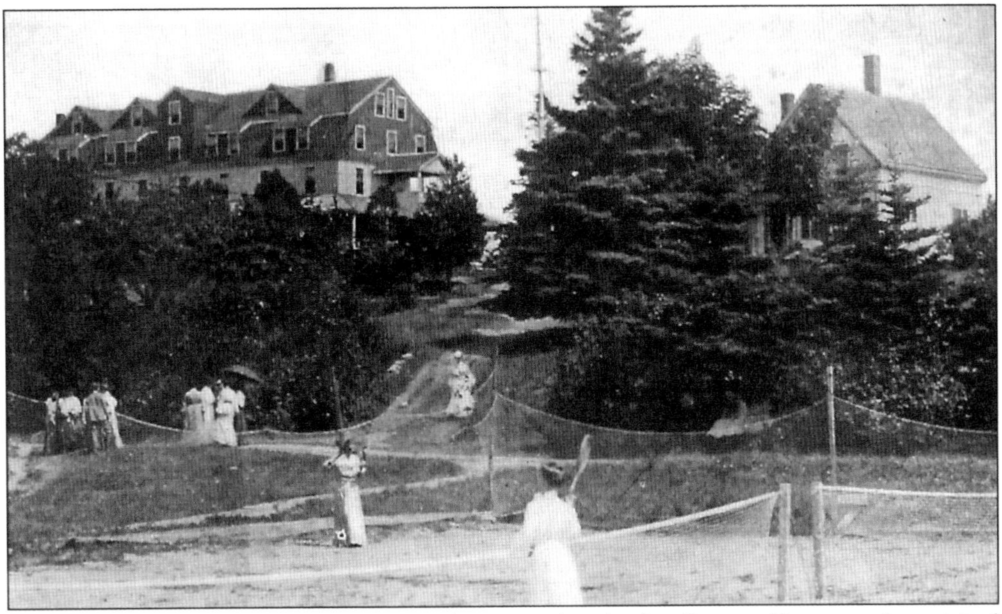

A ladies tennis match is in progress on the courts beside the Casino. Guests at the original Holly Inn, at top left, were also allowed to play on the courts maintained by the Christmas Cove Improvement Association. (William Kelsey)

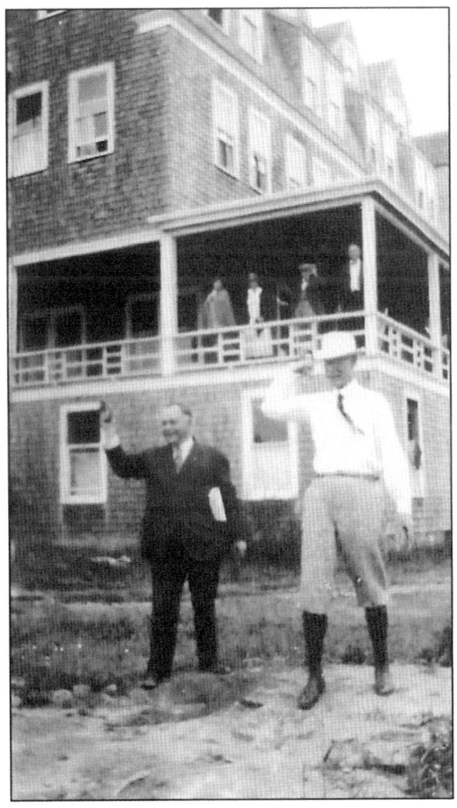

Holly Inn owner, Albert T. Thorpe (on the left), and an unidentified man wave to a crowd gathered at the inn *c.* 1920. Mr. Thorpe and his father, Edward, built the first hotel in 1904, a forty-room inn which burned three years later. The ninety-room hotel (above), boasting its own electric generating plant, was built to replace it. (William Kelsey)

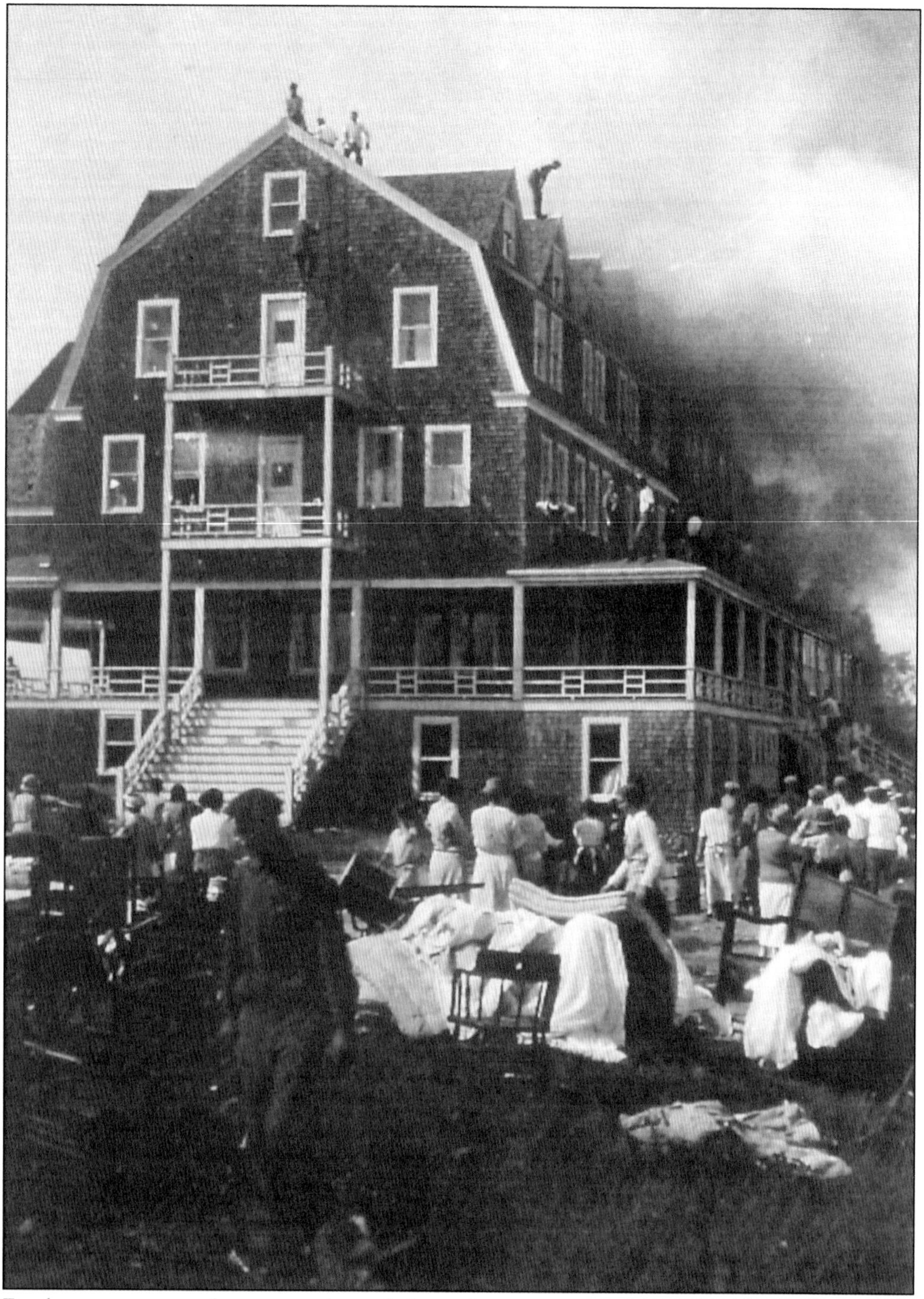

Employees, guests, and townspeople work furiously to remove belongings and furnishings from the burning Holly Inn, as others try to contain the flames that quickly overspread the building. The August 10, 1923 blaze marked the second time the inn had burned, and for the second time the building was a total loss. Mr. Thorpe, securing the backing of three wealthy summer residents, again rebuilt the hotel, expanding it to include one hundred rooms. (William Kelsey)

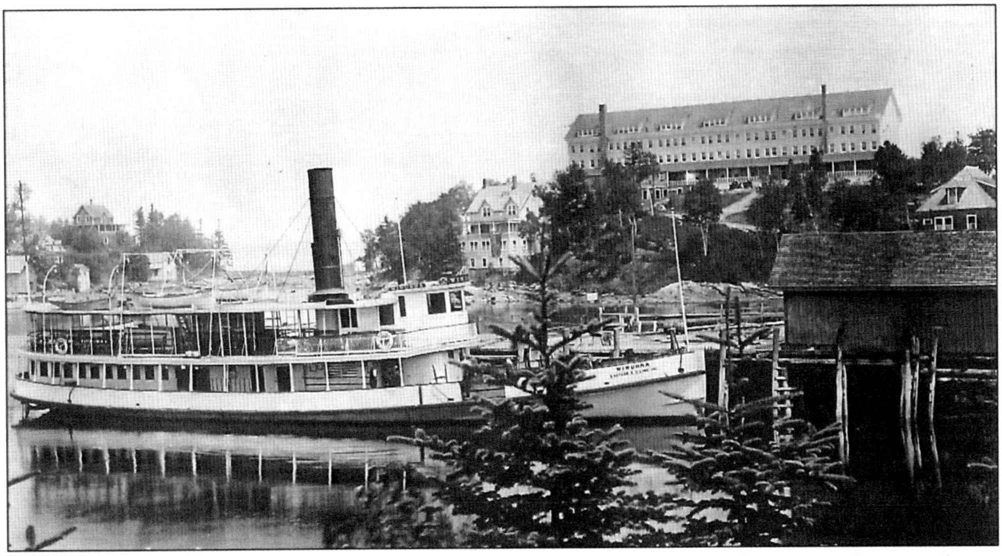

The recently completed third version of the Holly Inn meant increased revenues for steamboats running regular routes and excursions to Christmas Cove. The *Wiwurna* made the run from Bath to Boothbay Harbor and Christmas Cove, and was the last vessel to remain in that service. (William Kelsey)

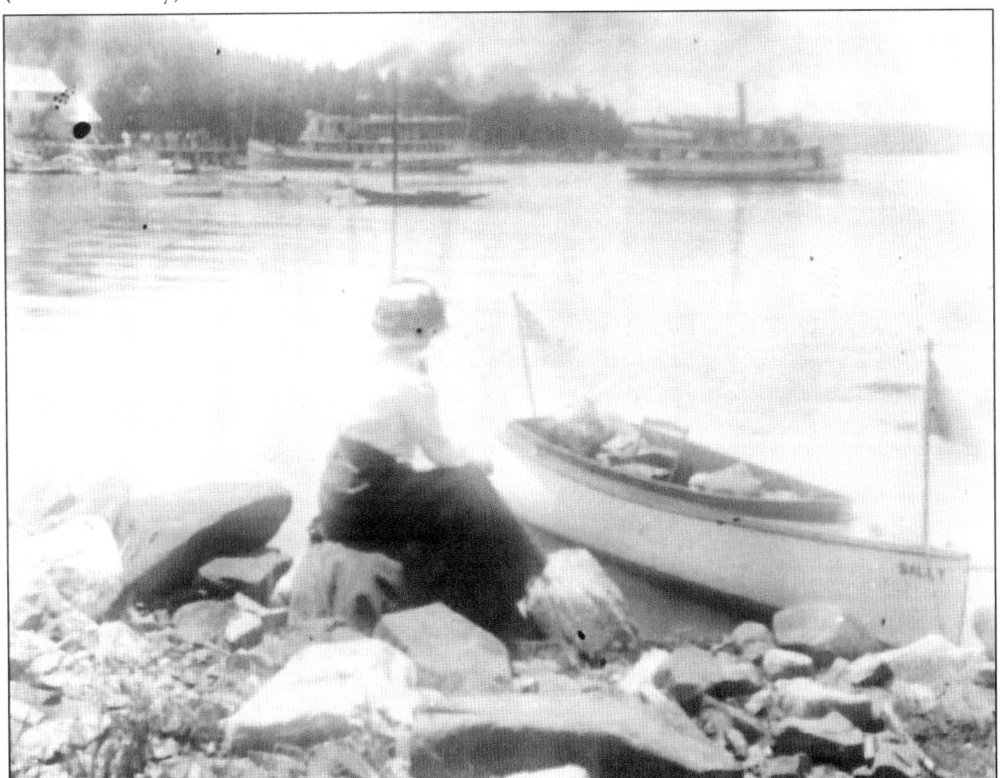

Watching the steamers move in and out of Christmas Cove on a Sunday afternoon was a pleasant pastime for Elizabeth Bryant, who made the trip down the river from Damariscotta Mills with her brother, Joe, in the *Sally*. (Bryant photograph, courtesy Arthur Jones)

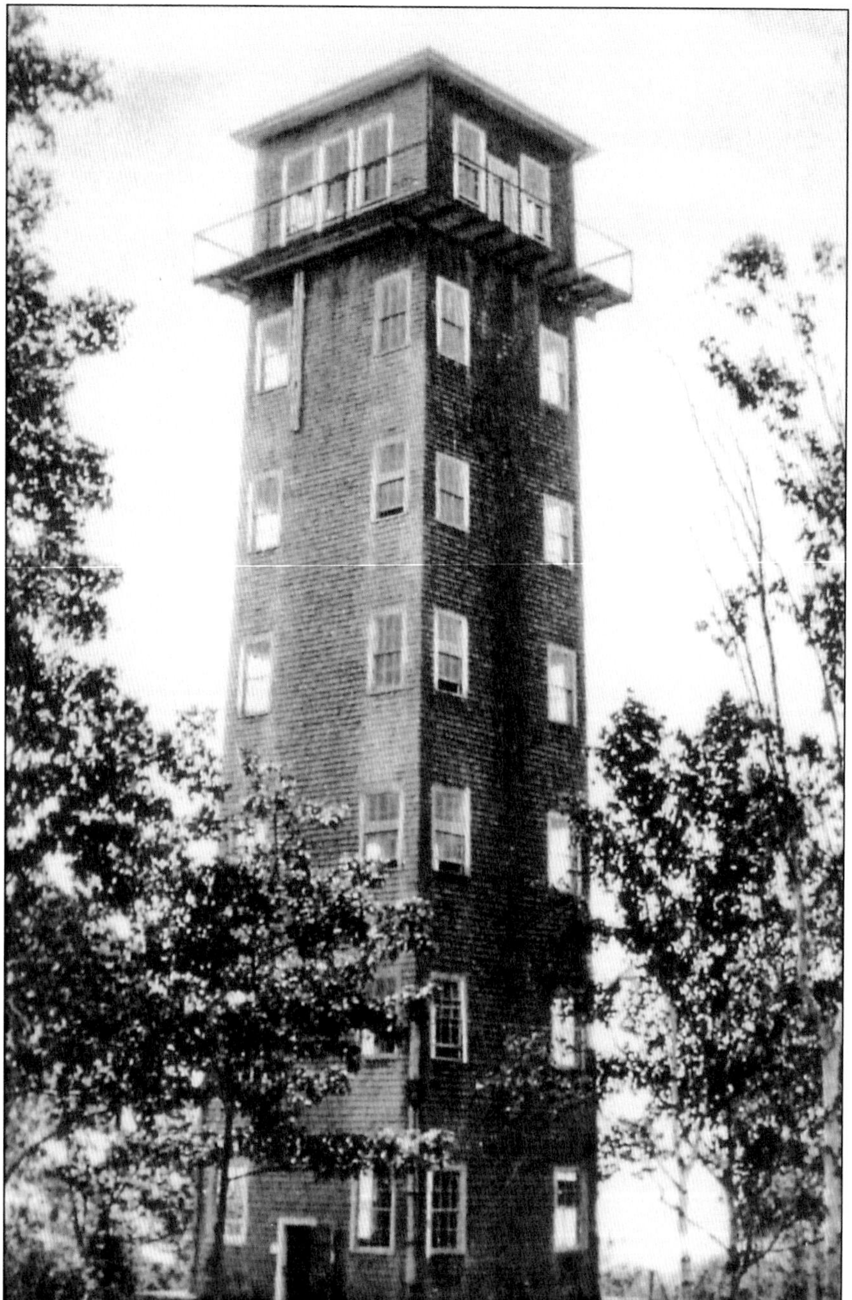

The 110-foot tower on the Miles estate has been an important mariner's landmark since its construction c. 1920. The original multipurpose tower which had a water tank on top and rooms on several levels, also had an observation deck with a viewing radius of 75 miles. A wealthy entrepreneur and a generous man, Samuel Miles also built a "Fresh Air Camp" on his property for disadvantaged Maine children, providing them with good food, wholesome recreational activities, and bringing in celebrities such as Babe Ruth to entertain them. Mr. Miles also included local children in the picnics and parties held at his estate. (William Kelsey)

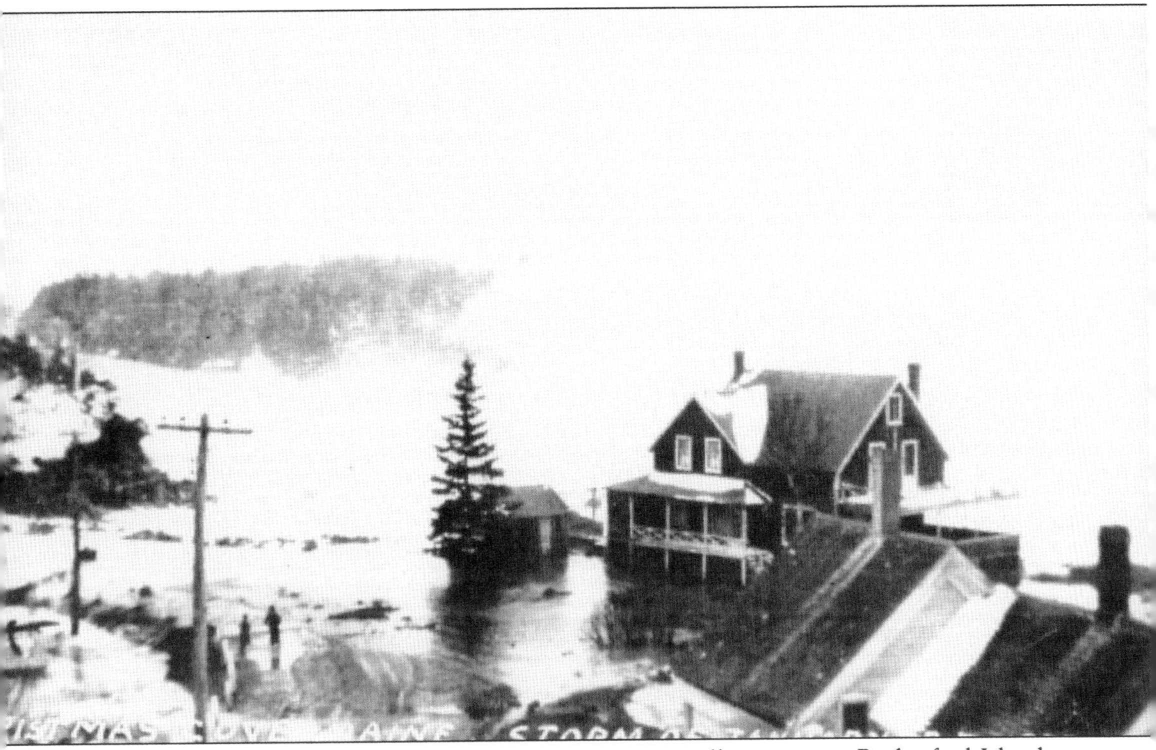

The weather is not always idyllic in Christmas Cove, especially in winter. Rutherford Island juts into the Atlantic and takes its share of damage from northeasters whipping wind and waves over the bar. This storm of January 25, 1933, is sending water and salt spray several feet into the air, almost obliterating Birch Island just offshore. The summer home in the center of the photograph (known as The Bar Cottage) has seen some damage over the years, but has managed to remain intact. The garage, however, has washed away several times. (William Kelsey)

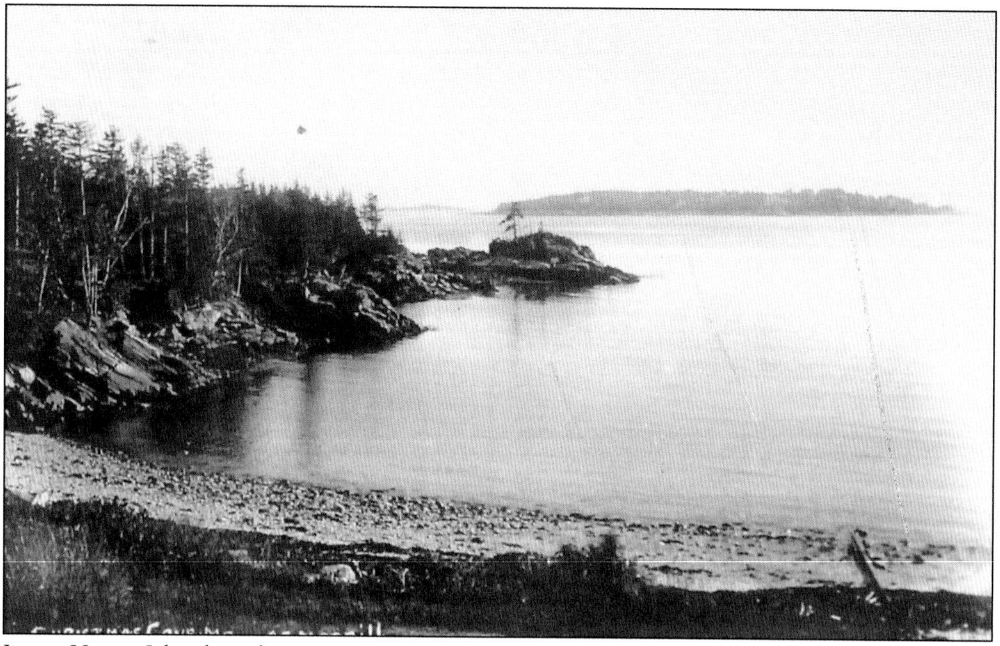

Inner Heron Island, with a summer cottage community of its own dating from 1886, stands offshore between Rutherford Island and Linekin Neck. Its cluster of homes seems to guard the entrance to the Damariscotta and to mark the end of this 26-mile fresh- and saltwater voyage to the Atlantic. Inner Heron, standing with purpose squarely at the mouth of the Damariscotta River, is appropriately cast as a sentinel to this delightful and historic waterway. (William Kelsey)

Bibliography

Biscoe, Mark. *No Pluckier Set of Men Anywhere*. Newcastle, Maine: Lincoln County Publishing, 1994.

Castner, Harold W. The Castner Papers (Unpublished manuscripts).

Clifford, Harold B. *The Boothbay Region: 1906–1960*. Freeport, Maine: Bond Wheelwright, 1961.

Dunbar, Robert E and Dow, George F. *Nobleboro, Maine—A History*. Nobleboro Historical Society, 1988.

Early Edgecomb, Maine. Compiled by Katherine Chase Owen, 1986.

Gamage, Nelson W. *A Short History of South Bristol, Maine*.

Jefferson—Touchstone of Democracy. Jefferson Historical Society, 1976.

Stevens, James P. *Reminiscences of a Boothbay Shipbuilder*. Boothbay Region Historical Society, 1993.

Vannah, Hudson. *Five Generations on a Maine Farm*. Nobleboro, 1984.